THE CHINA HUMAN DEVELOPMENT REPORT

Published for the
United Nations Development Programme (UNDP), China

New York   Oxford
Oxford University Press
1999

Oxford University Press

Oxford   New York
Athens Auckland Bangkok Bogotá Buenos Aires Calcutta
Cape Town Chennai Dar es Salaam Delhi Florence Hong Kong Istanbul
Karachi Kuala Lumpur Madrid Melbourne Mexico City Mumbai
Nairobi Paris São Paulo Singapore Taipei Tokyo Toronto Warsaw

and associated companies in

Berlin   Ibadan

Published by Oxford University Press, Inc.,
198 Madison Avenue, New York, New York 10016
http://www.oup-usa.org

Although the Report is commissioned by UNDP, the analysis and policy recommendations in this report do not necessarily reflect the views of UNDP China Country Office. The independence of views and the professional integrity of its authors ensure that the conclusions and recommendations will have the greatest possible audience.

The exposition of China in this report does not include Taiwan Province, Hong Kong Special Administrative Region, and Macao. The related tables and data do not include those about the three regions either. Information and data about Chongqing municipality under the central government are included in the part about Sichuan Province. This note applies to all the chapters and sections of this book.

Cover photograph by Mobo Gao.

ISBN   0-19-513210-6 (paper)
ISBN   0-19-513211-4 (cloth)

9 8 7 6 5 4 3 2 1

Printed in the United States of America
on acid-free paper

T a b l e   o f   C o n t e n t s

Introduction

Since the Copenhagen Declaration and Programme of Action promulgated at the World Summit on Social Development in 1995, UNDP has focused its efforts on helping to implement the goals and objectives of the Summit, first and foremost the alleviation of absolute poverty. China's State Planning commission, then to become the State Planning and Development Commission, has taken responsibility for devising follow-up programmes to promote social development, which China regards as the ultimate goal of economic development. There is a long record of cooperation between the Chinese government and the United Nations and other international organizations in designing and implementing effective social development programmes.

The publication of this first National Human Development Report (NHDR) for China is an important step in realizing that objective. The production of the Report was organized by UNDP, with full cooperation from the State Planning Commission. We hope this Report will pave the way for others to come that will deal with the signal issues of the future.

The purpose of this Report is to summarize the history and current status of sustainable human development in China, focus attention on the outstanding challenges to be overcome, and make broad policy recommendations for tackling them. Special attention is given to the theme of poverty reduction, which was the annual theme of the 1997 global Human Development report. Because this is the first NHDR undertaken for China, it also tries to establish a baseline for future such efforts by discussing in some detail a wide spectrum of human development issues, including the distribution of income, health care, education and nutrition, population and migration, the status of women, employment, social security provision, and the state of the natural environment. There are many causal inter-connections among these various issues, which the Report tries to highlight.

The Report finds that China has compiled an admirable record of promoting human development, with falling poverty rates and improvements in the health and educational status of the population. Major human development indicators, such as longevity, approach the levels of economically advanced countries. Much of the population has successfully completed a first "health care revolution" essentially eliminating mass infectious diseases that used to ravage the whole country. School enrollment rates are high, and adult illiteracy low and declining. China's people are, on the whole, healthier, better educated and longer-lived than ever before.

Yet China also faces enormous human development challenges. Some of these are left over from the past, others newly created or complicated by the process of transition from a planned to a market economy that has been in place for the past two decades. Threats of growing unemployment, rising social and economic inequality, the absence of a safety net adequate to cope with changing conditions, the unequal burden of change borne by women, and the grave and growing destruction of China's natural environment are among the most serious. The difficult reform of state enterprises, ongoing as this Report is published, is bringing several of these problems to a head.

Moreover, China has become increasingly integrated with the world market. While this has worked to its advantage, on the whole, it has also subjected China to the potential instability of world market forces, such as those involved in the Asian financial crisis. The Report points out that achieving human development objectives is easier in the high growth environment that has existed for most of the two-decade transition period. China now faces the further challenge of maintaining a healthy growth rate in a less favorable regional environment, while spreading the gains of reform more widely over its huge and diverse population and preserving its threatened natural environment. None of this will be easy. But, as the Report states, China's achievements to date and the extraordinary capabilities of its people provide firm hope that these challenges can be overcome, and that China will enter the new century providing a model not only of fast economic growth, but also of human development that promotes the well-being of people and the natural balance of the earth.

We sincerely hope the publication of this first China National Human Development Report will be of help to the government and people of China in realizing their social development goals.

Arthur N. Holcombe
Resident Representative
United Nations Development Programme
Beijing
February 1998

Preface

The social development of China, the largest developing country with a population of 1.2 billion, is of great importance to the development and progress of mankind. China's average expected life span has reached 70, its literate rate has exceeded 80%, its poor population has dropped from 250 million in the 1970s to 50 million at present, and its population accounting for 22% of the world's total are being supported by a farmland acreage accounting only for 7% of the World's total. These achievements have been made despite acute shortages of per capita resources. China's successes have attracted worldwide attention and provided helpful experience for numerous developing countries, and have benefited from experiences in other countries.

The achievements China has made in the social sector in the recent decades are based on its rapid economic growth and at the same time determined by its correct development goals and social policies. Always aiming to improve people's welfare and living standards and to realize social prosperity, justice and civilization, China has adhered to economic and social coordination as well as the strategy of sustainable development. President Jiang Zemin has pointed out time and again that we should regard the promotion of social development and overall social progress as one of strategic importance while maintaining sustained, rapid and sound economic development with economic construction as the pivotal task. The Chinese Government must enable the whole population to enjoy within a reasonable period of time the fruitful results of economic growth and create more stable, liberal and harmonious social environment for sustained economic development.

In March 1995, Premier Li Peng attended the World Summit on Social Development on behalf of the Chinese Government. Together with government leaders of other countries, he signed the Copenhagen Declaration and Program of Action. In the subsequent three years China has convened a series of important conferences on poverty alleviation, employment, education and health. Especially the PRC's Ninth Five-Year Plan for National Economic and Social Development and Outline of Long-Term Goals Through 2010 examined and adopted at the National People's Congress session held in March 1996 has set forth the overall goals for future social development, discussed at length the development orientation and policy measures regarding poverty eradication, labour employment, social security, education and health.

The tasks facing China are arduous and complicated.

There is no ready model or pattern to go by. The only thing we can do is to keep on searching for a road of development suitable to China's national condition in the practice of reform and development. While summing up its own experience, China will continue to learn from the good experiences of other countries, strengthen the exchanges and cooperation with other countries and share with them the useful experiences. The Chinese Government has always supported the UN in its effort to promote global development, and carried out broad and effective cooperation with various international organizations.

To prepare for the World Summit on Social Development, in October 1994, China's State Planning Commission (SPC) sponsored together with UNDP and the UN Social Development Summit Preparatory Committee the Beijing International Workshop on Social Development which conducted extensive discussions on social development and poverty eradication, yielding positive results for the Summit preparations.
After the Summit China carried out even more comprehensive and practical cooperation with UNDP. In February 1998 China's SPC and UNDP again co-sponsored in Beijing an International Workshop on China's Social Development during the Period of Economic Transition, which had deep discussions on China's development in late 20th and early 21st centuries, especially on poverty eradication, employment, social security, education and health care. The workshop was one of the actions in support of the UN work and in promoting global social development in view of the 2000 Special UN Conference on Social Development.

I attended the two workshops and I deeply believe that UNDP should maintain close and long-term cooperation with China's SPC in social development.

The Annual UNDP Report on Human Development is not foreign to the Chinese reading public. This time the National Human Development Report for China is the UNDP's first-ever comprehensive report about China; it is a form of exchange between UNDP and China on issues of social development which will be of interest to all parties, especially conducive to deepening exchanges between Chinese and foreign experts on issues of social development. Although we do not share all the views or agree to all the conclusions and analytical techniques applied in the report, the cooperation will provide space for future sincere and prudent discussions. I hope that the report will be of help to the Chinese reader.

Chen Jinhua
February 1998

P R E F A C E

Paying close attention to human development and promoting social progress will become an inexorable trend when the economy of a country reaches a certain stage. After half a century of construction and 20 years of reform and opening to the outside world, China has now reached the stage where accelerating human development has become an important item on her agenda. At this very moment, the publishing of UNDP's national report on social development - China: National Human Development Report - is obviously of great significance.

Nowadays, all of the world's advanced nations have made human development of their own countries an item of top priority on their development agenda. The reason for this is manifold: first, at the preliminary stage of economic development, the majority of people in the society find it difficult to feed and clothe themselves. Under such circumstances, the society cannot but concentrate mainly on the establishment of its economic foundation, so that the majority of people may lift themselves from poverty. Only when industrialization has been realized and a nation has acquired solid economic strength will it be able to put forward the task of eliminating poverty among all residents, realizing full employment, universalizing education and establishing a social security system covering the whole society. Second, the post-industrialized society has, at the turn of the century, entered a new epoch, in which the rise of the "knowledge economy" will become its main symbol and human capital will assume a dominant position in economic development. During this new epoch, no sustained economic growth is possible without the development of humankind itself. Therefore, not only industrialized nations, but many newly industrialized economies (NIEs) have put the realization of human development at the top of their work list.

This is exactly why China only very recently put accelerating human development in an important position even though she has regarded, right from the founding of the People's Republic, satisfying the material and cultural needs of the people as the aim of the state. The task of accelerating human development has become particularly prominent when the People's Republic of China fulfilled, ahead of schedule, the task of quadrupling the national GDP during the Eighth Five-Year Plan period (1991-1995). Looked at from this point of view, it is no coincidence, but a matter of course and something inevitable, that China signed the "Copenhagen Declaration and Programme of Action" on human development in March 1995 and, in the "PRC's Ninth Five-Year Plan for National Economic and Social Development and Outline of Long-term Goals through 2010" drafted in 1996, emphasis is placed on poverty elimination, labour employment, social security, education and health development.

Since human development assumes such an important position in China's economic and social development, in order to formulate the rules and regulations in this field, we must first of all give a matter-of-fact assessment of the present status and problems of human development in China. Only then will we be able to make realistic plans for future goals and ways of development. In order to do a good job in this respect, UNDP's "China: National Human Development Report" will provide important assistance. Taking advantage of knowledge on human development that developed countries have accumulated during long historical periods and using rich data, the report has analyzed the present status, existing problems and development prospect of China's human development. Due to differences in theoretical concepts and analytical methods and availability of data, there may be disagreements on certain problems. But the report's role in helping to deepen the study cannot be doubted.

W u   J i n g l i a n
F e b r u a r y   2 8 ,   1 9 9 8

Team for the Preparation of China National Human Development Report 1997

Senior Editorial Advisor

Wu Jinglian, Professor, Development Research Center, State Council of the PRC

Editor and Principal Author

Carl Riskin, Professor, Queens College and Columbia University, International Consultant for UNDP

Authors of Background Papers

Cai Fang, Deputy Director, Population Institute, Chinese Academy of Social Sciences, on population and migration.

Du. Hu Shanlian, Professor, Shanghai Medical University, on health and nutrition.

Feng Yuan, China Women's Daily, on the status of women.

Li Zhibao, State Education Commission of PRC, on education.

Li Shi, Professor, Institute of Economics, Chinese Academy of Social Sciences, on regional disparities and the Human Development Index.

Meng Xianzhong, Professor, Jilin University, on government policies toward human development.

Dr. Pan Jiahua, UNDP Beijing, on environmental problems and programmes.

Shang Xiaoyuan, Institute for Development Studies, University of Sussex, on reform of the social security system.

Zhu Ling, Professor, Institute of Economics, Chinese Academy of Social Sciences, on poverty and poverty alleviation programmes.

UNDP Beijing

Arthur Holcombe, Resident Representative (August 1992- February 1998)

Romulo Garcia, Deputy Resident Representative (August 1991- October 1997)

Chingboon Lee, Deputy Resident Representative (August 1994- March 1998)

He Jin, Chief, Division of Social Development

Guo Ying, Programme Assistant, Division of Social Development

UNDP New York

Saras Menon

Donna Seon

A c k n o w l e d g e m e n t s

The State Planning Commission of the People's Republic of China and, in particular, its Department of Social Development, offered assistance, cooperation and encouragement to this project. They provided extensive comments on earlier drafts, which led to substantial improvements in the Report. They are Yang Qingwei, Wang Dongsheng, Wang Wei, Su Guo, He Ping and Ding Yuanzhu.

Other helpful comments were given by Nay Htun, Sakiko Fukuda-Parr, Stephen Browne, Yannick Glemarec, Trine Lund-Jensen, Wang Yue, Shi Han, Zhu Min, Wang Xiaoping and participants in a UNDP seminar on an early draft of the Report in September 1997.

Susan Greenwell compiled the bibliography and served as a liaison among members of the preparation team. Justin Yifu Lin, Cai Fang and Li Zhou kindly made available an early version of their research on regional disparities in China. Invaluable early help in planning the Report was received from Alan Brody, Moez Doraid, Stephen J. McGurk, and Terry McKinley.

The human development record in China begins with the overwhelming reality of a nation of 1.23 billion people struggling to build a modern economy and society with a scarcity of the most basic resources, land and water. These are handicaps that people who live in an entirely different environment can hardly begin to appreciate. Yet, through the extraordinary ingenuity, resourcefulness and diligence of its own people, China has made remarkable progress in overcoming these obstacles and achieving modernization despite them. Without substantial progress in human development, it is unimaginable that China could have already accomplished the economic growth that it has. Its Human Development Index rank of 108 out of 175 countries (Human Development Report, 1997, based on 1994 data) is three places higher than its rank with respect to GDP per capita, and puts it firmly in the "medium human development" category.

Yet its especially challenging conditions as well as its unique history and culture dictate that China will modernize differently, with "Chinese characteristics". In this respect it will be no different than the early comers to development, each of which had to find a modernization path that fit its conditions.

China's big successes in human development begin with completion of the demographic transition from a high fertility, high mortality state to one of low fertility and mortality, an accomplishment of great import for the world's most populous nation. Most basically for human development, China's vital statistics approach the levels of highly developed countries. Life expectancy at birth of the average Chinese now exceeds 70 years, according to official statistics. Much of the population has passed through the first health revolution, is relatively free of the scourge of infectious diseases, and now faces the "second health revolution" of taming the non-communicable and chronic diseases that are the main causes of mortality in economically advanced countries. Many basic health indicators have improved well beyond the global average. Diet and nutritional status have likewise improved and malnutrition receded. The first capability people must have, that of living a long and healthy life, has been basically realized for most of the population.

Moreover, the population that is living longer and healthier is also smarter. With a school population of over 230 million students, China has the most educated and literate population in its history. The illiteracy rate has been reduced to 12 percent (or 16.5 percent of the adult population). Only in the enrollment rates at college level and above has China lagged somewhat behind some other developing countries. Thus, an increasingly long-lived population is also increasingly empowered by learning.

Although "women hold up half the sky" in China as elsewhere, the importance of the female half of the population has not always received the attention due it. Yet Chinese women have made great advances in recent decades. Their life expectancy (officially put at 73 years) considerably exceeds that of men; and, although their educational level on average lags behind men's, it has continued to advance. Women are economically and socially active in virtually all fields of endeavor. In the state sector, they have been recipients of generous labour protection laws, including maternity leave. China espouses the principle of equal pay for equal work. In practice, pay differentials between men and women exist, although they are small relative to many other countries, both developed and developing.

Many extraordinary changes have occurred in China since the transition to a market economy began almost two decades ago. These changes have resulted in a much wider distribution of initiative and greater autonomy for families and individuals than during the era of central planning (a misnomer in some respects, since the central planning practiced in China was notoriously weak and defensive). People have access to a much broader array of information from all over the world and are incomparably freer in their everyday lives. The opening of space for greater participation in decisions affecting their lives, which is central to the empowerment of people envisaged by the concept of human development, is still at an early stage in China. Further progress in this regard would reinforce the other positive developments in the political-economic landscape.

Thus, on balance the Chinese people have made remarkable progress in human development, especially given the fundamental handicaps of their size and resource limits. Not only the Chinese people but the people of the whole world benefit from the progress made by one-fifth of their number. In the long-run, international political tensions as well as global environmental stresses can be successfully addressed only by a healthy, prosperous and educated people.

China's successes to date are a source of confidence that the big obstacles to further progress in human development can be overcome. That there are such obstacles cannot be doubted. These are posed by the fragile and over-burdened environment, by the legacy of poverty, by the sheer numbers of people who must be fed and productively employed, by the centrifugal forces set in motion by economic reform, and by the difficulty of formulating policies and strategies to deal with the enormously varied conditions of the nation as a whole.

The transition to a market economy has occasioned major institutional upheaval. In the pre-reform era, a set of collective institutions in the countryside and public enterprises in the cities provided the population with a large measure of security and education in a surplus labour, low income environment. This was reflected in the relatively long life and high literacy rate achieved for the population by the mid-1970s. But those institutions have all been dissolving to one degree or another as China steps off the familiar shore of planning and collectivism into the unfamiliar ocean of the market economy. In comparison with many other transition economies, China's transition has been cautious and partial. Its maintenance of a high growth environment has minimized social dislocation by providing jobs and income while many of the former security institutions were being withdrawn.

High growth, especially of personal incomes, has been unevenly distributed over the country, however. In much of rural China, income grew very slowly from the mid-1980s until the early 1990s. Meanwhile, rural families found that their health care and the education of their children were requiring more and more out-of-pocket expenditures. The poorer among them often could not afford to send their children to school. Girls in particular have suffered in this regard; attendance and completion rates among rural girls, especially in poorer regions, are well below those of boys. Poor families have also experienced difficulty getting basic preventive health services, as well as pre-natal, maternity and post-natal care. Under these circumstances it is very difficult to overcome the great regional disparities in the health and educational status of children, the key to their regions' future.

While much of China has completed the "first health revolution" of virtually eliminating mortality from infectious disease, large parts of the countryside continue to be burdened with malnutrition, high infant and maternal mortality rates, and victimization by infectious and endemic diseases. There is a clear need for the rural health program to return to a preventive care orientation and to build an appropriate modern version of the cooperative health care and insurance network that did so much to protect the rural population before de-collectivization.

The uneven distribution of the benefits of reform manifested itself in rapidly increasing inequality along several dimensions. Overall inequality in China, as expressed in the Gini coefficient of the national income distribution, rose unusually rapidly in comparison with international experience, and attained a relatively high level (between 0.42 and 0.45). Inter-provincial differences widened quickly, as did broader regional differences, especially between the advanced east coastal provinces and the economically less developed west of China. An already substantial urban-rural gap widened even more during the transition period, although this trend has been offset somewhat by the decline in urban subsidies, which constituted a large share of urban income in the mid-1980s. And within both the rural and urban sectors individually, inequality has grown.

Viewing inter-regional inequality from the perspective of the Human Development Index yields additional insights. By and large, in China, human development is correlated quite closely with economic development as represented by GDP per capita. Therefore, overcoming regional polarization in human development will require finding ways to make economic advance more widespread. However, there is some divergence of provincial HDI ranking from that of GDP per capita: a few provinces, most of them poor, such as Ningxia, Tibet, Jiangxi and, especially, Qinghai, fall even farther behind the average in human development than in per capita GDP, whereas others -Shanxi, Hunan, Sichuan - do better in human development than in GDP. This divergence between GDP and HDI suggests that opportunities exist for translating low income into better human development outcomes in poor western regions.

The increasing role of market forces inevitably caused some kinds of inequality to widen. In addition, some development strategies, such as the mid-1980s shift in emphasis away from agriculture and the rural economy and toward the coastal regions and industry, also inadvertently widened inequalities. One result was that rural incomes stagnated until the early 1990s, even while GDP per capita continued to grow. It was in this context that the decline in poverty, which has been concentrated in the countryside, slowed. Since poverty incidence depends upon family income rather than GDP, when the two diverge, as in recent years, it is the former that is the relevant factor. When China's high growth has reached farm incomes, as in the early 1980s and the years since 1992, poverty incidence declined. When it has not, poverty has persisted. This experience should inform poverty alleviation strategy in future years. The Chinese government is certainly right to emphasize the importance of agriculture for general macroeconomic health, avoiding polarization and fighting poverty. The acceleration of farm income growth in 1992 was owed in large part to the government's decision to increase grain prices. The above example is but one case illustrating the strong influence of macroeconomic events, strategies and policies upon poverty, an influence that often exceeds that of the poverty alleviation programme itself.

China's poverty alleviation programme has gathered momentum since its establishment in the mid-1980s. The National 8-7 Plan announced in 1994 constitutes a commitment, rare among the world's nations, to basically eliminate absolute poverty by the end of the century. Increasing amounts of resources are being thrown into this effort, the seriousness of which is clear. In addition to the central government, provinces, localities and the general public are all joining the effort to lift poor areas out of poverty. The "twinning" of rich and poor cities, localities and enterprises, by which the better off help the less well off, has been spreading throughout the country.

There is some evidence, however, that the program's exclusive focus upon poor counties, rather than poor people, has led to the neglect of numbers of poor living outside the designated poor counties. The national 8-7 programme specifically stipulates that PA plans "reach poor households and bring benefits to them" and the search should continue for ways of accomplishing this goal, wherever the poor are located. With the transition to a more market-oriented economy and society, population mobility is increasing and local population homogeneity decreasing. New kinds of poverty are cropping up, including in the towns and cities, which entirely escape the purview of the PA programme, although they are to some extent addressed by new unemployment relief and other social welfare program's.

Within the poor areas, the focus has been upon economic and infrastructure development; there has been little information about the effects of such projects on the lives of poor families themselves. The central PA agency has not had the authority to draw up and implement comprehensive, multi-dimensional program's that simultaneously address the economic, infrastructure and human resource needs of the poor households. Recidivism remains a problem. There is thus room for further improving China's approach to poverty elimination, as well as incorporating the anti-poverty dimension in broader economic strategy.

In October 1996, the Central Committee of the Communist Party and the State Council convened the highest level meeting ever held in China on eliminating poverty. The meeting, which signaled China's continuing strong commitment to the 8-7 Plan and its goal of eliminating absolute poverty, addressed some of the problems encountered by the poverty alleviation programme in the past. From this meeting came decisions substantially increasing the resources to be devoted to poverty elimination and improving the program's focus.

Among the new kinds of poverty alluded to above is urban poverty, a relatively new phenomenon. Most of it is associated with growing unemployment, due both to anti-inflationary macro-economic policies and to the difficulties of the state operated enterprises which have been undergoing reform. In a market-determined environment, the state enterprises can no longer keep the large corps of surplus workers that they carried as part of the old income maintenance regime. Moreover, the demand-driven structural readjustments that are part of a market environment give rise to layoffs of workers in shrinking industries. Women, in particular, have furnished a disproportionately large proportion of the layoffs. The challenge for China is to build the institutions that must back up full labour mobility, such as a complete social safety net substitute for the old enterprise-based one, as well as training and job placement units that can promote the re-employment of increasing numbers of workers laid off by state enterprises. While some progress has been made on both counts, the discussion in this report makes clear that many hard questions remain to be resolved.

Perhaps most fundamental among these in the long run is the issue of the rigid urban-rural divide that has characterized China. Two different societies with two different institutional set-ups have existed under the same national roof. Of the two, the urban society has enjoyed privileges that could be maintained only under the divided regime. With the spread of markets and the rapid increase in population mobility, including tens of millions of rural-urban migrants taking jobs in the towns, this wall is crumbling. City dwellers and rural labourers will increasingly compete in the same job markets and live side by side. The inequity of providing social services and insurance to one sub-set of this population while denying it to their neighbors is likely to become increasingly apparent. And the spread of market relations will also make it less and less feasible, as capital flows from high-cost to low-cost areas.

Thus, in re-designing its social security set-up, China will have to come to grips with the increasing futility of maintaining the walls between city and countryside and between migrants and formal residents. This is apt to mean gradually supplementing the family-based social welfare system of the countryside with social security and social insurance in various forms. Such a development would also be conducive to further lowering the rural fertility rate by providing a social alternative to the still-essential role of the son as provider of security in old age, and by lowering the opportunity cost of women's education and participation in the labour force. Finally, erosion of the rural-urban divide would enhance overall social integration of the population, which would be consistent with the increasing empowerment of people to utilize their growing capabilities constructively and democratically.

As China proceeds with the difficult process of reforming state owned enterprises, it is crucial that viable social insurance systems be built to relieve the SOEs of their social insurance responsibilities and to cope with the problems of unemployment and the aging of the working population. There is an urgent need for rapid completion of a new unified pension system embodying pay-out rates and retirements ages that are viable in the long run, and based upon a combination of mandatory contributions from employers and workers, supplemented by voluntary worker savings. In the shorter run, a crucial issue is to make adequate arrangements for financing growing pension obligations during the transition from the current system to the new one. In the longer run, the system must be prepared financially to handle the growing retirement burden of an aging population.

China, which has done so well in overcoming its poverty and advancing the human development of its people under adverse circumstances, thus faces a full agenda of policy issues for continuing that progress. None of these issues will be easy to address; each involves costs and benefits, and the solution to each will redistribute both costs and benefits over large portions of the population. One of the most economically dynamic countries in its region, China is faced with the task of continuing the upward momentum while maintaining social and economic integration, spreading the gains of reform more widely over its immense and diverse population, and preserving the fragile natural environment. Human development in the broadest sense thus now depends upon both reinforcing China's orientation toward equity, community and environment, and at the same time continuing to mobilize the immense energies and talents of its people.

CHAPTER I

The Concept & Measurement of Human Development

Introduction. This first Human Development Report for China aims to do three things: first, give a comprehensive account of the status of human development in the world's largest country; second, to explain how that status has come about by reference to the particular conditions of China, and to the development strategies and policies followed by the government over the years since the People's Republic was established in 1949, and especially since the transition from central planning to a market economy began in the late 1970s; and third, to examine in some detail the issue of poverty, the theme of this year's global Human Development Report, as it pertains to China. This opening chapter briefly discusses the concept of human development and of ways of measuring it. Chapter II presents a historical overview of the achievements and problems in human development during the first three decades of the PRC, before the transition to a market economy began. Chapter III looks at the interactions between human development and that transition over the almost two decades during which it has been in progress. The question of poverty and its alleviation gets separate attention in Chapter IV, but is also integrated into the discussion of other outstanding human development issues. A brief final chapter draws conclusions about the outstanding human development challenges facing China today.

 ## What is Human Development?

1.1. Human Development and Economic Growth. The concept of human development was developed in order to focus attention upon the impact of economic change on human capabilities, such as the capability of living a long life (life expectancy at birth), enjoying good health, and acquiring knowledge, in addition to having the ability to obtain goods and services in general. Human development is concerned with the conditions of life of the entire population, not just the statistical average citizen, and therefore is sensitive to matters of income distribution, poverty, and the situations of women and of minorities.

The term "human development" is not commonly used in China. The preferred term is "social development", which is understood as the end in improved popular well-being for which economic development is the means. In practice, and in the range of issues included under their auspices, the two terms are very similar in meaning, except that "social development" perhaps connotes a greater emphasis on the well-being of the community and "human development" on the capabilities of the individual.

If economic growth always brought human development as defined above in its wake, there would have been no need to invent the latter term, and to have devised methods for measuring it. However, decades of experience with economic development since the end of World War II have shown that economic growth and human development can follow divergent paths. There is of course a longrun correlation between the two, in that the populations of highly industrialized countries generally enjoy higher human development status than do the populations of low-income developing countries. Even that generalization needs qualification, however, to account for the fact that many residents of inner cities in the U.S. have lower HD status than, say, the residents of Shanghai or of the Indian state of Kerala. In the short and medium run, moreover, the post-war world has seen a wide variety of relations between economic growth and human development. This is shown by the fact that international rankings of countries by GDP per capita differ substantially from rankings by Human Development Index (HDI, see below). In 1994, for example, Singapore's Human Development rank of 26 was fifteen places lower than its rank in terms of real GDP per capita, whereas Vietnam's HD rank of 121 was twenty-six places above its per capita GDP rank. It turns out that the degree to which growth is -- or is not -- translated into advances in human development depends greatly upon the way development is undertaken -- general strategies of development -- as well as upon government policies toward, inter alia, income distribution, health and education, gender equality, national minorities and the environment.

China's 1994 rankings by HDI and GDP per capita are fairly close: its HDI rank of 108 is three places above its rank by GDP per capita. Ten years ago the gap was much greater -- i.e., China's relative accomplishments in human development were much farther ahead of its economic growth status, and China's rank in the HDI list was higher. There are several reasons for the change. First and foremost, a number of middle income countries with middle human development status, which were formerly part of the Soviet Union, entered the list during the intervening years. These have pushed China's rank lower. Also, China's very rapid economic growth since its reform period began in 1978 has forged ahead of the growth in other components of the HDI, such as life expectancy and school enrollment rates. These indicators, which were already quite high at the beginning of this period, have continued to rise, but at rates well below that of income.

1.2. Human Development and Human Resource Development. It is generally recognized that the levels of health, education and skills of the population are major determinants of economic growth. Those countries that have grown fastest in the post-war period, such as Japan and South Korea, have done so in part because of the resources they put into human capital development. However, the concept of human capital or human resources treats people as inputs into a production function whose outputs are goods and services. In contrast, the concept of human development treats people as the output and organizes our view of the development process to focus on its impact on human beings.

1.3. Human Development, Welfare and Human Capabilities. There is a clear relation between human development and human welfare, or well-being. A population with high human development status will also enjoy a high level of well-being. But the converse is not necessarily true. The difference has to do with the agent of change. Welfare or well-being concerns a population's attainment of some objective status, such as the achievement of basic needs. It is possible to imagine a benevolent slave society with a high level of well-being thus defined, i.e., in which the slaves are well-fed, well-housed and receive good medical care and some education. In contrast, human development implies that people are free to employ their talents as they decide. Such an objective requires not only

China's 1994 HDI rank is three places above its rank by GDP per capita. Ten years ago, the gap was much greater.

that people be able to live long and healthy lives and educate themselves fully, but also that their society provides them with sufficient space for full participation in its social, economic and political life. This participatory quality of human development, which sees empowerment of people as a fundamental value, distinguishes it from such concepts as basic needs or human welfare, and focuses attention on prejudice, discrimination or political restraints that interfere with the full development and exercise of human capabilities.

② *Measuring Human Development*

2.1. The Human Development Index. The Human Development Index (HDI) was developed by the United Nations Development Programme to provide a relatively simple measure of human development status, using data that are available for most countries. It consists of a simple average of three measures: income, longevity and education. Income is measured by a purchasing power parity (PPP) estimate of real GDP per capita. Longevity is life expectancy at birth. Education is measured by a weighted average of the adult literacy rate (two-thirds weight) and combined school enrollment rates at primary, secondary and tertiary levels (one-third weight). For each variable, the actual value used is the distance traveled from a specific international minimum value toward a specific international maximum value, as a percentage of the entire distance from minimum to maximum. The minimum and maximum values established for each indicator is as follows:[1]

---

[1] See UNDP, Human Development Report, 1997, Technical note 2, for a detailed discussion of the derivation of the Human Development Index.

Real GDP per capita ($PPP): $100 and $40,000

Life expectancy at birth: 25 years and 85 years

Combined gross enrollment rates of 0% and 100%

However, in calculating the formula for HDI, real GDP per capita above the world average in 1994 (PPP$5,835) is discounted increasingly heavily as it rises, to reflect the diminishing marginal utility of income. China's GDP per capita in 1994 of PPP$2,604 was below this threshold, and thus not subject to discounting. Among the provinces only Shanghai's per capita GDP was higher than the 1994 international average, and thus had to be adjusted.

Table 1.1. Human Development Index by Province in 1995

Province rank	HDI rank	GDP rank	Life expectancy index	Education index	GDP index	Human development index (HDI) value
Shanghai	1	1	0.84	0.85	0.969	0.885
Beijing	2	2	0.81	0.86	0.960	0.876
Tianjin	3	3	0.80	0.83	0.954	0.859
Guangdong	4	4	0.80	0.79	0.850	0.814
Zhejiang	5	5	0.79	0.75	0.814	0.785
Jiangsu	6	6	0.79	0.77	0.724	0.760
Liaoning	7	8	0.76	0.80	0.708	0.756
Fujian	8	7	0.76	0.72	0.709	0.729
Shandong	9	9	0.77	0.74	0.604	0.704
Heilongjiang	10	10	0.72	0.78	0.526	0.676
Hainan	11	11	0.79	0.75	0.488	0.674
Hebei	12	12	0.78	0.77	0.464	0.670
Jilin	13	13	0.72	0.80	0.451	0.659
Shanxi	14	17	0.74	0.79	0.352	0.627
Xinjiang	15	14	0.67	0.75	0.438	0.619
Henan	16	16	0.75	0.74	0.358	0.618
Hubei	17	15	0.71	0.73	0.388	0.609
Guangxi	18	18	0.74	0.75	0.332	0.605
Anhui	19	19	0.75	0.72	0.328	0.600
Hunan	20	23	0.71	0.75	0.320	0.592
Sichuan	21	24	0.70	0.74	0.308	0.582
Inner Mongolia	22	25	0.70	0.74	0.296	0.578
Jiangxi	23	20	0.70	0.73	0.327	0.577
Ningxia	24	22	0.72	0.67	0.323	0.571
Shaanxi*	25	27	0.72	0.73	0.259	0.570
Yunnan	26	26	0.65	0.64	0.289	0.526
Gansu	27	29	0.71	0.62	0.216	0.514
Qinghai	28	21	0.61	0.57	0.326	0.503
Guizhou	29	30	0.67	0.64	0.172	0.494
Tibet	30	28	0.58	0.36	0.226	0.391

Sources: (1) Lu Lei, Hao Hongsheng and Gao Ling "Table of Provincial Life-expectancy in China in 1990", Population Studies in Chinese, May 1994. (2) SSB, China Regional Economy: A Profile of 17 Years of Reform and Opening-Up, China Statistical Press, 1996. (3) Data of National 1% Population Survey 1995, China Statistical Press 1997. (4) China Education Commission, Statistical Yearbook of China Education 1995, Press of People's Education, 1996. (5) China Population Yearbook 1996.

Notes: (1) GDP per capita is in 1990 prices. (2) Provincial price indices used for adjustment of GDP per capita are those of retail prices. (3) Life expectancy index is based on figures of provincial life expectancy in 1990. Since life expectancy changes very slowly, this should have little impact on the HDI estimates.

* The formally correct romanization of the name of this province is "Shanxi". The variant "Shaanxi" is commonly used outside of China to distinguish this province from its eastern neighbor, "Shanxi". In Chinese, the two names are distinguished by different tonal pronunciations and different written characters.

In this Report, Human Development Index numbers are presented for the first time for all of the provinces of China (see Table 1.1) for the year 1995. As can be seen, among China's 30 provinces and province-level regions,[2] there is considerable variation in human development level, whose explanation must involve many factors, including historical, geographic and cultural ones. The HDI value of the top-ranking province (Shanghai) more than doubles that of the bottom-ranking one (Tibet). It is also apparent that, while HDI and GDP are clearly correlated, there are some fairly large departures from that correlation, the most conspicuous example being Qinghai, whose HDI rank is eight places lower than its per capita GDP rank. In Chapter III (sec. 4.4) the provincial HDI rankings serve as one basis of an analysis of regional disparities in human development.

2.2. Broader Composition of Human Development: The Gender-related Development Index, Gender Empowerment Measure and Human Poverty Index.

The HDI is a relatively narrow measure of human development, which attempts to capture the most crucial aspects of it in a way that permits easy measurement and international (or inter-regional) comparability. It leaves out many important aspects, including those stressed above of empowerment of the population to participate fully in social, political and economic life. The components measured by the HDI are perhaps necessary conditions for such empowerment and participation, but they are not sufficient in themselves.

For instance, the HDI does not encompass the concept of sustainability. Because the HDI attempts to measure the average HD status of individuals at a given point in time, it would be difficult to build into it an indicator of environmental status, even though this is an important determinant of the longterm sustainability of income, health and general well-being. In some respects the HDI contradicts the principle of sustainability. For instance, growth in one of its components - GDP per capita - causes HDI to increase even if the GDP growth comes from environmentally destructive practices. Thus, deforestation will raise GDP and therefore HDI, as will intensive farming methods that destroy soil quality. Both happen to be acute issues in China, as they are elsewhere in the world.

China's GDI number in 1994 had a global rank of 90 among the 146 countries for which the GDI was calculated.

China's GEM rank is 26 out of 94 countries for which the GEM was calculated.

The same general problem attends the standard treatment of growing social costs as increments to GDP. For instance, the growing incidence of traffic accidents in cities raises GDP by the cost of medical care, burials, and police investigations that they entail. This in turn raises HDI.

The ways in which the income and longevity components of HDI are distributed over the population are also not captured by the averages used in the index. The degree of gender equality or inequality is left out, as is the question of discrimination against minority populations. Thus, a full discussion of human development requires that the HDI be supplemented by consideration of poverty and poverty alleviation efforts, of income distribution, of gender equality, and of environmental degradation and protection.

The global Human Development Report has created specific indices to measure progress in some of the dimensions omitted from the HDI. For instance, a Gender-related Development Index (GDI) uses the same variables as the HDI, but adjusts each variable for the disparity in achievement between men and women.[3] China's GDI number in 1994 (presented in the 1997 HDR, p. 150) had a global rank of 90 among the 146 countries for which the GDI was calculated. This is three ranks above China's HDI position among the same 146 countries.

Still another measure, the Gender Empowerment Measure (GEM), aims to measure the relative empowerment of women and men in political and economic spheres of activity. It makes use of the following variables: the percentage shares of women and men among parliamentary representatives, administrative and managerial personnel, and in professional and technical positions; and the percentage shares of earned income received by women and men.[4] In the 1997 global HDR (p. 41), the GEM is estimated for 94 countries. China's

---

[2] Taiwan, Hong Kong and Macao are not included in the HDI ranking of China's administrative regions.

[3] See Human Development Report for 1995, Technical Note 1, for a detailed discussion of the method of computing the GDI.

rank is 26, far above its HDI rank (among the same 94 countries) of 63, and above Japan, Israel and France.

In the 1997 global HDR a new index was presented for measuring poverty: the Human Poverty Index. The HPI measures "deprivation in three elements of human life already reflected in the HDI - longevity, knowledge and a decent standard of living" (HDR, 1997, p. 125). Deprivation of longevity is measured by the percentage of the population not expected to survive to age 40, deprivation of knowledge by the adult illiteracy rate, and deprivation in living standards by a composite of three variables-the percentages of people without access to safe drinking water and without access to health services, and the percentage of moderately and severely underweight children below the age of five.[5]

The HPI was estimated for 78 developing countries having the requisite data (1997 global HDR, p. 21). China ranks 18th among these countries, eleven places higher than its HDI rank among the same 78 countries.

In the following chapters of this national Human Development Report the issues of gender and poverty in China are given full discussion, despite the fact that gaps in available data prevent the calculation of regional estimates of the GDI, GEM or HPI.

2.3. Special Concerns of China.

The issues concerning Human Development that loom large at any given time in a particular country necessarily reflect that country's specific history and conditions. China's specific conditions include the world's largest population, numbering over 1.23 billion people, living on a limited amount of arable land and with very scarce fresh water resources. China in 1997 is heir to serious problems of pollution of air, water and land. It finds itself in the middle of a lengthy and complex transition from a centrally planned, state-dominated economic system to a mixed economy in which the market plays the major role in the allocation of resources. In the course of that transition,

China has achieved very rapid economic growth and with it widespread improvements in living standards. However, inherited regional imbalances have also worsened, huge temporary migrations have occurred, and the former social security arrangements of the urban population are having to be replaced by new institutions, as yet incomplete. These issues, so important to China's human development status at present, are given extended treatment in the chapters that follow.

2.4. Poverty.

In particular, special attention is given to the issue of poverty in China and the efforts to eliminate it. This reflects a convergence of emphasis between the global Human Development Report, of which the 1997 theme is poverty eradication, and a national effort that began in 1995 to eliminate the most abject poverty in China by the end of the century. Chapter IV of this report is devoted to a comprehensive account of the problem of poverty in China and of the efforts to solve it. In addition, however, each of the other sections gives substantial attention to the relevance of its particular topic to the problem of poverty alleviation. Thus, to take one example, the discussion of health focuses especially on the health needs and problems of the poor population in the context of China's transition.

However, this Report is not limited to a discussion of poverty and poverty alleviation in China. Because this is the first national Human Development Report undertaken for China, the authors have attempted to make it a comprehensive introduction to the state of human development there, analyzing as fully as possible China's accomplishments as well as the outstanding problems still faced. The discussion of poverty and poverty alleviation is placed in the context of this comprehensive discussion. ¡

China in 1997 is heir to serious problems of pollution of air, water and land.

---

[4] Technical Note 2 of the 1997 Human Develpment Report contains a detailed discussion of the method ov computing the GEM.

[5] Technical notes 1 and 2 of the 1997 Human Development Report provide detailed discussion of the HPI and its properties.

Historical Overview of Human Development in China

The first three decades of the People's Republic of China after its establishment in 1949 were marked by repeated campaigns of economic construction and of class struggle

The first three decades of the People's Republic of China after its establishment in 1949 were marked by repeated campaigns of economic construction and of class struggle, and by the virtual disappearance of private ownership of productive resources. Industry was organized entirely under state or collective ownership, while all farmers were brought into producer collectives in a series of convulsive campaigns ending with the formation of rural people's communes in the late 1950s. Most markets were eliminated and production was coordinated by central and provincial planning that was repeatedly disrupted by political campaigns. Planning in China thus remained quite crude and never advanced even to the level of proficiency achieved in the former Soviet Union and some East European countries. Nevertheless, measured growth of GDP was quite rapid over the three decades as a whole, averaging perhaps 6-7 percent per year. However, the economy fluctuated widely around this trend, with strong upswings alternating with periods of stagnation and even depression, as in the "three hard years" (1959-61) that ended the "great leap forward" (1958-60) and saw a famine of major proportions in much of rural China.

There are several things that can be said of the human development implications of economic growth during those three decades. First, the growth that occurred included increases in public consumption that translated into major improvements in the health, nutrition and literacy of the Chinese people; the status of Chinese women also greatly increased as a result of strong public commitment (see below). Second, a very large portion of that growth was devoted to continuous development of heavy industries, and progress was made in creating a heavy industrial base. Major advances produced by China's skilled and dedicated scientists and technicians also date from that period.

Third, the private consumption needs of the people - including the most basic ones, such as food and shelter - got little attention. This was due to the pattern of allocation of investment, which emphasized heavy industry and public consumption and neglected agriculture and consumer goods industries, as well as to agricultural policies that discouraged specialization in accordance with regional comparative advantage and deadened incentives to increase production. As a result, by the end of the period in the late 1970s, the food consumption standard of much of the population was no better than the meager standard of the mid-1950s, and the per capita housing space available to the urban population was lower than it had been twenty-five years earlier.

Fourth, the weak planning mechanism and the lack of markets caused much of the growth to be wasted in the production of goods for which there was no demand. Finally, the restriction of population movement and the narrowing of public discussion to the expression of approved points of view limited people's ability to participate fully in the social and political arenas.

Population

Some anti-natalist measures were taken by the Government in certain areas of the country as early as 1950 when it was realized that rapid growth of the population would hamper socio-economic development of the country. However, these measures went into abeyance after the mid-1950s when they appeared to conflict with the labour-intensive orientation promoted by Mao Zedong for the "great leap forward". Not until the early 1970s was a nationwide government-sponsored family planning program launched in the country, and it was in 1979 that the well-known anti-natalist policy came into being.

At the foundation of the People's Republic of China, due to the backward economy and chaos caused by wars, medical services were inadequate for most people, public health conditions were very poor and nutritional standards very low. China was then in the initial stage of population transition -- high mortality, higher fertility and high natural growth rate. In 1950, the crude death rate (CDR) was 18% the crude birth rate (CBR) 37% and the natural growth rate 19% From then until the beginning of the 1970s, the death rate declined steadily but the birth rate remained high, except for the demographic crisis that occurred during the famine of the late 1950s and early 1960s, when the death rate rose sharply and the birth rate dropped precipitously (see Figure 2.1.).

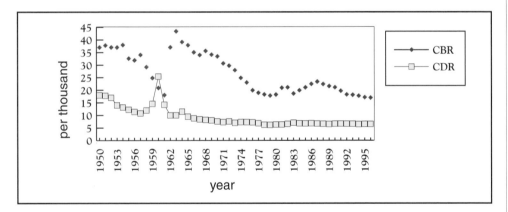

Figure 2.1. Crude Birth and Death Rates, 1950-1996
Source: Cai Fang, 1997

In 1970 the total fertility rate was still close to 5. With the recommencement of emphasis on family planning in the early 1970s, however, it fell steadily to below 3 by 1978 (see Figure 2.2.).

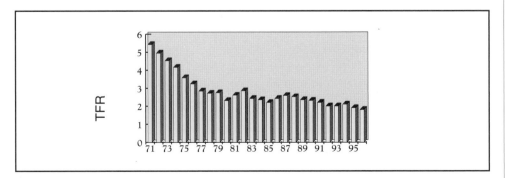

Figure 2.2. Total Fertility Rate, 1971-1996
Source: Cai Fang, 1997.

Health and Education

Since 1949, much of China has successfully gone through "the first health revolution". Many serious infectious and parasitological diseases were controlled and wiped out. Smallpox was eradicated in China in 1961, ten years earlier than in other countries. The average death rate dropped by 63 per cent between 1949 and 1978. At the foundation of the People's Republic, the average Chinese citizen could at birth expect to live only about 40 years. By 1975, life expectancy at birth had reached about 65 years (Table 2.1.). The number of health care providers, hospital beds and clinics all multiplied.

Table 2.1.: Infant Mortality and Life Expectancy, 1949-1975

Indicators	Years						
	1945-	1950-	1955-	1960-	1965-	1970-	1975-
Infant mortality	265.0	195.0	179.0	121.0	81.0	61.0	41.0
Life expectancy	30.5	40.8	44.6	49.5	59.6	63.2	65.8
Male	--	39.3	43.1	48.7	58.8	62.5	65.5
Female	--	42.3	46.2	50.4	60.4	63.9	66.2

Source: United Nations population database.

Before 1949, China's educational system was undeveloped. Over 80 percent of the country's population were illiterate and only about 20 percent of school-age children attended school. While ethnic minorities accounted for 6 percent of China's population, their children accounted for only 2.2 percent of the total number of primary school pupils. The geographical distribution of schools in China was also greatly uneven.

Immediately after the founding of the People's Republic, the Government set up a Ministry of Education to exert centralized management of education. It began to reform the old educational system in an effort to raise the overall cultural level and train the technical personnel so badly needed for national reconstruction. As a matter of policy, it was required that education should disseminate knowledge of science, be targeted to the general population, particularly workers and farmers, and should meet the needs of production.

In accordance with the above policy, regularized primary, secondary and higher education systems were developed, along with spare time literacy and technical training programs. Special emphasis was laid on providing educational opportunities to disadvantaged groups. For instance, the unbalanced geographical distribution of schools was attacked and local school budgets were increased to speed up the development of education in the hinterland, in remote areas and in places inhabited by ethnic minorities. Scholarships were provided to students who were unable to pay for their schooling.

By 1956, the enrollment rate of school-age children in China had risen to 63 percent, and the number of ethnic minority primary school students had gone up to 5 percent of the national total. However, owing to the high dropout rate among primary and middle school students and to the unsound approach taken in conducting literacy campaigns, 78 percent of China's population remained illiterate.

The Second Five-Year Plan period began in 1958. To speed up the development of education, the Government pursued an educational policy known as "walking on two legs". This policy encouraged local governments and the general public, as well as the central government, to run schools. Equal emphasis was placed on government-run schools and on those run by the public; on both basic and vocational education; on education of school-age children and on adult education; on both full-time and part-time schools; on formal education as well as self study; and on both free schooling and that requiring tuition.

At the same time, however, China's education began to be influenced by repeated political campaigns, which disrupted normal schooling and lowered educational quality. The "Cultural Revolution", launched between 1966-1976, adopted an ideology of denigrating formal learning. The literacy campaign came to a halt and illiteracy increased (World Bank 1983, p. 135); schools were shut down for long periods of time; college enrollment was suspended for four years. The closing of a large number of vocational schools weakened secondary education. All this led to deterioration in education and an acute shortage in well trained workers. The gap in education between China and the advanced countries, which had begun to narrow, widened again.

In short, between 1949 and 1978, education in China at first made considerable progress but then was compromised by the impact of the repeated political campaigns to which it was subjected. Relative normalcy returned to education only in 1977 and 1978. Yet between 1949 and 1978 as a whole, the number of teachers and of schools had multiplied and the primary school enrollment rate rose from only one in four school-aged children to over 90 per cent.

Table 2.2. Health & Education Resources, 1949 and 1978

	1949	1978	Percent change
Doctors per 1000 population	0.67	1.07	60.00
Nurses (1,000)	33.00	407.00	1133.00
Hospital beds per 1000 pop	0.15	1.93	1187.00
Number of hospitals	2600.00	64,421.00	2378.00
Number of health clinics	769.00	94,395.00	12175.00
Death rate (per thousand)*	17.00	6.25	-63.00
Primary school teachers (mills)*	1.44	5.23	263.00
Secondary school teachers (mills)*	0.13	3.28	2423.00
Primary school enrollment (mills)*	51.10	146.20	186.00
Primary enrollment as percent of age cohort (%)	25.00	94.00	276.00
Secondary school enrollment (mills)*	3.15	66.37	2007.00
No. of primary schools*	526,964.00	1,093,317.00	107.00
No. of regular secondary schools	4,298.00	162,345.00	3677.00

Note: (*): first column is for 1952
Sources: State Statistical Bureau 1996; Pepper 1990

The State Statistical Bureau later estimated that some 250 million people, or 31 percent of the rural population, lacked adequate food and clothing in 1978.

These accomplishments in health and education are summarized in Table 2.2. They indicate that there was great progress in the most fundamental aspects of human development during the PRC's pre-reform years. This progress exceeded that of the growth in per capita incomes, judged in international comparative perspective. One reason was an effective if simple public finance system. The state mobilized resources by simply claiming all profits made by state enterprises, which, after the mid-1950s, totally dominated the nonagricultural economy. Prices were kept low for labour, food and raw materials, which allowed light industrial sectors, especially those producing nonessential consumer goods, to be very profitable. These sectors were used by the government as the main source of revenue.

This scheme, while providing no incentive for enterprises to seek profitability, did effectively control the surpluses that were produced, discourage consumption, favor investment and avoid the need for a costly tax administration. It siphoned resources from the rural economy, and therefore from the rural majority of the population, to support industrialization and defense, but also to finance the basic social development achievements listed above. China's budget was highly centralized, with the budgets of lower levels of government included in the national budget. The center determined the relationship between a locality's revenue and expenditures, and through most of the period, the center redistributed revenues from richer to poorer provinces. This was a principal reason for the higher relative growth rates of low-income regions and for their ability to finance social sector spending.[1]

At the same time, as already suggested, the two decades from the mid-1950s to the mid-1970s were a period of great political and economic instability. This was the period of collectivization, the "great leap forward", a major famine, and the "Cultural Revolution". One feature of the last was Mao Zedong's condemnation of urban bias in public health work, which led to a substantial redistribution of health care resources toward the countryside. Paramedical workers ("barefoot doctors") proliferated by the millions in rural areas along with a system of local basic clinics and cooperative insurance programs within the rural people's communes. With the exception of the famine years, health status and life expectancy on the whole improved during this period in spite of the turmoil, but education, as suggested above, was very seriously disrupted.

The social turmoil destroyed the effectiveness of the central planning system without actually dismantling it, but a network of schools, hospitals, and clinics survived, although their mode of operation changed and, in some cases, their geographical location as well. The ideology of the times was strongly egalitarian and income inequalities within villages and towns narrowed to an extraordinary extent. Yet a ban on population movement and the weakening of the capacity of central planners to redistribute grain and other resources over provincial lines led to widening regional and urban-rural inequalities. Slow agricultural growth and the suppression of markets allowed rural poverty to burgeon; the State Statistical Bureau later estimated that some 250 million people, or 31 percent of the rural population, lacked adequate food and clothing in 1978. Yet the emphasis given to putting health resources in the countryside also greatly increased the rural population's access to basic primary health care in the form of paramedical "barefoot doctors" and rural health clinics.

The result of these various trends were contradictory. On one hand, the rural population in particular remained very poor in terms of measured per capita income, and as many as 30 percent may have lacked adequate food and clothing. Average per capita food consumption had not improved since the 1950s, and the diet was spartan, based overwhelmingly on cereals. Housing conditions had if anything deteriorated since the 1950s in both quality and per capita availability; average per capita living space in urban areas in 1980 was only 3.9 square meters, and in some cities, such as Shanghai, it was considerably less than

---

[1] *The classic discussion of public finance in the pre-transition period is Lardy 1978.*

that.

On the other hand, this same population enjoyed high life expectancy and high levels of literacy for its income. Over these decades there were rapid increases in the average height of Chinese (World Bank 1984, p.20).[2] Life expectancy at birth of around 65 (in the mid-1970s) was made possible in part by a broad and publicly financed health policy making primary health care widely accessible, especially for mothers and children. Infant mortality had fallen steadily from 250/1000 in 1950 to between 40 and 50 per 1000 in 1980, according to the best estimates.[3] Thus, the level of the most basic human development, in the form of health and education, was quite high. Moreover, women had greatly improved their economic and social status in comparison with the pre-Communist past. The urban minority of the population enjoyed full job and income security, including generous health coverage and pensions. The rural majority had far less in the way of social welfare coverage, but even they were generally assured of some protection against the most extreme effects of illness, injury and other misfortunes through commune insurance schemes and the collective distribution system (see section 3 below). For instance, commune members could borrow grain from the collective, if necessary, and many did so indefinitely, never able to repay. Such security was obtained at the cost of personal freedom of movement (migration being prohibited) and stagnation of real incomes.

Yet, the population enjoyed high life expectancy and high levels of literacy for its income.

---

[2] *The combination of stagnant food intake with increasing anthropomorphic status is a puzzle that requires explanation. The World Bank (1984, p. 20) gives several possible explanations, including the possibility that improvements in health, especially reduction in diarrhea infections, improved the efficiency of a given nutrient intake.*

[3] *UNICEF (1995 pp. 21-22). Other studies have produced lower estimates. The ones cited in the text are UNICEF's best guess after taking into account the problem of under-reporting encountered by most surveys.*

Women's Status

The situation of Chinese women has undergone a sea change in this century. In the first decade, women were given the right to an education, although its aim was to produce "a good wife and loving mother (xianqi liangmu)"; in the second decade, feminist pioneers fought for the right of political participation; in the third decade, several women were for the first time elected as provincial government delegates, and a generation of "new women" grew up who were independent and freethinking. In early 20th century, women workers made up 35-45 percent of all workers[1], although this percentage often fluctuated during the eventful period of initial modernization of China.

With the founding of the People's Republic in 1949, women formally became entitled under law to equal rights in politics, economics and family affairs; and to equal pay for equal work. In the land reform of the early 1950s, woman farmers got their own land, a woman became vice chairperson in the central government, and women's school enrollment rates jumped significantly. Since then women have made inroads in all walks of life. The majority of female workers in urban areas enjoy 90 day's maternity leave with salary, and other forms of social protection and security. Women's lives on average last much longer, their educational levels are higher, their employment opportunities more numerous, and their role in public life more noticeable than in the past.

By 1978, women made up 43 percent of the labour force and 33 percent of "workers and staff" (essentially, nonagricultural employment). Women began to make progress in politics, as well: in the early 1950s, women comprised 22 percent of township representatives and 15 percent of county level representatives.[2] In

The situation of Chinese women has undergone a sea change in this century.

---

1 *Calculation from Encyclopedia of The Chinese Working Class, p.165.*

2 *The History of the Chinese Women's Movement, Northern Publishing House for Women and Children, 1989, p289.*

the First National People's Congress in1954, they made up 12 percent of deputies; and in 1956, among 756 thousand Agricultural Cooperatives, 70-80 percent had women as president or vice president. But the road has been uneven; in 1978, only one in twenty People's Communes had a woman leader.[3]

The waves of radical political mobilization that marked the first three decades of the People's Republic produced similar waves of progress and regress for women's social status. The more radical periods tended to emphasize gender equality and mobilize women to move into the social labour force and political activity. They also provided more opportunities for women to enter management levels in the Party and government. The less radical periods saw pressures mount for women to return to more traditional and supportive roles. But the picture is more complicated than this, because the more radical periods also severely limited social spheres and activities which had been sources of economic opportunity for women, such as markets, handicrafts, and family sidelines. And the enforced ideological uniformity that characterized much of the period put great restraints on the exercise of independent thought by women as well as men, in that fundamental way limiting the development of the capabilities of both.

---

[3] *Report of ACWF, 1979, p.10.*

Institutional Features of the Social Security System[1]

China's social security system is in the midst of a great change as the transition to a market economy has undermined the basis of the past system. Because this process concerns the social safety net of the population and thus has great relevance for human development status, we will devote some space to the features of the inherited system, and to the changes taking place.

Dominant values of the pre-reform era included social equality and the planned allocation and compensation of labour. The social security system before 1978 was very much oriented towards these social values, which had much to do with both the failures and achievements of the previous system.

4.1. The Urban-rural Divide.
The Chinese social security system was a dualistic one. It was characterized by institutional divisions between rural and urban areas, and between relief, social welfare and the social insurance systems. The last was implemented only in the urban public sector. By providing every one with a job in urban areas and to the use of land under the people's communes in rural areas, the system successfully placed most Chinese people under some form of protection until the onset of the economic reforms in 1979.

However, the institutional patterns and dominant principles of social provision differed between urban and rural areas. In urban areas, the main system was one of social insurance. Social relief and social services only played complementary roles. The state, usually acting through the residents' work units (danwei), took a disproportionately greater responsibility for social provision for urban residents than for rural inhabitants. In towns and cities, the functions of support for the elderly, traditionally borne by families and kinship networks, were largely transferred to employers and the state. In the countryside, however, there was almost no social insurance, with the exception of a cooperative health programme that was established in the 1960s and 1970s. The traditional family based protection system was dominant and a community based mutual help system protected people who lost such family support. The family bore the main responsibility for the aged in

---

[1] *This section relies on Shang 1997.*

terms of both financial support and caring duties.

The urban welfare system as a whole was a protected and privileged part of a wider dualistic divide based on a strongly enforced administrative distinction between 'urban' and 'rural' sectors. The rural population received far fewer welfare benefits per capita from the government and had to rely on the economic strength of their own communities and families in the context of collective provision through the people's commune system. From a national point of view, therefore, although the urban welfare system, organized around each resident's danwei, was impressive in its range of benefits, it covered only a small proportion of the population. In the late 1970s only about 18 percent of the total population and 23.7 percent of the total work force were classified as urban.

4.2. The Urban Social Insurance System.

The urban social insurance system was based on the public sector (state and collective) work unit and covered most of the urban work force. Welfare benefits were provided by individual enterprises or units to their own workers and functioned in effect as a social wage to compensate for stringent constraints on cash wages. On the surface there were no individual contributions. Social insurance benefits included pensions, health, work-injury, maternity, sick leave, hardship relief and subsidies for surviving dependents. The most fundamental benefit of all was job security - later called the 'iron rice-bowl' for manual workers and the 'iron armchair' for managerial staff.

The relationship between the state and enterprises was key. On the one hand, the state bore neither financial responsibility nor responsibility for actually providing security benefits to urban public employees. It only played the role of organizer and made policies and regulations. On the other hand, the state bore responsibility for any loss or profits made by the state enterprises. Enterprises enjoyed almost no autonomy from the state: wages and welfare standards were decided by the state, profits were taken by

it, and any financial responsibility enterprises bore would ultimately fall to it, as well. Thus, although the social insurance system was work unit based, it was actually government-administered, and the regulations, entitlements and benefit standards were unified across all of China. Employees could move from one enterprise to another without losing their entitlements as long as the job transfer went through formal administrative procedures.

4.3. The urban non-public sector.

The urban welfare system was dualistic because the relatively small proportion of the urban population that fell outside the unit-based system did not qualify for social insurance, but only for state social relief and welfare services, which were provided on a means-tested basis. Thus, this part of the population were forced to rely much more heavily on their own and their families' resources. Permanent state relief came only when all other collective or private arrangements had failed.

State social assistance was the prime responsibility of the Department of Civil Affairs and was mainly been targeted at the disabled, elderly, orphans and other hardship cases with neither work units to rely on nor relatives who could look after them. Assistance to the last category was based on the principle that state aid should be only supplementary to reliance on individual/family self-help. Relief funds were means-tested and kept at very low levels.

Another important category receiving social assistance more recently is the 'Five Guarantees Households', which were previously mainly confined to the rural areas. But during the reform era, along with changes in formal government arrangements, some rural regions have merged with urban areas, and the category has appeared in urban areas as well.

4.4. Main Forms of Social Assistance:

Social assistance for the above groups of urban residents has mainly taken two forms: centralized and dispersed provision. Centralized provision operates

Although the social insurance system was work unit based, it was actually government-administered.

through welfare institutions, including children's homes, old people's homes and special facilities for people with various forms of disability, including mental disorders. Dispersed provision means that services and financial help are provided in the home. This includes minimum income support (permanent or temporary), free health services, free rent, or water and electricity bill exemption, etc. It can also include help organized through neighbors or local 'volunteers' (such as 'learn from Leifeng teams'), but this varies considerably from place to place and is not always reliable.

The third method of provision, targeted specifically to assist disabled people, has been through special welfare factories (fuli qiye). Most of the disabled have retained some work capability and have thus been provided with work in welfare factories. This reflects the wider commitment of the government to encourage people to help themselves, in this case by helping those capable of working to find gainful employment.

4.5. Commune based collective social security system in rural areas. The institutional achievements of the rural social security system under the rural

people's communes had four main aspects. First, it guaranteed the rural population equal rights of access to land and farm work. Second, the 'Five Guarantees System' was originally based on the economic capability of the people's commune. This was the first system in Chinese history to provide systematic collective protection to vulnerable rural people, in particular the aged, orphans and the sick who were not capable of supporting themselves and who had no family to rely on. These people were given free food, fuel, clothes, health care and funeral services, hence the term 'Five Guarantees Households'. Thirdly, a collective health service system, making use of rudimentarily trained paramedics known as 'barefoot doctors', was established in the 1960s, which provided basic preventive and primary health care to the rural population. However, the system was unevenly applied throughout the countryside.

Thus, the pre-reform system of social security was able to furnish a measure of security, in varying degrees, to most people. Its erosion under the reforms, and the attempts to replace it with institutions more consistent with a market economy, are a major part of the contemporary human development story, and will be taken up in Chapter III.

 Environmental Degradation

During the first three decades of the PRC, the attention of leaders and population was focused on the problems of economic development and on various pressing domestic and international political issues. Protection of the natural environment was not recognized as a priority, and it received little attention in the public policy arena. As a result, there was little consideration of industrial structure, pricing and management issues from an environmental perspective.

Prior to 1978, the industrial structure closely followed the Soviet model, characterized by an emphasis on heavy industries. Natural resource prices were

kept very low as a means of maximizing the profits of state-owned enterprise profits, which constituted the principal source of state revenues. As a result, there was profligate use and consequent serious depletion of natural resources, growing pollution and lack of attention to creating environmental infrastructure, such as facilities for waste water treatment and solid waste disposal.

The natural environment suffered especially grievous losses during the "great leap forward" of the late 1950s, when the proliferation throughout the country of small iron and steel furnaces and small coal mines brought considerable destruction to land vegetation as well as widespread deforestation - a serious problem in a country that had already lost much of its original forest cover.

In agriculture, as well, a lack of environment-consciousness led to policies that were ecologically unsound. The heavy emphasis on achieving local self-sufficiency in grain production caused large areas of grasslands and hillsides to be plowed up and planted, which contributed to growing problems of soil erosion and desertification. During the "great leap forward", the construction of many poorly planned water projects on the North China Plain resulted in widespread salinization and alkalization of that crucial grain basket area, which seriously affected agriculture for years afterward. Yet not everything done in agriculture was environmentally unsound. China continued to stress age-old practices of nutrient recycling and use of organic and green manure that preserved the structure and organic content of the soil. This was not done for overtly environmental reasons but because, in the absence of a developed chemical fertilizer industry or access to the world market, it was the only way to provide the plant nutrients crucial to feeding China's expanding population. Yet, it had benign environmental consequences that have become increasingly apparent to Chinese farmers, planners and scientists as some of the untoward consequences of the later wholesale shift to chemical agriculture have made themselves felt.

 ## Conclusion

The first three decades of the People's Republic were a period of almost continuous change, characterized by repeated mass campaigns that brought both considerable industrialization and enormous institutional transformation to the country. In 1949, China was a nation of small family farmers and urban handicrafts, whose people had an average life expectancy of 40 years, and 80 percent of whom were illiterate. Thirty years later, the family farms had given way to some 70,000 rural people's communes, China had a substantial industrial base, nuclear weapons and earth satellites, life expectancy had reached 65 years and 80 percent of the people could read and write. But the turbulence had been very costly in lives, careers, basic liberties and peace of mind. A generation had lived through a major and largely man-made famine (1959-61) and repeated social conflict, culminating in the near civil war of the "Cultural Revolution". The country's ineffective central planning system, originally modeled on that of the Soviet Union, had been crippled by an ideology hostile to its basic technocratic principles. Production was wasteful, energy-inefficient, polluting and not oriented to demand. Independent expression was just beginning to be possible again after being severely curtailed for two decades by a rigidly enforced ideological orthodoxy.

In the starkest terms, human development had made great progress despite the turmoil. The Chinese people lived much longer, were much healthier, and were better educated. The urban population enjoyed economic security; the rural majority did not, but they had in the commune system a safety net stronger than any most had had access to in the past. Women's status and opportunities for education and employment had greatly improved. But many of these gains had occurred during the first decade of the PRC, and had then fluctuated back and forth during the chaotic second and third decades. And material consumption had hardly progressed at all. Food intake was at the meager level of the mid-1950s, per capita housing space had declined, trade and services in general had declined, people counted themselves lucky to own a wrist watch or a bicycle. There was a great deal of poverty in the countryside, some of it produced artificially by the government's eradication of markets and insistence on local foodgrain self-sufficiency. The challenge before China was to preserve the considerable progress in human development achieved by the previous system while moving to solve the great problems it had left behind.

The challenge before China was to preserve the considerable progress in human development achieved by the previous system while moving to solve the great problems it had left behind.

CHAPTER III
Human Development in the Transition Period

The dramatic change in China's approach to development is generally dated to the Third Plenum of the 11th Central Committee in December 1978, which set the stage for the rural reform of the early 1980s. But it might really be dated back to Mao Zedong's overtures to the United States in the early 1970s that culminated in Richard Nixon's trip to Beijing in 1972. China at that time began opening its doors to the world and re-thinking its own development path, a process that accelerated after Mao's death in 1976, and became dominant at the Third Plenum in late 1978. The people's communes were dismantled and the land leased out to families. Foreign trade was promoted and foreign direct investment first permitted and then promoted in earnest. The government allowed a non-state sector to take root and begin growing up outside the central plan, still dominated by state owned enterprises. "Township and village enterprises" (TVEs) proliferated, especially in the more advanced parts of the country, and soon absorbed a substantial fraction of the rural labour force. The fiscal system was decentralized and much of the center's previous share of the economy was turned back to the provinces. Economic growth boomed at unprecedented rates and living standards soared while many of the institutions that had been providing economic security and social welfare to the population melted away.

The human development implica-tions of all these changes are many and complex. The material base, the distributive mechanisms, and the institutional structure of China's human development situation circa 1978 have all been changing radically in ways that have contradictory effects on human development. One particular change that has affected virtually all human development issues in China is the decentralization of the fiscal system. This has occurred in part because of a deliberate effort to spread investment initiative more widely throughout the country in the wake of China's abandonment of the rigid central planning system of old. In part, however, it has occurred spontaneously because of changes in the economy that have made it harder for governments in general to collect revenue, and, among governments, harder for the central government in particular. The state enterprises that were the main source of state revenue in the past have become increasingly less profitable because of wage and raw material price increases and increasing competition from the ebullient non-state sector and imports. Faced with declining revenues relative to GDP, China has been slow to reform its tax system to tap potential new sources of revenue. The result, as shown in Table 3.1 and Figure 3.1, has been a continuous fall in the government's share of GDP. By 1996, the government was claiming only 11 percent of GDP, an extraordinarily small share by comparative international standards.

Table 3.1. Fiscal Decentralization, 1979-1996: Government Revenue and Expenditure as Percent of GDP

	1980	1982	1984	1986	1988	1990	1992	1994	1996
Revenue	30.6	29.1	25.2	24.0	18.8	19.2	14.7	12.0	11.4
Expenditure	34.1	30.6	26.6	25.8	21.0	21.1	17.0	13.6	12.9
Balance	-3.5	-1.5	-1.4	-1.8	-2.2	-1.9	-2.3	-1.6	-1.5

Source: International Monetary Fund 1997

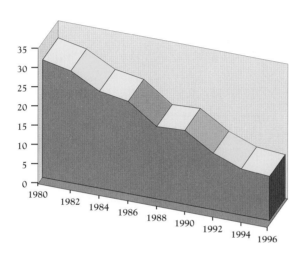

Figure 3.1. Government's Declining Share of GDP (%)
Source: Table 3.1.

This naturally affected Beijing's ability to implement its priorities, whether in development planning or social spending. Indeed, the pre-reform practice of redistributing some of the richer province's revenues to shore up investment in both human and tangible capital in the more backward provinces was greatly weakened, with predictable consequences for the latter.[1]

We begin considering these changes by looking at the effect of the transition on the health of the Chinese people.

1 This is argued persuasively in Wong et al. 1997.

Health and Nutrition in the Transition Period[1]

1.1. The Demographic Transition.
Of great relevance to the health status of the Chinese people is their basic accomplishment of the demographic transition from high to low birth and death rates. This is pictured in Figure 3.2. Compared to other low income developing countries China completed this transition faster. Consequently, the average annual growth rate of China's population for the period of 1990-1994 was less than half that

1 This section relies on Hu 1997 and Cai Fang 1997.

of the weighted average of the total population in the developing world, excluding China and India.

Most experts expect China to realize zero population growth around the year 2040-2050 with a maximum population size around 1,550 -1,600 million, if the total fertility rate remains around 2.0. Obviously, this trend in population growth is quite conducive to the relief of demographic pressure on employment, resources and environment in China.

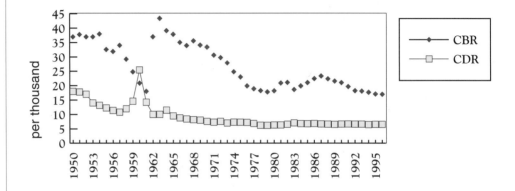

Figure 3.2. The Demographic Transition: Crude Birth and Death Rates, 1950-1996

1.2. Fertility in the Context of Transition. In the changed conditions of transition to a market economy, the administrative approach to fertility control has become less efficient, and this has resulted in an unbalanced population growth among regions and between rural and urban areas.

Fertility is determined by social and economic factors, and so differences in socio-economic development will translate into differences in fertility and thus in population growth. Hence, it is not surprising to witness increasing discrepancies among the provinces in their natural growth rates as the national average declines in the 1990s.

For instance, as early as 1993, Shanghai City realized negative population growth with a natural growth rate of -0.78(. This achievement came about 40 years ahead of the expected date for the country as a whole. Meanwhile, a number of provinces, containing perhaps 30 percent of the total population, still have high rates of

natural increase. These provinces are mainly located in central and western China and include Jiangxi, Guangxi, Yunnan, Guizhou, Tibet, Ningxia, and Xinjiang. The percentage of women in their most fertile age range in these provinces will peak during 1997-2000. Similarly, for the nation as a whole the natural increase rate of the rural population is higher by a fourth than that of urban residents.

Economic reform also raises challenges to family planning policy, especially in the rural areas. The economic functions of the family have been resurrected, and farmers are now likely to want more children, whose costs are low and benefits high in rural areas. At present, China's rural situation in this regard is as follows:

1) Under the Household Responsibility System, contract land is distributed according to size of household: the larger its size the more land it will get. Farmland is regarded as both a basic source of income and as insurance against the risks

of engaging in non-agricultural activities. Therefore, many farmers will have more children in order to increase their allotment of contract land.

2) The incentive for rural families to invest in their children's education is constrained by two factors: (1) agriculture is still quite backward, which limits the demand for high quality labour; and (2) rural/urban segregation and employment discrimination against rural workers in the towns channels rural migrants into low quality jobs.

3) Social security has been concentrated in urban areas. Although that is changing, the social security system is still neither comprehensive nor adequate even in towns and cities. Without an effective social insurance network, farmers must still rely on children as their main source of old age security and, in this respect, the more children the better.

4) The sacrifice of women's economic opportunities involved in having more children is very small in rural areas where the surplus labour force exceeds 30% .[2]

In the context of the economic transition, family planning programs are changing gradually, and becoming integrated with rural development programs. They are providing comprehensive maternal and child health care. These programs are geared to serve the needs of women, as indicated in the accompanying box.

---

[2] Colin Carter, Zhong Funing, and Cai Fang: China's Ongoing Agricultural Reform, San Francisco, The 1990 Institute, 1996.

The Community Development-Family Planning Nexus.

In China, neighborhood and village or township are the basic units of community in urban and rural areas, respectively. People in the same community are closely linked in their daily life and work. They tend to influence each other's habits and customs, consumption style and values. Attitudes toward fertility are also influenced by the socio-economic settings of the community, such as level of economic development and prevailing norms. Hence, development of the community economy, introduction of modern culture, increasing educational investment, and improving the level of social insurance are all apt to lead to fertility decline.

Up to 1995, community development networks have been set up in 23 counties of 18 provinces. These networks aim to reduce fertility by improving women's status and changing socio-economic conditions. Common methods include:

1) finding income-generating opportunities for women, and providing the necessary training courses and production-related services to promote women's participation in community economic activities.
2) Adopting preferential policies in housing, land area distribution, loan provision, fertilizer supply, local welfare services and old age insurance policies for those women and households who have accepted family planning;
3) Providing women with maternal and child health care services;
4) Enhancing family planning education by increasing investment in cultural infrastructure, disseminating knowledge of family planning methods and maternal and child health care to women.
5) Organizing cultural activities in the community to counter fertility related tradition and customs and create an environment of equality for women and men.

1.3. Health Status of the Chinese People. The life expectancy of Chinese has continued to rise during the transition period (Table 3.2), reaching 70.8 years in 1996, according to official data. Life expectancy of women reached 73. The infant mortality rate officially fell from 39 to 32 per thousand births in 1990. However, some observers, such as UNICEF,

believe this to be an underestimate and put the IMR in the 40s.

According to the reports from national surveillance areas, the maternal mortality rate has improved significantly in both urban and rural areas. The national maternal mortality rate declined to 67.3 per 100 thousands in 1993 (Table 3.3).

Table 3.2. Demographic Indicators, 1980-90

Indicators	1980-	1985-90	1996
Crude birth rate (per thousand)	19.0	20.5	17.0
Crude death rate (per thousand)	6.7	6.7	6.6
Total fertility rate (per thousand)	2.4	2.4	n.a.
Infant mortality (per thousand)	39.0	32.0	31.4*
Life expectancy (years)	67.8	69.4	70.8
Male	66.7	68.0	68.7
Female	68.9	70.9	73.0

* 1995 figure.
Source: United Nations' population database

Table 3.3. Maternal Mortality Rates (per 100,000) in National Survey Localities: Urban and Rural Areas, 1989-1993

Year	Total	Urban	Rural
1989	94.7	49.9	114.9
1990	88.9	45.9	112.5
1991	80.0	46.3	100.0
1992	76.5	42.7	97.9
1993	67.3	38.5	85.1

Some 85 percent of children are now getting immunized, and the incidence the major childhood diseases prevented by immunization -- measles, pertusis, diphtheria and tetanus -- has declined by more than ninety percent compared with the pre-vaccination era. Filariasis was almost eliminated by 1994. Although the control of schistosomiasis (snail fever) suffered some setbacks, the incidence rate has now dropped to a new low. In 1995, 278 out of 391 schistomosomiasis-endemic counties, or 71%, had eliminated or basically eliminated the disease. China is now approaching the critical stage in the eradication of polio.

Great progress has been made in combating infectious diseases. The total incidence of infectious disease declined from 7061 per 100,000 in the 1970s to 176.2 per 100,000 in 1995. To prevent iodine deficiency disease, eighty percent of provinces have used iodine-supplemented salt in China. The areas where Kaschin-Beck, Keshan, and iodine deficiency diseases are endemic have gradually shrunk, the size of the threatened population is declining and the prevalence of these diseases has decreased significantly. Water supply engineering has made great progress in the rural areas, allowing some 800 million people, or 87 percent of the rural population, to obtain improved water. Half this number now have access to tap water.

Many of these basic health indicators have improved well beyond the global average, and even reached the advanced levels of developed countries. The government has set goals for the year 2000 in implementing its Health for All programme, and has signed on to the strategic targets announced by the World Summit on Children. In recent years, the achievements in eradicating polio, controlling iodine deficiency disease, expanding the national program for immunization, and promoting the short regime for treatment of tuberculosis in China, have all gained international attention.

World Bank analysis indicates that non-communicable and chronic diseases and injuries are now responsible for almost two-thirds of disease incidence in China.

Life style issues such as smoking (an especially pernicious problem in China) and environmental problems of pollution are coming into focus as major health issues of the future. Having made major inroads against infectious diseases, China is thus now facing the so-called "second health revolution", which addresses such non-communicable and chronic diseases and their varied causes. Among these are sexually transmitted diseases; in 1995 there were 362,000 reported cases of all kinds, but experts estimate that the actual numbers are several times higher. The first case in China of HIV/AIDS was identified in 1985; there are now an estimated 200,000 Chinese who are HIV positive. Addiction to narcotics is a problem estimated to affect several times the 520,000 reported drug users. All these are relatively new social/health problems to which China has begun formulating responses.

With rapid economic development and improvement in living standards, the diet and nutritional status of the Chinese people have greatly improved. The dietary pattern has become more diversified. Consumption of cereals has fallen while the intake of animal food and fat has grown. The body height and weight of children have increased significantly, and the body mass index (BMI) of adults is increasing gradually.

China has 5.4 million health care workers, comprising 0.8 percent of the total labour force, and including 1.9 million doctors, averaging 1.6 doctors per thousand population. More than half of health care workers are employed by various government health institutions under the Ministry of Health. Another 1.4 million work for state owned enterprises, which provide health services to their employees, retirees and their families. There are almost three million hospital beds, averaging 2.4 beds per thousand population. This is a high rate by the standard of low-income countries.

The achievements of China's health care system have not only been impressive, they have also been very cost effective. In 1990, China's spending on health care came to about 3.5 percent of its gross national product, and accounted for about one percent of global health care spending, according to the World Development Report (1993). The average health expenditure per capita was only 11 US dollars.

Since 1991, China has invested RMB10 billion yuan to support a construction program for rebuilding 23 thousand county sanitation and anti-epidemic stations, maternal and child health stations and township hospitals. In 1996, the central government allocated 60 percent of program funds to less development areas. More than 40 percent of funds have been used in the nationally designated poor counties.

The major principles characterizing government policy toward health have been defined as follows: "Setting rural health as the priority, putting prevention first, giving equal attention to both traditional Chinese medicine and western medicine, relying on advances in medicine, education, science and technology, mobilizing social participation, serving the people's health and the modernization and construction of society." The basic characteristics of China's approach to rural health care, in particular, have included construction of a three-tier medical, preventive and health care network; reliance on village doctors and paramedics; and the spread of a rural cooperative medical system (RCS) to provide health insurance to the rural population at low cost. However, these institutions have melted away in most of the Chinese countryside as a result of the changes of the transition period. As a result, rural access to health care has become increasingly uneven, and there is now belated recognition of the value of the RCMS and attempts to re-establish it throughout the rural areas.

1.4. Health and Poverty.

For all the gains that have been made, the health status of the Chinese people is extremely uneven, and there is some indication that the transition period has witnessed an increase in this unevenness. Major differences exist between urban and rural areas, and between the eastern coastal provinces, the midlands and the western interior areas. Table 3.4 summarizes these

The achievements of China's health care system have not only been impressive, they have also been very cost effective.

differences in the mortality rates of newborns, infants, and children under 5 years old. The infant mortality rate of the remote interior regions is 2 1/2 times that of the coastal areas, while the rural rate is three times as high as the urban. Clearly, bringing the levels of maternal and child health in the poorer inland and western areas up to those of the cities and richer coastal areas is a key to further improving the health status of the population as a whole.

Table 3.4. Comparison of Child Mortality Rates in Urban and Rural Areas and in Coastal, Interior and Remote Areas

Areas	Neonate			Infant			1-4 years			Under five years		
	1991	1992	1993	1991	1992	1993	1991	1992	1993	1991	1992	1993
Coastal	18.7	17.5	19.5	27.4	23.6	25.3	1.1	1.2	0.8	33.7	30.6	30.0
Inland	36.9	35.6	37.9	55.4	49.9	51.2	2.1	1.9	1.9	66.3	60.1	62.4
Remote	47.6	50.7	42.9	78.2	80.4	67.3	4.1	3.6	2.7	100.2	99.4	80.5
Urban	12.5	13.9	13.2	17.3	18.4	16.1	0.6	0.5	0.5	20.9	20.7	19.7
Rural	37.9	36.8	34.5	58.0	53.2	48.8	2.5	2.3	1.8	71.1	65.6	59.0
Total	33.1	32.5	32.9	50.2	46.7	45.7	2.1	1.9	1.6	61.0	57.4	55.2

Source: Hu 1997

A program of "Strengthening maternal and child health and family planning in the grassroots" was conducted by the government in collaboration with the United Nations Children Fund (UNICEF) and United Nations Fund for Population Administration (UNFPA) between 1990 and 1994. This project created demonstration programs in 300 remote, minority and poor counties in 27 provinces and autonomous areas. Based on a baseline survey carried out in 1990, the average infant mortality rate was 68 per 1,000 live births; the under five mortality rate was 84.4 per thousand; and the maternal mortality rate was 202.3 per 100,000. The main causes of death in infants, children aged below five years and pregnant women are shown in Table 3.5.

Table 3.5. Causes of Death in Infants, Children and Pregnant Women in Poor Rural Areas

Rank	Infant		Children at age 1-4		Pregnant women	
	Cause	%	Cause	%	Cause	%
1	Pneumonia	24.4	Pneumonia	24.7	Hemorrhage	44.9
2	Neonate suffocation	16.4	Diarrhea	22.5	Complication with diseases	21.2
3	Stillbirth	14.3	Injury	22.4	Postpartum fever	9.8
4	Neonatal tetanus	8.8	Infectious diseases	11.8	Obstetric toxemia	7.1
5	Diarrhea	8.4	Congenital abnormality	4.6	Others	17.0
6	Congenital abnormal	6.6	Others	14.0		
7	Injury	6.1				
8	Birth injury	1.8				
9	Others	13.2				

Source: Hu 1997

Figure 3.3. presents a graphic picture of the disparities in under-five mortality rates between city and countryside, between large and small cities, and among four classes of rural counties, classified in descending order of socioeconomic development, as shown in Table 3.6. The third and fourth categories include rural areas with high rates of birth and death and high infant mortality. Between the urban and Class IV rural counties there is an enormous gap (of five times) in child mortality that presents a solid target for social policy.

Table 3.6. Socioeconomic Characteristics of Rural Counties at Four Different Levels of Development.

Indicators	Urban	Rural			
		Category 1	Category 2	Category 3	Category 4
No. of counties		468 (0.22)	681 (0.32)	776 (0.36)	213 (0.10)
Per capita ind'l & ag'l output value (yuan)	2010	850.0	470.0	330.0	250.0
Secondary industry Employment (%)	-	17.3	10.6	6.0	3.9
Population density (Person/km)	-	330.0	243.0	260.0	59.0
Share of children in population(%)	8.0	5.0	34.9	36.6	40.8
Share of aged in population(%)	6.0	5.4	4.8	4.7	4.3
Illiteracy & semi- illiteracy rate(%)	20.0	29.3	30.4	38.3	64.0
Crude birth rate (%)	17.3	19.2	21.1	23.0	25.2
Crude death rate(%)	6.4	6.3	6.8	8.0	10.9
Infant mort. rate(%)	21.5	36.1	41.0	65.71	24.6

Source: Ministry of Health, Health Statistics Information Center, cited in Hu, 1997.

Table 3.6. also makes clear the complex relationship between population and poverty in China. The poorest category of rural area has by far the lowest population density. These areas tend to be remote upland counties with poor soil, inadequate rainfall and no access to markets. No simple and na?ve argument for a demographic cause of poverty will stand up. Population density that would be very sparse in the Yangzi delta constitutes overpopulation for Gansu or Ningxia's Class IV counties, where terrain, rainfall and low socioeconomic development all cooperate to reduce the carrying capacity of the land. The relation between poverty and population is a mutual one: poverty prevents the creation of technological and employment solutions to the poor local ecology and creates disincentives to lower population growth, which, in turn, puts even greater pressure on the already stressed local environment.

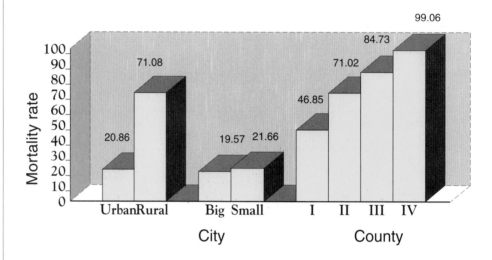

Figure 3.3. Under-five Mortality Rate by Type of Region

Nutritional status of the poor population. Two national surveys, conducted in 1982 and 1992, showed that the nutritional status of children generally improved over that decade. Only 3.5 percent of children below age six were found to be acutely malnourished (very low weight for height) in 1992 (2.7 percent in urban and 3.6 percent in rural areas). Under less severe standards of nutrition, however, one fifth of children below six years of age were found to have a low height for age (13.9% urban, 21.5% rural) and 14.5 percent (9.0% urban and 15.8% rural) a low weight for age. Thus, while severe malnutrition among children is not widespread in China, there is still a fairly wide incidence of growth retardation and low weight indicating some chronic malnutrition (Hu 1997).

Malnutrition among adults has decreased over the past decade but has not been eliminated. According to WHO standards chronic malnutrition affects some 9 percent of rural adults and 8 percent of urban.[3] In poor areas of the country, iron deficiency anemia is a major problem along with other nutrient deficiencies, especially retinal, riboflavin and calcium.

The health and nutrition status of poor rural residents is generally well below the average for China. Time lost from work due to health problems in poor counties averages 2.5 times the national rural average. This suggests that residents of poor areas should be making greater use of health services than the national average, but in fact the opposite is the case. Utilization of medical services is much lower in poor areas. For instance, rates of prenatal and postnatal care in 30 poor counties in 1993 were only half the national average (see Table 3.7.). 86 percent of pregnant women in the surveyed counties delivered babies at home, of whom only 25 percent were assisted by a village doctor. Rates of dystocia, puerperal fever and neonatal tetanus were high, as a result.

While severe malnutrition among children is not widespread in China, there is still a fairly wide incidence of growth retardation and low weight.

---

[3] *Ge Keyou, 1996. The standard used is the BMI index, which is body weight in kg divided by the square of height in meters. People with BMI below 18.5 are judged to be chronically malnourished.*

Table 3.7. Maternal and Child Health Services in Poor Rural Areas (1993)

	30 poor counties	Rural average	3rd category rural areas	4th category rural areas
Prenatal care rate (%)	32.9	60.3	54.8	28.5
Township clinics (%)	45.1	46.7	44.6	40.6
Village stations (%)	28.2	30.9	32.8	35.1
Birth at home	86.7	76.6	80.9	92.7
at hospital	13.3	14.5	12.7	2.8
Delivery by scientific midwifery	41.2	42.0	42.5	24.8
by non-professional	6.5	14.6	15.2	31.7
by self-delivery	46.1	10.8	13.6	30.0
Postnatal visit rate (%)	22.6	48.3	39.0	30.0
Midwife (%)	-	58.0	60.2	59.0
Hospital (%)	-	40.0	36.8	41.2

Source: Hu 1997.

A principal reason for this situation is the inability of poor people to pay for health care. The national health services survey found that fewer than 3 percent of the residents of third and fourth categories of poor rural areas (see Table 3.6. and preceding text) were covered by medical insurance of any kind, that from 82 to 95 percent had to pay their own medical bills. Most patients who did not go to hospital also gave up medication for lack of funds. The same economic problem affects use of maternal and child health services. In poor areas, pregnant women must pay their own expenses for pre- and postnatal care and for delivery and, if unable to do so, go without these services. Lack of basic MCH services is a major factor causing the infant and maternal mortality rates to remain high in poorer rural regions. Thirty-eight percent of maternal mortality associated with home delivery from 1989-1993 occurred during the delivery process because of the absence of timely emergency treatment, and another nineteen percent occurred on the way to hospital. Poverty, illiteracy and lack of MCH services all contribute to these results. Analysis has shown that a woman's educational level and own health, as well as her family income, have much to do with her choice of prenatal care, postnatal care and hospital delivery.

1.5. Financing of Health Care. A breakdown of sources of total health expenditure is given in Figure 3.4. Out-of-pocket payments by the urban and rural population constitute no less than 42 percent of total expenditures, a big change from the past.

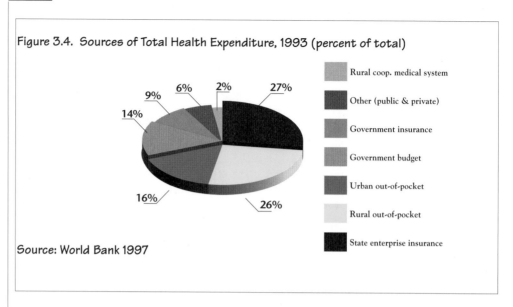

Figure 3.4. Sources of Total Health Expenditure, 1993 (percent of total)

9%
6%
2%
14%
27%
16%
26%

Rural coop. medical system

Other (public & private)

Government insurance

Government budget

Urban out-of-pocket

Rural out-of-pocket

State enterprise insurance

Source: World Bank 1997

China's rural majority gets health care through a three-tier system, starting at the village level with some 1.44 million village doctors, many of whom have only rudimentary training and who are not included among the 5.2 million health care workers enumerated above. These doctors diagnose and treat patients and make referrals to higher levels. They charge fees for their services and also get part of the price of the medicines they prescribe. The second tier is the township hospital or health center, of which there are some 52,000, which operate about one fourth of the total number of hospital beds in the country. These hospitals deliver babies, treat infections and perform some basic surgery. The third tier is the county hospital, some 4,000 in all, which constitute the highest level of medical care available to most rural residents.

In rural areas, in addition to self-paid medical care, there are several routes for financing health care:

* Government paid medical service. This is funded by county and township government appropriations and covers the medical expenses of employees of government and public institutions. Only a small minority of the rural population, and 2.8 percent of the rural poor population, is covered by this channel.

* Labour health insurance, financed from enterprise welfare funds and worker contributions, covers employees of state-owned enterprises. Because most rural resi-

dents do not work in state enterprises, this channel, too, applies to only a minimal percentage of the rural population (and 0.5% of the poor rural population).

* Cooperative medical service. This is now jointly financed by local government, collective enterprises, individual contributions and other sources. It is divided into two types of coverage: the first type (risk coverage) covers catastrophic events, such as those requiring hospitalization. The second type (mutual assistance) covers minor medical needs that can be treated by ambulatory visits to the local health clinic or county hospital. Both types of coverage have set reimbursement structures, including co-payments, deductibles and payment ceilings.

* EPI Contract Service. Under this Expanded Programme of Immunization, provincial and county governments provide the capital cost of immunizations, while user fees pay for recurrent costs of maintenance, administration and medical personnel. Parents usually pay the contract cost as a lump sum at the birth of their child, and receive six vaccines in 13 doses before age 7.

* MCH contract service. This is a kind of rudimentary health maintenance scheme in which women and children prepay a lump sum or installment fee which makes them eligible for certain medical services if needed.

Of these various sources of funding for health care, by far the most important for rural residents has been the cooperative medical system (CMS). This was an important health security system in rural China in the 1960s and 1970s and was instrumental in upgrading rural medical facilities and improving the health of the rural population. With the introduction of rural economic reform in the mid-1980s and the resulting disappearance of the rural communes, the cooperative medical system disintegrated in most areas. Recently there have been efforts to resurrect the CMS, but at present it covers only about 10 percent of the rural population (see Figure 3.5.).

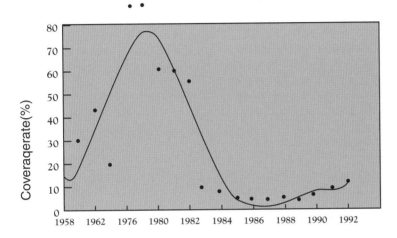

Figure 3.5. The Village Coverage Rate of Cooperative Medical System in Rural China, 1958-1992

The decline of the CMS and its replacement by private payment for medical care in rural areas is the single most important change in the health care financing system during the transition period. From 20 percent of national health spending in 1978, the CMS share declined to 2 percent in 1993. Correspondingly, out-of-pocket payments increased from 20 percent of total spending in 1978 to 42 percent in 1993. This change probably impacted most sharply on the poor rural population, which has the least ability to afford private health care. The current structure of health financing in poor areas is suggested by Table 3.9., which shows the coverage of the various forms of financing in 30 poor counties.

The decline of the cooperative medical system and its replacement by private payment for medical care in rural areas is the single most important change in the health care financing system during the transition period.

Table 3.8. Different Forms of Health Financing in 30 Poor Counties (1993)

	No. of villages covered	Village coverage(%)	Pop. coverage (%)
Health contract service	58	10.9	6.4
EPI service	110	20.7	13.0
Cooperative medical service	88	16.5	11.6
Risk coverage	29	5.4	4.4
Mutual assistance	59	11.4	7.2
Self paid health service	445	83.5	88.4

Note: There was a total population of 673,797 in 534 villages in the 30 poor counties.

The transition period has seen a continued and substantial improvement in the health and longevity of the average Chinese.

At the same time, there has been increased inequality of access to health care.

The problem of health care in poor areas of China is not primarily due to lack of facilities. In fact, the number of health care facilities, hospital beds and health professionals per thousand population in poor counties is similar to the national rural average. The ownership structure of village health networks has changed, however, with the share of collective-run village health posts dropping from the 1980s to the mid-90s and that of private clinics rising. Quality of health services is also a serious problem. Not only is equipment often poor and outdated, but the economic compensation mechanism of rural hospitals and clinics, which depend greatly on sale of medicines to patients, has resulted in inappropriate use of expensive pharmaceuticals and irrational and escalating costs for patients.

The main problem for China's rural poor, however, is the disappearance of the social, risk-sharing funding mechanism represented by the CMS, and its replacement in large part by private out-of-pocket payment for medical services. As in the case of China's poverty alleviation effort, the focus upon putting facilities in poor areas does not necessarily ensure that poor people will benefit. Rapid growth and rising averages have been accompanied by increasing inequality,[1] while government fiscal decentralization has weakened the transfer of fiscal resources from richer to poorer areas.[2] The net result for the health care of the rural poor is that they have been left increasingly on their own, struggling to pay for medical treatment. The same tendencies are at work in the towns and cities, where the proportion of health care spending in total annual consumer expenditures increased 140 percent over the past decade, from 1.2% in 1985 to 2.9% in 1994. For the poorest five percent of households the increase was from 1.53% in 1986 to 3.48% in 1994.

Surveys indicate that the presence of CMS makes a major difference in utilization of medical services. CMS increases the demand for clinic care and hospitalization. It also reduces the burden on medical facilities at county level and above by making adequate provision for health care at the village and township level. This has made medical services less costly as well as

more easily accessible.

The introduction of CMS also has a significant impact on health care provision. It encourages preventive care, which has been discouraged by the trend toward out-of-pocket payment. It brings down the per visit cost at village clinics. The structure of service earnings becomes more rational. In the anti-risk type of CMS, for example, hospital bed turnover and number of outpatient visits at township clinics both increase, the cost per visit and per bed decrease and the proportion of earnings from drugs falls.

Although CMS is still not in place in most of China's poor rural areas, MCH and EPI contract insurance schemes have existed to varying degrees, encouraging some preventive care. These can noticeably increase the utilization of maternal and immunization services, bring down infant mortality rates, and increase the use of prenatal and postnatal care and the number of hospital visits.

In sum, the transition period has seen a continued and substantial improvement in the health and longevity of the average Chinese. Rapid growth in real income, increasing expenditures on health care, and growing access to modern medical technology have all contributed to this improvement. At the same time, the rapid growth of inequality associated with the market transition, the disappearance of the cooperative medical system in the countryside, and the reduction in fiscal redistribution of resources from better off to poorer provinces and localities have all contributed to increasing inequality in access to health care. As a recent World Bank study observes,

"Government spending on health has not been effective in reaching China's poorest residents. . . . An analysis of public expenditure over eleven years shows that the allocation of public expenditure is

---

1 *In addition to the above material on inequality of access to health care services, see the discussion in section 4 of this chapter regarding the increase in income inequality.*

2 *See introduction to this chapter and Wong 1997.*

skewed toward richer regions and, within regions, to the provinces growing fastest" (World Bank 1997).

For a large piece of China the first "health care revolution" has already taken place, and the main concerns have progressed from malnutrition and infectious and parasitological diseases, which have largely been controlled, to the chronic diseases and injuries associated with life style and environmental conditions. However, for another big part of the population, the first health care revolution is far from over, and chronic malnutrition, infectious and endemic diseases, and high infant and maternal mortality remain potent threats to longevity and health. The main reason, as we have seen, has less to do with medical supply conditions than with demand for health care, which has been compromised for poorer Chinese by the transition of the health care system from a public health to a fee for service orientation. The challenge for China is to make the health status gains of better off Chinese more broadly available. In the countryside, this can be done through the encouragement of some kind of cooperative health care system, similar to the CMS of the past but consistent with contemporary conditions, to cover the majority of low income rural residents and to regenerate the public health and prevention orientation that China did so much to pioneer.

The challenge for China is to make the health status gains of better off Chinese more broadly available.

 # Education during the Transition Period [1]

2.1. Main Trends. China currently is educating the world's largest school population, a total of 234 million students of whom some 136 million children are enrolled in primary schools (1996).[2] Basic data on China's education system are presented in Table 3.9. The government reports that 98.8 percent of children between the ages of 6 and 12 were enrolled in primary schools in 1996, and over 78 percent of those between 12 and 16 were in middle schools (1995).[3] However, the enrollment rate in post-secondary educational institutions was only 1.6 percent in 1992, well below the 4 percent level of other developing countries.[4] Actual school enrollment rates may be somewhat lower than these officially reported rates. For instance, the Sample Survey on the Situation of Children for 1993 reported that primary school enrollment rates were 96 percent in urban areas and 91 percent in rural. The same survey found that rates were higher for boys (94 percent) than for girls (91 percent). About three-quarters of children not enrolled were girls, mostly in poor and national minority regions. By 1995 the national illiteracy rate had been brought down to 12 percent, amounting to 16.5 percent of the adult population, which still left 145 million illiterates. Illiteracy increases sharply with age, however; in 1995, the illiteracy rate was over 70 percent among those older than 68, but only about 5 percent for those 21 to 25 years old.

Education and science and technology are regarded in China both as priorities in the modernization process and as key aspects of the national development strategy. During the transition period, and especially since the mid-1980s, Chinese education has undergone reform in distinct stages. In 1984 and 1985, several decisions were announced to undertake basic improvements in both quantity and quality of the system of education, including strengthening of basic education, universalizing nine-year compulsory schooling, increasing the emphasis on vocational and technical training, reforming the content and methods of teaching, and improving college curriculum. In addition, separate channels of community and privately run schools have opened. In 1996, there were 1,453 private primary schools, 1,467 private middle schools and 568 private vocational schools in China.

China currently is educating the world's largest school population.

[1] This section relies on Li Zhibao, 1997.
[2] Li Zhibao, 1997; ZTZ 1997, p. 140.
[3] Beijing Review, 39, 19, May 6-12 1996.
[4] Beijing Review, 39, 10, March 4-10 1996.

Table 3.9. Basic Statistics of Regular Schools in China by Level and Type (thousands)

	Schools	Graduates	Entrants	Enrollment	Teachers, Staff and Workers	
					Total	of which full-time
Total	934,470	38,181.0	70,421.5	234,566.7	14,393.5	11,210.5
1. Graduate Education	(740)	39.7	59.4	162.3		
(1) Institutes of Higher Learning	(419)	36.8	54.8	149.9		
(2) Research Bodies	(321)	2.9	4.6	12.5		
2. Regular Institute of Higher Learning, Undergraduates	1,032	838.6	965.8	3,021.1	1,035.8	402.5
Enrolled According to State Plans		544.1	758.4	2,280.6		
Enrolled by Contract		182.9	107.6	397.2		
Tuition-paying Students		110.2	97.7	338.8		
In-service Teachers in Training		1.4	2.1	4.5		
3. Regular Secondary Schools	98,705	17,937.7	24,585.0	68,248.9	5,758.4	4,156.6
(1) Specialized Secondary Schools.	4,099	1018.7	1,523.4	4,227.9	542.8	267.4
-Secondary Technical Schools.	3,206	737.9	1,207.7	3,347.8	429.8	204.3
-Teacher Training Schools.	893	280.8	315.7	880.1	113.1	63.1
(2) Skilled Worker Schools.	4,507	681.5	740.5	1,885.9	336.7	115.4
(3) General Secondary Schools.	79,967	14,839.7	20,429.3	57,396.8	4,424.4	3,464.8
-Senior	13,875	2,049.3	2,822.3	7,692.5		572.1
-Junior	66,092	12,790.4	17,607.0	49,704.3		2,892.7
(4) Vocational Schools	10,049	1395.5	1,889.1	4,732.7	451.7	307.6
-Senior	8,515	1,207.9	1,582.3	3,957.5		268.5
Junior	1,534	187.6	306.8	775.2		39.2
(5) Correctional Work-Study Schools.	83	2.3	2.7	5.6	2.8	1.4
4. Primary Schools	645,983	19,340.8	25,246.6	136,150.0	6,385.8	5,735.8
5. Special Education Schools.	1,426	23.8	48.2	321.1	39.7	27.0
6. Kindergartens	187,324		19,516.5	2,6663.3	1,173.8	888.6

The most pressing problem faced by education in China is that of inadequate resources. Increased investment is a necessary condition for improving education. The Education Law of the People's Republic of China adopted in 1995 contains the following provisions on increasing expenditure for education:

The State shall gradually raise the proportion of educational expenditure in gross national product (GNP) as the national economy develops. The proportion of educational expenditure in the total fiscal expenditure of governments at various levels shall be gradually raised along with national economic development.

The rate of increase of educational expenditure allocated by the people's governments at various levels shall be higher than the growth of general financial revenue.

Specifically, the government stipulated that spending on education should be raised to 4 percent of GNP by the end of this century. Even if this target is attained, the situation will still be very tight because the number of students attending school will continue to rise. However, even though overall government expenditure on education has gone up by a fairly large margin in recent years (see Table 3.10.), and both GNP and government revenue have been growing, the share of government expenditure on education in China's GDP has nevertheless continued to fall, accounting for only 2.0% of GDP in 1995.[5]

After 1985, the State Education Commission advocated a "multi-channel" strategy for educational financing so as to tap various sources of funds. This policy included levying an educational tax, charging tuition for non-compulsory, developing school-run enterprises, encouraging social donations, and various kinds of fund raising. Responsibility for education has thus been devolved to the localities with primary schools being sponsored by villages, junior secondary schools by townships, and senior secondary schools by counties. Various subsidy programs exist to help the poorest areas manage.

Nonetheless, resources for education have continued to be lean. This is due in part to the steady decline in government's share of GDP, and in part to the fact that some government departments have neglected education. Educational spending has not always grown in accordance with the law, nor have local officials been held fully accountable for its growth. Misappropriation of educational funds has also been known to occur. Despite the continued expansion of China's economy, these phenomena have compromised progress toward achieving universal compulsory education, causing delays in teachers' salary payments, shortages of funds for running schools and imposition of excessive student fees in some places. The government should take effective steps to address these problems, including exercising strict budgetary management, setting goals for increasing educational expenditure on an annual basis, and vigorously enforcing laws. The fact that despite economic difficulties and budgetary constraints, some local governments have been able to increase the resources devoted to education indicates that the problem can be solved if addressed forthrightly.

The most pressing problem faced by education in China is that of inadequate resources.

---

[5] *Zhongguo tongji zhaiyao, 1997, pp. 2, 48.*

Table 3.10. Sources of Educational Spending, 1994-1995 (Billions of yuan)

	1994	1995	1995/1994 (%)
<u>Total</u>	148.88	187.80	126.14
Budgetary Expenditure on Education	88.40	102.84	116.34
Taxes or Fees Collected by Governments of Various Levels for Educational Purposes	13.28	18.91	142.41
Education Spending by Enterprises	8.91	10.49	117.69
Education Funds Derived from School-run Industries, Work-study programs and Social Services	6.07	7.68	126.62
Other Education Funds Derived from State Finance	0.82	1.23	150.43
Education Funds from Social Groups and Individuals	1.08	2.04	188.96
Education Funds Raised Within Communities	9.75	16.28	167.10
Tuition and Miscellaneous Charges	14.69	20.12	136.97
Other	5.89	8.20	139.21

Source: Zhongguo jiaoyu jingfei niandu baogao 1996 (Annual report on educational spending in China) 1997

Out of every 1000 children starting school today, only 275 will go beyond lower-middle school.

Perhaps the second most serious problem affecting education is the unevenness of the distribution of educational resources and opportunity. For instance, school enrolment rates vary widely by region, with the lowest rate being 46 percent.[6] Another and perhaps more telling indicator is completion rate. The 1991-92 national average for the completion rate, which is the proportion of students entering first grade who will eventually graduate from primary school, was estimated at 91percent. This average reflects a wide range of rates, however, from 78.6 percent for Jiangxi to 99.7 percent for Beijing (Table 3.11). Out of every 1000 children starting school today, only 275 will go beyond lower-middle school, and almost the same number will end their education with primary school.

In one of China's poorest provinces, Guizhou, one-third of counties had not achieved universal six-year primary education by 1985. The national illiteracy rates in 1990 were 12 percent for urban areas and 26 percent for rural, but in Guizhou, the corresponding rates were 21 percent and 41 percent.

[6] UNICEF 1994, pp. 87-89.

Table 3.11.: Primary School Completion Rates, by Province, 1990-1992

Shanghai	100	Hainan	91
Beijing	100	Gansu	91
Tianjin	99	Inner Mongol	91
Jilin	98	Sichuan	90
Hebei	98	Anhui	89
Liaoning	97	Guangxi	88
Guangdong	97	Ningxia	88
Jiangsu	95	Henan	86
Heilongjiang	94	Fujian	86
Zhejiang	94	Yunnan	84
Shaanxi	94	Guizhou	84
Shandong	94	Qinghai	83
Hubei	93	Jiangxi	79
Shanxi	93	Tibet	n.a.
Hunan	92	CHINA	92
Xinjiang	92		

Source: UNICEF 1995

Part of the reason for the persistence and even widening of regional disparities and urban-rural differences in educational services, as in other public services, is the decentralisation of China's fiscal system during the transition period. This has reduced the redistribution of budget resources - long a hallmark of Chinese fiscal policy - from developed, coastal areas to the poor interior.[7] In 1990 some 87 per cent of budgeted expenditures on education, and virtually 100 per cent of those on primary education, came from local government. Off-budget expenditures, which have come to play an increasingly dominant role in local finance, are almost entirely local in origin (Cheng 1995 p. 57).

In 1990, Beijing's budgeted expenditure per student for primary schools came to

[7] Wong et al. (1997: 23-24). On the redistributive role of China's national budget in the pre-transition era see Lardy 1978.

290 yuan, while Hubei's was 61 yuan. Capital expenditure per capita on education was fourteen times greater in Beijing than Shandong (Cheng 1995 pp. 59-60). On the other hand, poor Shaanxi's residents contributed 78 per cent more per capita, and Hubei's 124 per cent more, than Beijing's much richer residents (Cheng 1995 p. 61). In other words, despite government aid programmes for the educational needs of poor localities, many of these have had to adopt surcharges, tuition, and other kinds of fees charged to pupils' families in order to finance educational costs in the face of a general decline in revenues from higher levels (Wong et al. 1997).

This has increased the financial burden of schooling on families to the point that such burden has become the single most important reason why children are not attending school (UNICEF 1995 p. 90). UNICEF reports that nearly all girls and as many as half of the boys in some poor areas do not attend school and will never learn to read. A 1993 study of schools in poor villages in relatively poor Shaanxi Province found that most were old and dilapidated, teachers were badly paid, and poor families had to devote from 5 to 25 per cent of their incomes to educational costs. Without employment opportunities for their children to look forward to, families had little incentive to spend so much on schooling, even if they could afford to.

Even within the richer provinces there are disparities between relatively rich and poor localities. For instance, in Guangdong, China's richest and fastest growing province (other than the province-level municipalities), annual per capita spending on education in 1989 was 1053 yuan in central Guangzhou (the provincial capital) and 397 yuan in the rural counties. Moreover, only residents of the central city may be admitted to the key schools, which are by design the best schools in the province (Lee 1995 pp. 72-73). These trends, like those affecting health care, involve the differentiation of opportunity by income class and region. They pose a serious threat to the progress of education in poor areas and more generally to the prospects for further improving China's admirable record in education. This threat

UNICEF reports that nearly all girls and as many as half of the boys in some poor areas do not attend school and will never learn to read.

has been recognised by many in China; at the March 1997 meeting of the Fifth Plenum of the Chinese People's Political Consultative Conference, an advisory body of prominent citizens, there were frank and open criticisms of inadequate funding of education, and a call for educational funding to grow faster than GNP in order to attain the target ratio of 4 per cent of GNP set by the State Council in 1993 (China Daily, March 8 1997).

Recognizing the imbalance in regional development, China follows the principle of conducting educational planning on a regional basis and of providing differentiated guidance with regional disparities in mind in carrying out its literacy and compulsory education drive. The country is divided into three broad macro-regions according to their different levels of socioeconomic development. The first region covers nine provinces and province-level municipalities along the east coast, the most highly developed region of the country. The second region covers twelve central provinces of medium relative development level, and the third consists of nine poorer provinces in western China. Different schedules are set for eliminating illiteracy and universalizing nine-year compulsory education in each of the above three regions. The first two regions are to meet these goals by 1997 and 1998, respectively. For the third region, the target of achieving nine-year compulsory schooling is limited to 65% of the regional population by the end of the century. The rest of the region is to work on the first step of accomplishing universal six-year compulsory schooling. For some poverty stricken areas, the first step is to universalize three-to-four year compulsory schooling. Compulsory junior middle school education in these areas can proceed only after compulsory primary school attendance has been achieved.

Higher education has been available to only a small minority of Chinese. In 1994, only 2.4 percent of the cohort aged 18-22 were enrolled in institutions of higher education, a very small percentage by the standard of other developing countries. Because of the suspension of universities during the Cultural Revolution years and the relatively small emphasis on higher education since, China's current stock of college and university graduates is aging rapidly and will soon be reduced through retirement. Replenishing it with new and well-educated graduates will require that the upward trend in enrolments that began in the late 1980s continue and perhaps even accelerate.

2.2. Promoting Education in Poor Areas

China faces two principal difficulties in universalizing compulsory education in poor areas: insufficient spending on education and outdated content and methods of teaching that do not meet the development needs of these areas. Therefore, the government is both increasing educational expenditure for universalizing compulsory education in poor areas and carrying out overall rural educational reform.

Since 1983 four types of special educational budget appropriations have been set up for compulsory education, vocational education, teacher's training, and ethnic education in ethnic minorities regions, old revolutionary base areas, and poor areas. These appropriations plus other government subsidies provide 300 million yuan annually for assisting educational development in poor areas. The State Education Commission and the Ministry of Finance have since 1995 been putting into effect a National Project for Implementing Compulsory Education in Poor Areas. Under this program a total of more than 10 billion yuan are earmarked –3.9 billion yuan from the central government and the rest from local governments – for promoting compulsory education in poor areas between 1995- 2000. This fund is to be reserved for the 592 poor counties designated under the National 8-7 Program for Poverty Elimination, and for some poor counties on the provincial lists. Appropriations will mainly be used for building schools, purchasing teaching equipment and books, and training school principals and teachers. This is the largest national project ever undertaken in China for eliminating poverty through education, with the largest central government appropriations ever allocated to that task.

In addition to domestic programs, China administers some foreign assistance it receives for educational development in poor areas. The State Education Commission has in the past few years used all or most of the educational loans provided to it by the World Bank and educational funds provided by UNDP and UNICEF to universalize primary education, improve basic education, ensure schooling for school-age girls and carry out labour skill training in poor areas and ethnic minority areas.

Also, the general public has played a big role in providing financial contributions for development of basic education and particularly the spread of universal primary education in poor areas. Project Hope launched in 1989 and Project Spring Bud for assisting school-age girls launched in 1989 have gained widespread support. By the end of 1996, Project Hope had raised a total of 978 million yuan, enabling over one and a half million children to continue their education. Assisted by the Spring Bud Project, several hundred thousand school-age girls have returned to school. Girls' education is most vulnerable to the pressures of poverty.

China has also been working to reform the approach to education in rural areas to make it more directly serve the needs of economic development in the countryside where the great majority of Chinese live. Basic education has been oriented toward passing entrance examinations for admission to higher levels of schooling, whereas a national average of only 49 percent of junior middle school graduates actually move up to senior middle school (1996), a figure that is lower in poorer regions. The majority of rural Chinese students still end their formal education at lower middle school level or below. The criticism is that they take away from school an inappropriate set of skills, designed to further an academic career they will not in fact follow. They do not acquire more practical skills that would help them in their family life and work.

Therefore, the reform is to give increased emphasis to vocational and technical training in rural education, for both

The government is both increasing educational expenditure for universalizing compulsory education in poor areas and carrying out overall rural educational reform.

children and adults, with a view toward making education a more forceful tool in local economic development and poverty elimination. Textbooks are no longer solely produced by the People's Education Press, allowing for more regional diversity in the curriculum. There have also been efforts to reform the curriculum in rural areas to better address the needs of rural students. One example is the Prairie Program, which integrates agriculture, science, and technology with education to promote a coordinated development of regular education, adult education, and vocational education in rural areas.

The challenge for China is to improve the relevance of rural education without tracking students so completely that their opportunities for going on to higher levels are cut off. As China becomes increasingly integrated into the world economy, its norms of rapidly changing technologies and tastes will play a greater role throughout the country in determining employment and income-earning opportunities. The most valuable characteristic of workers will be their capacity to adapt to new conditions, master new technologies, think critically and solve problems. These are characteristics that are best imparted by general education, rather than by narrower technical training. Therefore, while experimenting with curricula that better serve the practical needs of students, China should be sure to include as the core of its new approaches these vital aspects of a good general education.

 # Women's Status[1]

About two-thirds of China's urban women and over three-quarters of rural women work outside the home. Chinese women participate in virtually all fields of endeavour, including science and technology, government and social organisations and business and financial enterprises. The Communist Party has consistently advocated gender equality, in general, and women's full participation in the social labour force as an important means of achieving it (UNICEF 1995). Women in the state sector have long benefited from labour protection laws, including generous maternity leave, and China officially espouses the principle of equal pay for equal work. Legal protection for women has continued to advance, most notably in recent years the Law on Protection of Women's Rights and Interests (1992), which provided for "equal rights with men in all aspects of political, economic, cultural, social and family life" (UNICEF 1995). Women have continued to increase their representation in occupations requiring greater skill, paying better salaries, and bringing higher social status. These facts alone establish that women have experienced much progress in recent decades with regard to living conditions, social status and opportunities to develop their abilities.

Despite this substantial progress, Chinese women, like women elsewhere in the world, do not yet participate fully and equally with men in economic, political and social life. Traditional cultural values still have a big influence on social attitudes toward women and their role in society, including those of women, themselves. Women constitute a very small percentage of senior government officials at all levels from the centre to the township and are generally under-represented in the political arena (see Figure 3.6.). In 1993, for instance, they made up only about one-fifth of the deputies to the top legislative body, the National People's Congress. Nor are women well represented in higher managerial positions. On the other hand, women are probably over-represented in jobs requiring heavy labour. In agriculture, the widespread out-migration of men seeking better-paying jobs in the towns and cities has left farming increasingly in the hands of women (see below).

---

[1] This section relies on Feng Yuan 1997.

Figure 3.6. Social and Political Participation by Women

Women in Trade Union Representative Conference and Executive Committee(%)

	Represent	Exec Com
1953	11.69	7.07
1957	9.81	6.57
1978	22.37	22.78
1983	29.43	22.82
1988	26.4	17.47

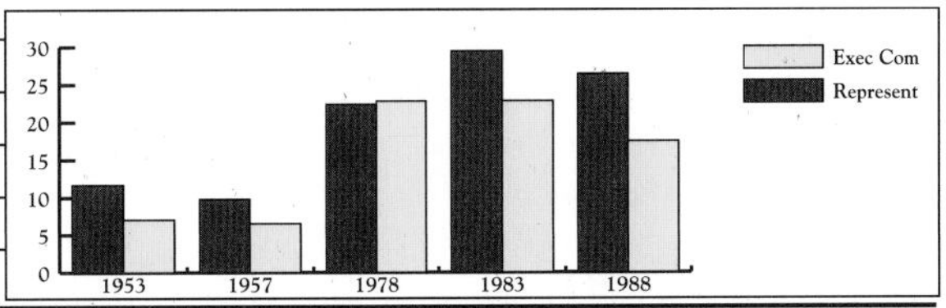

Members and Alternate Members of Central Committee of Communist Youth League(%)

	Members	Altern Mem
57	16.78	30.65
64	16.29	33.78
78	21.89	27.27
82	25.1	33.33
86	13.3	35.71
93	15.15	32.72

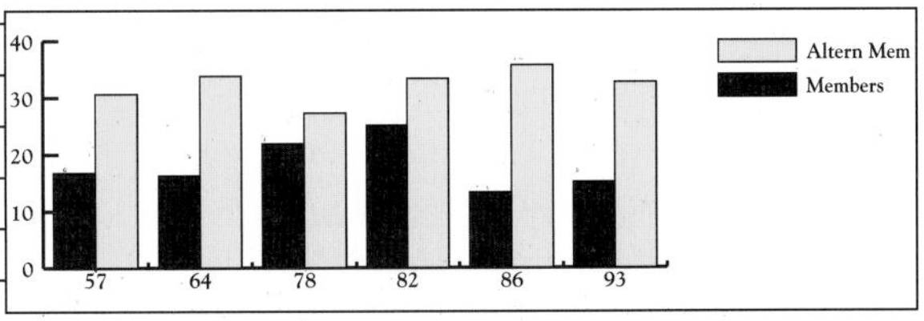

Women in Chinese People's Political Consultative Conference and its Standing Committee(%)

	Members	Stand Mem
1949	6.6	6.9
1954	14.3	6.5
1959	8.1	5.0
1964	6.3	5.6
1978	14.5	7.6
1983	12.5	11.0
1988	13.6	9.7
1993	13.52	9.7

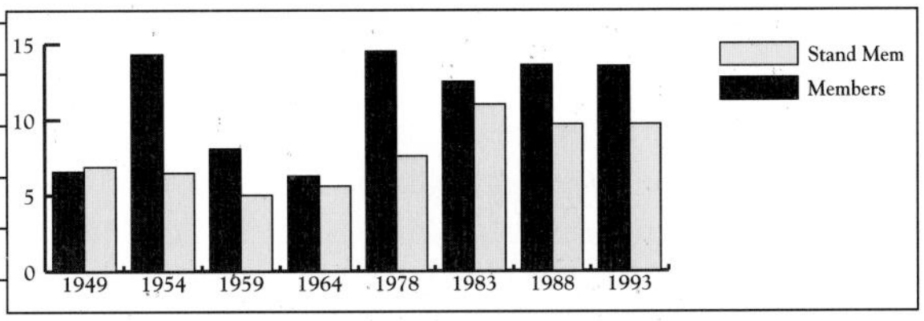

Women's Prop. of Reps and Standing Committee Members, Natl People's Congress(%)

	Reps	Stand Mem
1954	12	5
1959	12.2	6.3
1964	17.8	17.4
1975	22.6	25.1
1978	21.2	21
1983	21.2	9
1988	21.3	11.6
1993	21.03	12.69

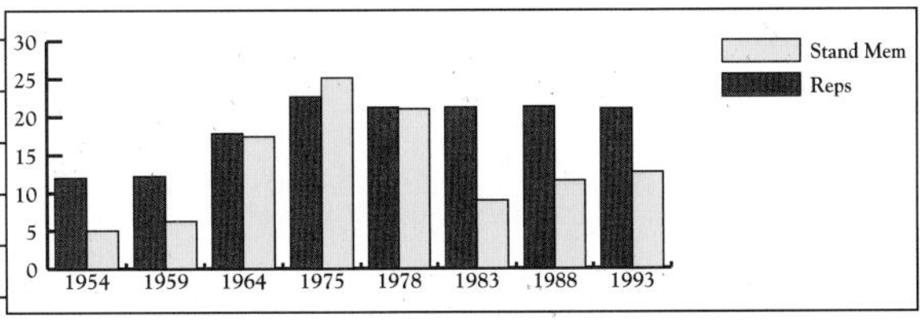

Woman Members and Alternate Members, Central Committee, CCP(%)

	Members	Altern Mem
1956	4.12	5.48
1969	7.65	9.17
1973	10.26	16.94
1977	6.97	18.18
1982	5.24	9.42
1987	5.71	10.91
1992	6.35	9.23

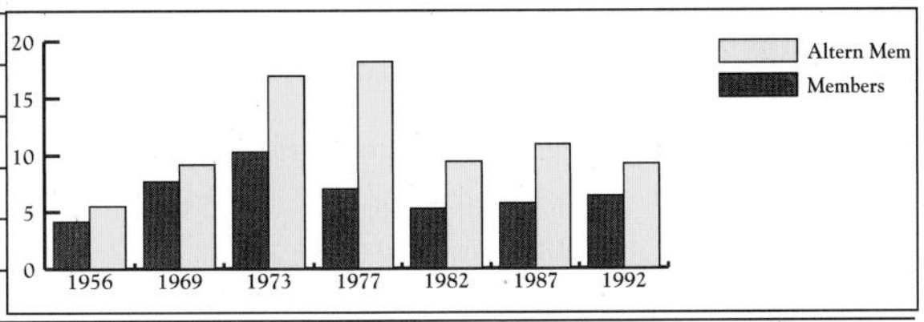

Source: Statistics on Chinese Women, 1949-1989; The Chronicle At Length of the People's Republic of China, vol. 4, p. 891, cited in Feng Yuan, 1997.

Most Chinese women still bear a triple burden, working outside the home and also assuming responsibility for housework and child and elder care.

While the latest demographic statistics indicate that the life expectancy of women, at 73 years, considerably exceeds that of men (68.7 years), some other demographic indicators attest to disadvantages still borne by women. The most dramatic is the sex ratio at birth. Under conditions of relatively equal treatment for both sexes, 105-106 males are born for every 100 females to compensate for the greater biological vulnerability of males. However, there is evidence that female infants have had higher mortality rates than male infants in recent years. The 1990 Census showed that female infants had an average mortality rate of 37 per 1000 live births, as against 32 for male infants - the opposite of what is expected. This disadvantage of infant girls is particularly marked in specific provinces, such as Jiangxi, Guangxi, Fujian and Gansu (UNICEF 1995). The 1994 national population sample survey revealed a sex ratio at birth in that year of 116.3 males to 100 females, substantially higher than the expected ratio (State Statistical Bureau 1995). According to the 1995 one per cent sample population survey, the overall female-male ratio for China was about 0.96, significantly below the ratio of well over 1.0 that would hold if both sexes receive equal care.[2]

These statistics highlight the continuing strength of male preference in large parts of rural China. Such attitudes have weakened greatly in the cities and towns; the three province-level municipalities (Beijing, Shanghai and Tianjin), for instance, all have the expected small excess of male mortality over female at birth. But more than just traditional attitudes are involved: in rural China, where very few people have pensions of any kind or health insurance, parents are dependent upon their children to take care of them in old age. In practice, this means their sons, since in the majority culture daughters marry out of the village and family and become responsible for their husbands' parents. Therefore, preference for sons is primarily not a matter of "backward attitudes", but of the requirements for survival in old age.

A second basic issue of well-being faced by many women, especially in rural areas, is physical abuse, including domestic violence and the kidnapping and sale of women. Abductions have been reported in a number of poorer provinces, such as Guangxi, Hunan and Anhui, usually for transport to other parts of the country for sale to men who lack wives. Such acts are of course strictly forbidden by Chinese law and also by government policy, including a Decision on Severe Punishment of Criminals Who Abduct or Kidnap Women or Children. Domestic violence, as elsewhere in the world, tends to occur in circumstances that make detection difficult. Moreover, as is true in other countries as well, many Chinese tend to regard domestic violence as a "family matter" to be handled within the familial community. Yet it has attracted increasing attention, and the Women's Federation as well as various independent groups have included violence against women on their agendas. A women's hotline has been established which provides telephone consultation, advice and support to women.

Most Chinese women still bear a triple burden, working outside the home and also assuming responsibility for housework and child and elder care. This of course considerably impedes women's ability to participate fully in social and political life.

3.1 Women in the Labour Force. The transition to a market economy has had multiple effects on the lives of China's women. Like men, they are subject to the dichotomization of life into urban and rural categories. As of 1995 there were 57.5 million "workers and staff members" (zhigong), mostly in the towns and cities, where they constituted 38.6 percent of employment in the formal economy. A majority of these women - 39.57 million - were employed in the state sector, where they made up 36.1 percent of employees.

In the countryside, the female labour force numbered 209.5 million in 1995, constituting 46.6 percent of the total rural labour force. In 1996, 54 million rural women worked in township and village enterprises (TVEs), or 41.4 percent of TVE employment. Although many rural women

2 Beijing Review 39. 22, May 27-June 2 1996.

have left farming for industrial or service sector employment or to join the flood of migrants seeking work in the towns, surveys have found that a smaller proportion of the female rural labour force (20.7%) than of the male (42.6%) have done so. Accordingly, there has been a "feminization of agriculture" in which women have been left to do an increasing share of the farm work. The 1990 national census found that, while women comprised 48 percent of farm workers nationally, their share was over 50 percent in developed areas such as Beijing, Shanghai, Jiangsu and Shandong (Feng Yuan 1997; UNICEF 1995). Since then, according to the Women's Federation, women may have come to constitute well over half of the agricultural workforce in the nation as a whole (Feng Yuan 1997).

Regional Differences in Women's Status. There are substantial regional differences in the overall socioeconomic status of Chinese women. Scholars have tried to measure this by means of "gender equality indexes" for health, economic and social status, comprising such sex-differentiated variables as infant mortality rates, employment rates, professional employment rates, literacy rates and marital status at age 15. They found that Beijing, Shanghai, Tianjin, Jilin, Heilongjiang and Xinjiang in the far west, score highest on these tests, while Anhui, Jiangxi, Hainan and Gansu scored lowest.

3.2 Women in Poor Areas.

Poverty is treated as a regional problem in China, and the statistical system focuses on the household rather than the individual. There is thus a lack of good information about the number and condition of poor women. Poor women outside of the officially designated poor areas, like their poor male counterparts, are not attended to by the policy makers. In 1987 there were about 107 million women living in officially designated poor counties, where they made up 48 percent of the local populations.

Poverty is a powerful impediment to progress for women. In 1989, the female adult illiteracy rate in poor areas was 49 percent. Only a third of poor area women had a primary school education and 2 per-

cent of them a high school education. Well over half had less than three years of formal schooling (compared with 31 percent of men). In general, remaining illiteracy in China is concentrated among women. 1 million of the 1.8 million children not in school in 1990 were girls, mostly in the poorer western provinces. A survey carried out by the State Education Commission in 1995 found that about half of girls not in school were not there because their families could not afford it; the second most common reason was hardly different - that their families wanted them to work. We have already seen (section 1) the serious effect poverty has on maternal and infant mortality rates.

3.3 Pay Differentials between Men and Women.

China is in principle committed to the idea of equal pay for equal work, but in practice there is a wage gap between the earnings of male and female workers. Women's wages in enterprises averaged 86.6 percent those of men in 1994. In non-economic organizations, however, women's wages were 97 percent of men's. As for women's salaries in administrative posts, a 1995 survey found that they averaged 83.4 percent of men's. Women are under-represented in most high-income occupations, and tend to be paid less within the same occupation, e.g., getting 90 percent of male salaries as managers and 64 percent of male salaries as factory chief engineers, chief economists or chief accountants. The gender gap was smallest in state-owned enterprises, government agencies, institutes and other organizations, and largest in joint ventures and foreign-invested enterprises.

The gender gap in earnings has always existed in urban China and it is difficult to say whether it has widened or narrowed over time, but some Labour Ministry data show it narrowing between 1978 and 1988. On the other hand, women have had increasing difficulty during the transition period getting and keeping jobs (see below). Rural China is harder to analyze because much income is earned by the family as a unit and cannot be ascribed to individuals. However, the Ministry of Labour in 1995 found that women in agriculture earned 80 percent as much as men, whereas in rural non-agricultural jobs they earned only 51 percent as much.[3]

Among the tens of millions of rural-urban migrants the earnings differential between men and women is also hard to get at, although some surveys have found that women tend to be concentrated in the lower ranks of the income distribution relative to men. Female migrants tend be employed in labour intensive manufacturing industries, such as toys and electronics assembly, or in domestic service, where there is neither social security nor channels for upward mobility. Of course, the same can be said of most male migrant workers, as well.

Earnings differentials can be the product of many different circumstances, of which the most frequently cited are differences in education and skill level. However, Chinese women have consistently registered high in relative human capital formation. The 1982 census found that among formal employees women on average had slightly more schooling than men. More than a decade later, in 1993, their advantage persisted. Among the administrative staffs of both enterprises and government organs, women had on average a third to a half year's more education than men (see Figure 3.7.).

[3] Liu Danhua and Chai Haishan, 1996, cited in Feng Yuan 1997.

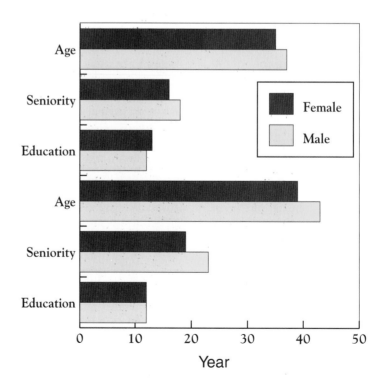

Figure 3.7.: Education and Sex Differentiation of Administrative Staffs, 1993
Note: The top bars refer to government organs, the bottom to enterprises.

3.4. Women and the Retirement System.

The retirement system at first blush looks favorable for women, for women workers retire at age 50, compared to 55 for male workers; and female cadres retire at 55 compared to 60. However, in another respect, this system puts women at a disadvantage because the pensions received by workers and cadres depend on the number of years worked. For instance, a work history of 35 years achieves a pension of 88 percent of the final wage, while a work history of 20-30 years earns a 75 percent pension. This structure enables men to start work at 20 (worker) or 25 (cadre) and still achieve the maximum pension, whereas a woman would have to start work at 15 (worker) or 20 (cadre), which would limit her educational opportunities and thus compromise her earnings. Under pressure from women's organizations and representatives, the Ministry of Human Resources decreed in 1990 that high ranking woman experts could continue to work until age 60, the same as men. In 1993 there were a total of 210,000 women in relevant job titles, constituting about 18 percent of people holding such titles and only 0.38 percent of women employees. Even so, there have been frequent complaints that the new policy has not been implemented in many work units.

3.5. Women and Housing.

Discrimination in housing is strictly contrary to law, specifically, the 1992 Law on Protection of Women's Rights, which guarantees women equality in access to housing. In urban areas of China, an employee's residence is usually assigned by his/her work unit. Although most women are employed, a common rule for allotting dwelling units is "for the man and not for the woman" (fen nan bu fen nu). Surveys have found that women often are in fact subject to discriminatory treatment (such as higher seniority requirements for housing eligibility) that in practice prevents them from having the same access to housing as men,[4] or from keeping their housing in the event of divorce. In many rural areas, where patriarchal traditions survive more strongly, divorce is likely to lead to loss of both land and home. With the rate of divorce increasing in China (1.06 million couples divorced in 1995 compared to 341 thousand in 1980[5]), more and more women need be assured of access to housing. The first local regulation attempting to do this was adopted in July 1995, in Qingdao, Shandong.[6]

The institution of the housing reform, designed to encourage privatization of the housing stock, has also brought complaints of discrimination. Some work units have charged women workers more than men to build houses for them, while other units have simply refused to allow their women workers to buy housing. Such institutional discrimination exists even in some government organs: to buy an allotted house a male employee might be charged only 10 thousand yuan while a female employee must pay 50 thousand yuan.[7] There is clearly a need to improve compliance with the laws banning sex discrimination in housing.

3.6. Women and the Transition: New Opportunities.

The development of a market economy has brought many new opportunities to women to use their talents and entrepreneurial abilities, and there are many examples of women who have succeeded in business or the arts. A characteristic of the transition is the emergence of a "new economy" consisting of ownership sectors other than the state and collective sectors, including individual and private ownership and TVEs, mostly considered collectives but of a different and more independent kind. Then there is the category called "other" in Chinese statistics, which includes various kinds of partnerships and jointly owned businesses, share holding corporations and foreign-invested enterprises, including those funded by overseas Chinese from Hong Kong, Macao and Taiwan.

Since 1994, a majority of new

The development of a market economy has brought many new opportunities to women to use their talents and entrepreneurial abilities.

---

[4] Union, 1993, China Women's News, February 11, 1994, p. 3, cited in Feng Yuan, 1997.

[5] Zhongguo minzheng tongji nianjian, Mingzhengbu Jihuacaiwusi bian, 1996, p228

[6] China Women's News, July, 1995, p1

[7] China Women's News, March 6, 1997, p2,

In recent years, old-fashioned sexist attitudes have re-emerged in public.

There is much room, therefore, for continued efforts to promote gender equality in China.

workers have gone to non state-owned units. In 1995, 4.24 million women formally worked in the "other" sector, making up 7.4 percent of formal female employment, whereas as recently as 1987 total employment in this sector had amounted to well under half a million. The proportion of women in the "other" sector was almost half in 1995, well above their 36 percent share in state enterprises, and even higher than their 45 percent share in urban collective units. In booming coastal Guangdong, over one million women work for over 18 thousand foreign-funded businesses (about 65 percent of their employees), and another five million work in TVEs, where they constitute 55 percent of TVE employment.

A rapidly growing and major source of jobs for women have been the TVEs, which employed 54.4 million women in 1996, some 41 percent of all TVE workers. Women constitute about 38.5 percent of the self-employed and 35.2 percent of owners of private and individual businesses in 1996. Clearly, the new era has brought considerably more choice and opportunity to women, as it has to men. Even in rural areas, women are no longer tied to the land and have begun to move to non-agricultural activities, even if more slowly than men. The ACWF even claims that TVEs run by women are almost all profitable, unlike many run by men!

3.7. Women and the Transition: Some New Problems.

In some respects, however, the transition has created additional difficulties for many women. The trend in China as elsewhere has been toward greater use of contingent labour - contract, temporary, part-time or seasonal - which lacks the social protection accorded to full-status state employees. Working conditions are poorer and labour protection weaker in the informal sector where increasing numbers of both men and women must find jobs.

Moreover, with the ideological relaxation of recent years, old-fashioned sexist attitudes have re-emerged in public, shouldering aside the principle of ensuring equal rights and opportunities for women. In a labour surplus economy, there have been constant calls - and some tangible pressures - for returning women to the home. Employers' want-advertisements frequently reveal bias, specifying "men only" or requiring that female applicants be young and attractive. Social gender roles reinforce such prejudices. With women still largely responsible for childcare and elder care, employers often avoid hiring women on the "efficiency" grounds that they will be absent more often. Thus, in a jobs fair for service sector graduates in January 1996, 27 of 42 central state units either declined to hire female graduates or restricted the job categories for which they would be considered. The grounds given were that women could not travel as easily as men, could not do various physical duties, and would be hampered by maternal duties. Such job discrimination is also in violation of the 1992 Law on Protection of Women's Rights.

Thus, despite the increase in employment rates among women, they still constitute a substantial majority of the jobless, as can be seen in Figure 3.8, which shows workers laid off by state enterprises in selected provinces, by sex, and the national percentage of women among young people awaiting job assignments.

There is much room, therefore, for continued efforts to promote gender equality in China. From the poor, rural hinterland, where girls are often kept from school, to the burgeoning cities, where women constitute more than their fair share of the unemployed, there is an agenda of issues that can be addressed by enlightened public policy. Ongoing improvement in conditions for women to fully develop their capabilities represents one of the biggest potential sources of talent and energy for China's future development.

Figure 3.8. Unemployment, by Sex, in Selected Regions

Total Number of Workers Laid Off, by Sex(thousands)			Percentage of Laid-off Workers in Total		
	Male	Female		Male	Female
Liaoning	282	470	Liaoning	4.6	10.8
Heilongjiang	214	186	Heilongjiang	5.7	8.9
Hubei	120	160	Hubei	2.6	5.3
Jiangsu	270	330	Jiangsu	4.9	8.9
Anhui	104	122	Anhui	4.8	5.6
Tianjin	80	180	Tiangjin	4.8	15.0

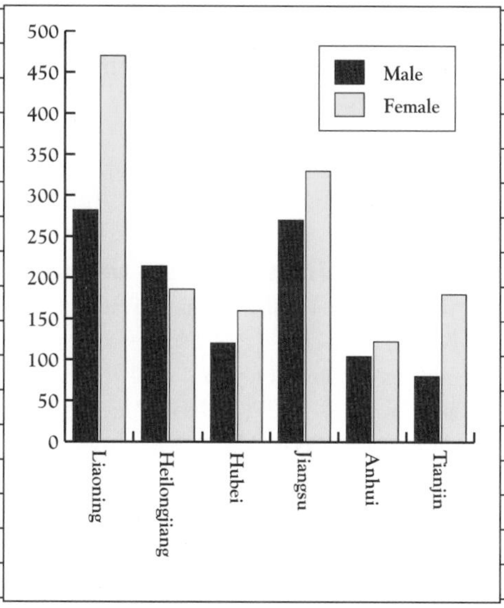

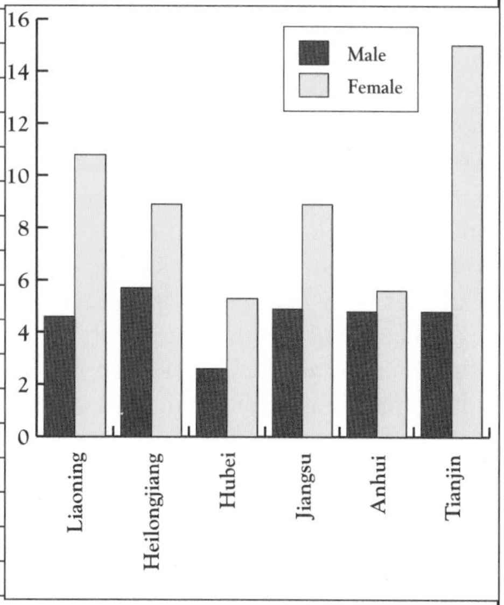

Percentage of Women among "Job-waiting Youths"

Year	Rate
1982	53
1985	60
1988	59
1992	57

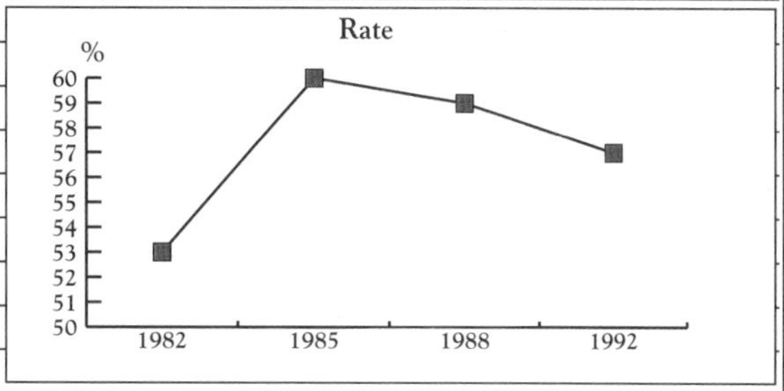

Source: ACWF survey, 1996, cited in Feng, 1997; Statistics on Chinese Women, 1949-1989, 1992, from National Report on Strategy at Nairobi, 1994, cited in Feng, 1997.

Income Distribution and Inequality

China's urban-rural gap was already substantial before the transition period began.

4.1. Overall Distribution.
At the beginning of the transition period which began in the late 1970s China was widely regarded as a highly egalitarian society. China's leaders and many academics criticized it for excessive egalitarianism, attacking the equality of wages ("everyone eating from the same big pot") as harmful to motivation and efficiency. All indications are that the urban distribution of income was extremely equal by international standards, that the range of wages and salaries within economic sectors was highly restricted, and that income differentials within rural villages tended to be small. However, some inequalities were quite great, even then. The policy at that time of local "self reliance", the sharp dichotomy between urban and rural residence status, and the prohibition of population movement all acted to magnify the urban-rural gap, as well as the differences between regions and localities.

In the early years of the reform period, overall inequality (as measured by the Gini coefficient[1]) changed little and may have fallen somewhat. The reforms began in agriculture and the countryside, where the great majority of the population and almost all households at the low end of the national income distribution reside, and led to widespread gains in income. The second half of the 1980s, however, saw a different pattern emerge, in which average incomes grew little but inequality rose sharply, the Gini rising from 0.30 in 1984 to 0.35 in 1989, according to World Bank estimates. In the first half of the 1990s, personal incomes have grown faster again, while inequality has continued to increase, the Gini reaching an estimated 0.415 (World Bank) in 1995. An independent study of income distribution that used a more comprehensive (and internationally accepted) definition of personal income, found somewhat greater inequality-a Gini ratio of 0.38 in 1988, rising to 0.45 in 1995.[2] This study also found that national inequality was about one-fifth higher than the average of

inequality in urban and rural incomes, taken separately, because of the substantial urban-rural income disparity in China. The sharp increase in inequality appears to have made China one of the more unequal of Asian developing countries.[3]

The burden of net rural taxes is largely borne by households that are poor in the rural context and extremely poor in the context of China as a whole. A reduction in net taxes/fees imposed on rural households would have a strongly favorable effect on overall income distribution.

4.2. Urban-Rural Inequality.
China's urban-rural income gap was already substantial before the transition period began, as indicated above. In 1988 this gap was about 2.4-to-1 (2.2-to-1 according to government statistics), which was very high by the standards of other Asian developing countries. Table 3.12 compares two estimates of the urban-rural gap in 1988 and 1995. The official SSB estimates show this already substantial gap widening by 20 percent in real terms, from 2.19 to 2.63, between the two years. The "Study Estimates", however, show no further widening over the period (242 in 1988 and 238 in 1995). The reason is that this source includes subsidies in personal income. These subsidies were a very high proportion of urban income (39 percent) in 1988, but as a result of the continuing institutional changes in China's transition to a market economy, they had melted away to 11 percent in 1995. The fall in urban subsidies offsets part of the rise in urban non-subsidy income, causing total urban income to grow more slowly than official statistics indicate, and keeping the urban-rural gap

---

[1] *The Gini coefficient is a common measure of inequality of distribution. It ranges in value from 0 (perfect equality) to 1 (absolute inequality).*

[2] *See Khan 1997.*

[3] *International comparisons of Gini ratios is subject to many difficulties, including differences in the exact variable being measured.*

from increasing. Nevertheless, this gap, already large in 1988 by international stan- dards, remains so today.

Table 3.12. Urban-Rural Income Inequality

	Study Estimates	SSB Estimates
Growth in Nominal Income (% per year):		
Rural	17.20	16.40
Urban	17.52	20.07
Growth in Real Income (% per year):		
Rural	4.71	4.00
Urban	4.48	6.74
Growth in Consumer Price Index (% per year)		
Rural	11.93	11.93
Urban	12.49	12.49
Urban Per Cap Income as Multiple of Rural:		
1988: Nominal	2.42	2.19
1995: Nominal	2.47	2.72
1995: At 1988 prices	2.38	2.63

Note: "Study Estimates" refers to an international collaborative study based upon two household income sur- veys, for 1988 and 1995. See Khan 1997.

4.3. Regional Inequality.

The transition period has seen the rapid widening of regional inequalities in development that reflect both the heritage of the pre-1949 past (when foreign capital focused on the eastern coastal areas) and the unequal present accessibility to the global market to which China has opened. Even before the transition period began, China's provinces experienced very different levels of development, including human development. A centralized fiscal policy that redistributed resources from richer coastal areas to the more backward interior at best kept such differences from widening even more, but did not succeed in narrowing them. With the adoption in the mid-1980s of a "coastal development strategy" designed to attract foreign direct investment and expand exports, the existing disparities began rapidly to widen.

Regional disparities are viewed first by examining the distribution of provincial average incomes. Table 3.13. shows the average per capita GDP and the average per capita personal income for China for the years 1978-95, and the Gini coefficients of the provincial averages for both. Figure 3.8. plots the trends in various measures of inequality. It is apparent that the disparity in provincial GDP per capita remained fairly constant over the entire period or even fell somewhat (if the coefficient of variation of provincial averages is used as the measure of inequality). However, a very different behavior characterizes the distribution of personal income (right-hand panel of Figure 3.9.).   After becoming more equal in the early reform years (roughly 1978-83), provincial average personal incomes diverged sharply thereafter, ending up considerably more unequal than they started.

Table 3.13. Inter-provincial Income Disparities

	Per Capita GDP	Gini Coefficient	Per Capita Income	Gini Coefficient
1978	359	0.2438	164	0.1261
1979	386	0.2394	197	0.1174
1980	414	0.2394	217	0.1119
1981	431	0.2391	248	0.0998
1982	465	0.2335	279	0.1003
1983	517	0.2404	311	0.1057
1984	580	0.2323	357	0.1123
1985	660	0.2324	376	0.1106
1986	700	0.2355	409	0.1198
1987	762	0.2467	423	0.1271
1988	847	0.2463	420	0.1326
1989	870	0.2419	408	0.1394
1990	892	0.2414	443	0.1452
1991	975	0.2436	464	0.1407
1992	1135	0.2538	509	0.1484
1993	1331	0.2613	551	0.1629
1994	1523	0.2695	607	0.1685
1995	1715	0.2747	656	0.1670

Source: Lin 1997

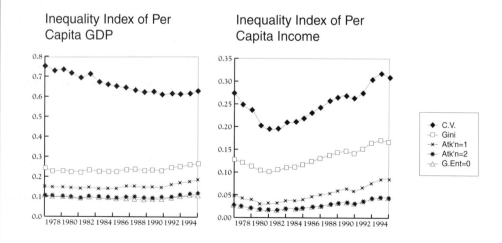

Figure 3.9.: Inequality in Provincial GDP per capita and Income per capita

The difference in behavior of provincial GDP and provincial income has been analyzed by Lin et al (1997). They find that the lack of increase over time in inequality of provincial GDP per capita is due to the mutually offsetting effects of two opposite trends. On the one hand, the disparities between eastern, central and western regions have widened quickly. But on the other hand, within each of these regions, the more backward provinces have grown faster than the more advanced ones. This relative convergence of provinces within regions has offset the divergence between regions, keeping the overall inequality of provincial GDPs from rising, even though inequality of regions has risen sharply. When it comes to personal income, however, this convergence factor is not present, and so provincial per capita incomes diverge steadily from about 1982.

The divergence of GDP from personal income, especially since the mid-1980s, deserves attention. According to the official estimates, per capita real GNP in China increased at an annual average rate of about eight percent between 1988 and 1995,[4] while the growth in real per capita household income was only about five percent.[5] This decline in the share of personal income in GNP was matched by a fall in government's share, government revenue dropping from 16 percent to 11 percent of GNP between 1988 and 1995 (State Statistical Bureau 1996). Even though a good deal of extra-budgetary revenue probably goes unreported, these omissions could not be large enough to reverse the strong trend toward a shrinking government share of GNP. However, if the shares of both the household and government sectors of the economy have declined, then business sector income must have risen very sharply during the period in question.

The difference between the behavior of personal income and that of GNP or GDP has important ramifications for human development in China. For instance, the incidence of absolute poverty is determined by the average personal income and its distribution. Holding distribution constant, a growth in per capita income will reduce the poverty rate; and holding per capita income constant, a deterioration in distribution will increase poverty. If income is growing while distribution is becoming more unequal, as in China, then the result for poverty depends upon the relative strengths of these two trends. A 4-5 percent growth in personal income, the relevant variable, will outweigh a much smaller adverse change in income distribution than would the 8 or 9 percent annual growth in GDP, which - although irrelevant in this context - is what usually comes to mind when economic growth is considered.[6] This subject will be discussed further in Chapter IV.

4.4. Regional Inequality and the Human Development Index.

One way of gauging the extent of inter-regional inequality in China is to compare the human development index numbers of China's 30 provinces, centrally-administered municipalities, and autonomous regions (hereafter all called "provinces").[7] This is done in Table 3.14, which shows that the province with the highest HDI rank is Shanghai, while Tibet has the lowest. The ratio between them is 2.3-to-1.

The HDI and its components are highly correlated with one another, the highest correlation being between the GDP index and HDI. That this correlation for China is even stronger than it appears in the table is indicated by the fact that the two provinces with the biggest gap between HDI and GDP ranks - Qinghai and Ningxia - are both very small provinces in terms of population, with fewer than 5 million inhabitants each. Thus, in China in general, provinces that are economically more developed have achieved higher human development level as well. This close correlation is important to take note of. As

Thus, in China in general, provinces that are economically more developed have achieved higher human development level as well.

---

[4] *This is based on the data in SSB, 1996.*

[5] *The annual growth rate in real per capita household income for China as a whole (the weighted average of rural and urban incomes) was higher than either the rural or the urban real income growth because there was a rise in the weight of the urban population, the richer of the two income groups, between 1988 and 1995.*

[6] *This point is made by Khan and Riskin 1997.*

[7] *Taiwan, Hong Kong and Macao are not included in this and other discussions in this Report of China's administrative regions.*

the various global Human Development Reports show, there is considerable divergence internationally between GDP and HDI ranks, indicating the existence of unexploited potential for improvements in human development at given levels of economic development. In China, in general, appropriate economic development must be seen as an essential ingredient in regional human development.

Table 3.14. Human Development Index by Province in 1995

Province	HDI rank	GDP rank	Life expectancy index	Education index	GDP index	Human development index (HDI) value
Shanghai	1	1	0.84	0.85	0.969	0.885
Beijing	2	2	0.81	0.86	0.960	0.876
Tianjin	3	3	0.80	0.83	0.954	0.859
Guangdong	4	4	0.80	0.79	0.850	0.814
Zhejiang	5	5	0.79	0.75	0.814	0.785
Jiangsu	6	6	0.79	0.77	0.724	0.760
Liaoning	7	8	0.76	0.80	0.708	0.756
Fujian	8	7	0.76	0.72	0.709	0.729
Shandong	9	9	0.77	0.74	0.604	0.704
Heilongjiang	10	10	0.72	0.78	0.526	0.676
Hainan	11	11	0.79	0.75	0.488	0.674
Hebei	12	12	0.78	0.77	0.464	0.670
Jilin	13	13	0.72	0.80	0.451	0.659
Shanxi	14	17	0.74	0.79	0.352	0.627
Xinjiang	15	14	0.67	0.75	0.438	0.619
Henan	16	16	0.75	0.74	0.358	0.618
Hubei	17	15	0.71	0.73	0.388	0.609
Guangxi	18	18	0.74	0.75	0.332	0.605
Anhui	19	19	0.75	0.72	0.328	0.600
Hunan	20	23	0.71	0.75	0.320	0.592
Sichuan	21	24	0.70	0.74	0.308	0.582
Inner Mongolia	22	25	0.70	0.74	0.296	0.578
Jiangxi	23	20	0.70	0.73	0.327	0.577
Ningxia	24	22	0.72	0.67	0.323	0.571
Shaanxi*	25	27	0.72	0.73	0.259	0.570
Yunnan	26	26	0.65	0.64	0.289	0.526
Gansu	27	29	0.71	0.62	0.216	0.514
Qinghai	28	21	0.61	0.57	0.326	0.503
Guizhou	29	30	0.67	0.64	0.172	0.494
Tibet	30	28	0.58	0.36	0.226	0.391

Sources: (1) Lu Lei, Hao Hongsheng and Gao Ling "Table of Provincial Life-expectancy in China in 1990", Population Studies (in Chinese), May 1994. (2) SSB, China Regional Economy: A Profile of 17 Years of Reform and Opening-Up, China Statistical Press, 1996. (3) Data of National 1% Population Survey 1995, China Statistical Press, 1997. (4) China Education Commission, Statistical Yearbook of China Education 1995, Press of People's Education, 1996. (5) China Population Yearbook 1996.

Notes: (1) Hong Kong, Taiwan and Macao are not included in this ranking of administrative regions. The same is true of all other tables in this Report. (2) GDP per capita is in 1990 prices. (3) Provincial price indices used for adjustment of GDP per capita are those of retail prices. (4) Provincial life expectancy estimates for 1990 were used in lieu of 1995 estimates, which were not available. Since life expectancy changes very slowly, this should have little impact on the HDI estimates.

* The formally correct romanization of the name of this province is "Shanxi". The variant "Shaanxi" is commonly used outside of China to distinguish this province from its eastern neighbor, "Shanxi". In Chinese, the two names are distinguished by different tonal pronunciations and different written characters.

However, there are some exceptions to this rule. Take, for instance, two contiguous interior provinces, Hubei and Jiangxi. Hubei's HDI rank (17) is two places below its per capita GDP ranking (15), and Jiangxi's HDI rank (23) is three places below its GDP rank (20). Moreover, all of the provinces whose HDI and GDP ranks differ by two or more places are among the poorer half of the provinces, except for Hubei, which is just at the halfway point.

Within the poorer half, some provinces - Shanxi, Hunan, Sichuan, Inner Mongolia, Shaanxi, Gansu - do better with respect to HDI than to GDP per capita, whereas others - Jiangxi, Ningxia, Tibet, and, especially, Qinghai - do worse. Given the varied and extensive historical, geographic, cultural and ecological backgrounds of these provinces, no simple explanation can account for the differences in ratios of HDI-to-GDP ranks.

Provincial HDIs were also computed for 1990 (Table 3.15.), and the changes in provincial HDI values between 1990 and 1995 are shown in Table 3.16. It is instructive to compare the results for the two years. Clearly, there is significant variation in provincial HDI growth. Among the 30 provinces there are nine with HDI growth above 10 points, and all of them are located in coastal areas. 13 provinces are in the range of growth between five and ten points, and eight provinces had growth below five points. Among the low-growth group, Shanghai is exceptional in that it had already reached the threshold level of GDP per capita at which further increases in this variable are discounted when calculating HDI (see Chapter I, section 2.1.). The other seven provinces are mostly located in western regions. Regression analysis also indicates that, consistent with the close correlation of per capita GDP with HDI, the difference in the per capita GDP index between 1990 and 1995 explains most of the difference in HDI between the two years.[8]

---

[8] The relevant equation is:
$$DHDI = 0.026 - 0.0184 \cdot HDI90 + 0.341 \cdot DGDPI$$
$$(3.12) \quad (-1.24) \quad (32.32)$$

Adjusted $R^2 = 0.977$.
    where DHDI is difference in HDI value between 1990 and 1995, HDI90 is the 1990 value of HDI, and DGDPI is change in GDP index between 1990 and 1995. This equation explains almost 98 percent of the variation in growth of HDI between the two dates.

Table 3.15. HDI by Province in 1990

Province	Life expectancy index	Education index	GDP index	Human Development Index (HDI) Value	HDI rank	GDP rank
Shanghai	0.84	0.80	0.949	0.862	1	1
Tianjin	0.80	0.80	0.799	0.798	2	2
Beijing	0.81	0.82	0.596	0.742	3	3
Liaoning	0.76	0.78	0.556	0.698	4	4
Guangdong	0.80	0.75	0.409	0.652	5	7
Jiangsu	0.79	0.70	0.431	0.638	6	5
Zhejiang	0.79	0.69	0.400	0.628	7	9
Shandong	0.77	0.68	0.421	0.625	8	6
Heilongjiang	0.72	0.75	0.401	0.624	9	8
Jilin	0.72	0.76	0.346	0.609	10	11
Shanxi	0.74	0.75	0.324	0.607	11	14
Hebei	0.78	0.69	0.320	0.598	12	15
Xinjiang	0.67	0.72	0.395	0.593	13	10
Fujian	0.76	0.68	0.331	0.688	14	13
Hainan	0.79	0.70	0.262	0.582	15	20
Hubei	0.71	0.68	0.343	0.578	16	12
Inner Mongolia	0.70	0.70	0.316	0.571	17	17
Henan	0.75	0.67	0.246	0.558	18	24
Shaanxi	0.72	0.67	0.253	0.550	19	22
Guangxi	0.74	0.72	0.189	0.548	20	29
Hunan	0.70	0.72	0.219	0.547	21	27
Ningxia	0.72	0.62	0.289	0.543	22	18
Anhui	0.75	0.60	0.251	0.533	23	23
Sichuan	0.70	0.68	0.217	0.532	24	28
Jiangxi	0.70	0.67	0.224	0.529	25	26
Gansu	0.71	0.57	0.235	0.505	26	25
Qinghai	0.61	0.56	0.319	0.498	27	16
Yunnan	0.65	0.58	0.258	0.496	28	21
Guizhou	0.67	0.58	0.159	0.470	29	30
Tibet	0.58	0.32	0.266	0.388	30	19

Sources: (1) Lu Lei, Hao Hongsheng and Gao Ling "Table of Provincial Life-expectancy in China in 1990", Population Studies (in Chinese), May 1994. (2) SSB, China Regional Economy: A Profile of 17 Years of Reform and Opening-Up, China Statistical Press, 1996. (3) Figures of the 1990 Population Cencus, China Statistical Press, 1993.
Notes: (1) Provincial price indices used for adjustment of GDP per capita are those of retail prices.

Table 3.16. Change in Human Development Index Values, 1990 to 1995, by Province

Province	Human development index (HDI) value	Education index	GDP index
Shanghai	2.2	4.7	2.0
Beijing	13.3	3.7	36.3
Tianjin	6.1	2.9	15.4
Guangdong	16.2	4.5	44.1
Zhejiang	15.8	5.9	41.4
Jiangsu	12.3	7.5	29.3
Liaoning	5.8	2.1	15.2
Fujian	14.1	4.4	37.9
Shandong	7.9	5.5	18.2
Heilongjiang	5.3	3.3	12.5
Hainan	9.3	5.2	22.6
Hebei	7.2	7.2	14.4
Jilin	5.0	4.6	10.5
Shanxi	2.1	3.4	2.8
Xinjiang	2.6	3.4	4.3
Henan	6.0	6.8	11.2
Hubei	3.1	4.7	4.5
Guangxi	5.7	2.7	14.3
Anhui	6.6	12.2	7.7
Hunan	4.4	3.1	10.2
Sichuan	5.0	5.8	9.1
Jiangxi	4.8	6.1	8.3
Inner Mongolia	0.7	4.2	-2.0
Ningxia	2.8	4.8	3.5
Shaanxi	2.0	5.5	0.6
Yunnan	3.1	6.1	3.0
Gansu	0.9	4.6	-1.9
Qinghai	0.5	0.8	0.7
Guizhou	2.4	5.8	1.4
Tibet	0.3	4.7	-4.0

Sources: Tables 3.13. and 3.14.

Source: Zhang Shikun: A Brief Introduction to the Network of Community Development and Population Control, China Population Almanac . 1995

It is significant that such close correlation exists between per capita GDP and HDI in China. In international experience, there is great diversity in the GDP/HDI relationship, indicating that some countries do a much better job than others of translating measured income into human development outcomes. In China, however, improving the human development status of relatively backward provinces would seem to depend heavily on increasing their per capita GDPs. In 1995 there were only two provinces - Jiangxi and Qinghai - whose HDI rank was lower than their GDP rank by three or more places.

The most important regional disparity in China is the gap between the eastern coastal provinces and those of the interior, especially the western interior. Eight of the top ten provinces in terms of HDI are located on the coast (Beijing and Heilongjiang are the exceptions). All of the western provinces except Xinjiang (15th) are in the poorest ten, where they are joined by one central province: Jiangxi. These regional gaps have been increasing, and there is the danger that they will continue to widen. Foreign direct investment is highly concentrated in coastal regions and township and village enterprises have grown fastest there. Sharp differences in educational opportunities among the provinces promise to extend regional inequalities indefinitely into the future. These differences are illustrated in Table 3.17, which shows provincial inequality in the education component of the Human Development Index by province.

Table 3.17. Education Index, by Province, 1995

Beijing	0.86	Shandong	0.74
Shanghai	0.85	Hubei	0.73
Tianjin	0.83	Sichuan	0.74
Liaoning	0.80	Fujian	0.72
Jilin	0.80	Henan	0.74
Heilongjiang	0.78	Shaanxi	0.73
Shanxi	0.79	Jiangxi	0.73
Guangdong	0.79	Ningxia	0.67
Hunan	0.75	Anhui	0.72
Guangxi	0.75	Guizhou	0.64
Xinjiang	0.75	Yunnan	0.64
Inner Mongol	0.74	Gansu	0.62
Jiangsu	0.77	Qinghai	0.57
Hainan	0.75	Tibet	0.36
Zhejiang	0.75		

Note: The variable measured is the education component of the human development index.

4.5. Inequality and Development Strategy.

We have seen that various dimensions of inequality narrowed somewhat in the early years of reform, and then began widening again in the mid-1980s. In the first period, reform was concentrated in agriculture and farm incomes - the lowest incomes in China — rose rapidly. After the mid-1980s, on the other hand, attention shifted to the cities and to reform of industry, and the "coastal development strategy" focused state financial and administrative resources on coastal cities with a view to attracting foreign direct investment there. Farm incomes stagnated for the second half of the 1980s and into the early 1990s. This shift in development strategy may well have had the unintended consequence of exacerbating income inequality. Other strategies and policies, such as the decentralization of the fiscal system, may similarly have had distributional consequences. For instance, a recent study of income distribution has found that the burden of rural net taxes and fees falls most heavily on the lowest income groups.[9] Such examples suggest that the public policy formation process should routinely review the distribution impact of proposed policies and, where necessary, formulate off-setting policies to counter unintended but anticipatable negative effects on distribution.

[9] Khan 1997

Problems of the Labour Market: Surplus Labour, Unemployment, Migration and the Social Security System.

5.1. Surplus Labour and Reform.[1]

China's is a labour surplus economy. The economically active population comes to more than 615 million people, including a rural workforce of 450 million, of whom 120 million are thought to be redundant. The problem of rural labour surplus has been partly offset by the rapid development of township and village enterprises (TVEs), which now employ over 135 million, or 28 percent of the rural labour force. TVEs have thus played a big role in providing rural employment opportunities and limiting the flood of rural-urban migration, but it is a role that is very unevenly distributed throughout the country.

The urban labour force came to 198 million workers in 1996, of which 57 percent worked in state enterprises, 15 percent in urban collective enterprises, and 12 percent in private or individual enterprises. The remaining 16 percent were distributed over a variety of ownership forms: domestic and foreign-domestic joint ventures and foreign-invested enterprises mainly. There were also 38.5 million workers in rural private enterprises or self-employed (State Statistical Bureau 1997).

Of the urban labour force, there are an estimated 28 million surplus state sector workers (including disguised unemployed and laid off workers). Over seven million new jobs per year have been created in the urban economy during the first half of the 1990s, including jobs filled by rural migrants. However, about the same number of young people have entered the job market annually. In addition, there are the millions of redundant state sector workers plus an increasing portion of the tens of millions of surplus rural labourers who are seeking urban jobs.

The Labour Ministry put the number of urban unemployed in early 1997 at 6 million, and the rate of registered unemployment in 1996 at 3 per cent of the urban labour force (China Daily, March 11, 1997). By October, 1997 the rate of registered unemployment had risen to 8 million (Figure 3.10). While the trend has clearly been upward through the 1990s, the absolute numbers greatly understate actual unemployment, because they include only those registered with local labour bureaus. Unemployed workers who have not registered are left out, including a large number of workers who have been laid off by state enterprises. Fully 87 percent of the urban poor are state sector workers and retirees and their families, according to the State Statistical Bureau (China Daily, August 6, 1997).

---

[1] This section relies on Shang Xiaoyuan 1997.

The Labour Ministry put the number of urban unemployed in October, 1997 at 8 million. The absolute numbers greatly understate actual unemployment, because they include only those registered with local labour bureaus.

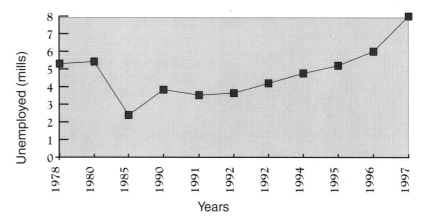

Figure 3.10. Urban Registered Unemployed, 1978-1997 (millions)
Sources: SSB, 1996; People's Daily (overseas ed.), 27 October, 1997; China Daily, March 11, 1997.

An estimate for Shanghai at the end of 1993 that attempted to include unemployed workers who are excluded from the official rate found that the actual unemployment level was 7 to 8 per cent, two or more times the official rate of 3.6 per cent (ILO 1994 p. 10). This unmeasured addition to unemployment will inevitably grow larger as the reform of state enterprises proceeds to completion and more of them close down or shed their unneeded workers. Moreover, the official rate covers only those with an urban hukou (household registration),[2] and thus leaves out the tens of millions of temporary migrant workers from the countryside (see sec. 5.2. below).

Under the planned economy labour surpluses were managed through such institutions as rural communes and state enterprises, which distributed available work more or less evenly over the labour force without concern for the relation between wage and marginal product; and also by severe restrictions on migration, which blocked movement of people from relatively low income to relatively high income sectors, and thus prevented the emergence of open unemployment. The urban labour surplus was contained by the population registration system, food rationing and the absence of a free market in food, and the administrative sanctions on population movement. Those lucky enough to be urban residents were almost certain to have lifetime job security. This system provided a mechanism of work distribution as well as of income maintenance for the working population.

With the coming of reform, however, this system has changed radically. State owned enterprises (SOEs) have been separated from direct control by government, and governments are no longer to bear direct financial responsibility for their performance or for labour insurance. SOEs now must face market competition, for which they are unprepared. They have traditionally provided a full range of benefits to their workers, including pensions, housing, schools, and medical insurance. Labour costs are thus much higher in the SOEs than in non-state sectors. Yet SOEs cannot divest themselves of these obligations until alternatives have been established. Among SOEs, labour costs are unevenly distributed because older enterprises with a larger corps of retired workers have heavier responsibilities for pensions and health care.

Moreover, market competition is forcing enterprises to adopt a more flexible employment and wage system. In a labour surplus economy, with an estimated one-fifth to one-third redundant workforce, the system of lifetime employment cannot last.

[2] All Chinese are assigned hukou or household registrations identifying their place of residence. Until recently, it was virtually impossible for people without an urban hukou to live in a town or city because all staple food was rationed and they would not be entitled to ration coupons. With the development of a market in food and a more relaxed official attitude toward population mobility, rural-urban migration has swelled rapidly.

Yet labour mobility is impeded by the fact that all entitlements to social insurance benefits have been tied to the enterprise. To leave one's work unit is to lose all benefits. Naturally, workers have resisted the threat to their employment and welfare entitlements, making deeper enterprise reform politically difficult.

For these reasons, and because the inherited administrative system of the SOEs cannot function well in a market economy, a large number of public enterprises have been making losses or becoming insolvent. The situation has been aggravated by concerted anti-inflationary policies which have brought down the real GDP growth rate from a high of 14.2 percent in 1992 to "only" 9.5 percent in 1997.[3] Some economists attribute growing unemployment as much to macro-policy as to the problems of SOEs. Whatever the causes, many employees of such enterprises are quasi-unemployed - that is, still on the books, but receiving only partial wages or none at all - or semi-employed (working only intermittantly). Their pensioners fail to receive their pensions, in part or in full; workers' medical expenses go unreimbursed; and the entire urban work unit-based social insurance system has been unraveling. Some laid off workers find work in the informal sector, but an estimated 74 percent of the urban poor population in 1994 and 1995 were public sector workers or their dependents (Fan 1996).

The previous urban social security system only covered state sector workers. This was not problematic when the urban non-state workforce was very small: in 1978 there were only 140 thousand self-employed people in China (Shi, 1993). But the proportion of non-state sector workers has risen rapidly, and in 1996 constituted 43 percent of the urban labour force. This raises the problem of how to provide social security coverage for the growing population outside the state sector.

Exacerbating the short-term problem of social welfare provision is the longer term challenge of an aging population, whose proportion aged 60 and above will grow from 7.6 percent of the population in 1982 to 9.8 percent in 2000. Between 2000 and 2020, the proportion of elderly will increase from 9.8 per cent to 15.2 percent. At the peak of the aging process, the proportion of old people is expected to reach 24.3 percent of the total population (CRCOA, 1994: 34). This trend is driving up the cost of health care and pensions. Thus, the cost of social insurance and welfare funds as a proportion of the total wage bill rose from 13.7 percent in 1978 to 34 percent in 1995. The ratio of current employees to pensioners of all kinds dropped from .26 in 1978 to .05 in 1995, and the total number of pensioners increased from 3.1 to 30.94 million.

The emerging market is having a complex impact on the urban social security system. On the one hand, the market provides new resources outside government budgets while on the other it throws up new economic and social problems, such as inflation, unemployment, income polarization, etc. These phenomena create difficulties for people on fixed government subsidies, and add new faces to the urban poor, including losers in the market, the unemployed and laid off (xiagang) workers.

In the countryside, decollectivization in the early 1980s completely changed the financial base of the rural social security system. The Five Guarantees System had to find a new financial base, and the collective health insurance system was dismantled (see sec. 1.3 of this chapter). A new land distribution system has provided a secure base for the re-emergence of the traditional family security system, but it leaves the rural population with little recourse other than to rely on family.

Second, the rapid rise of rural industry has presented new problems, such as the provision of social security for rural industrial employees, a rise of the number of work-related disabilities, etc. Third, demographic changes - including both migrations to urban areas and the aging of the population - are particularly important in

The emerging market is having a complex impact on the urban social security system.

---

[3] *Chinese growth rates are commonly regarded as containing a certain percentage of "water" - i.e., somewhat exaggerated. Moreover, growth rates have different implications in a labour surplus country like China. The sharp and painful recession of 1989-90 registered 4 percent real growth of GDP, a rate that would be considered inflationary in the U.S.*

terms of their long-term impact. The decrease in the proportion of younger age groups in the rural population, and the decline in household size will together work to weaken the main support for the elderly traditionally provided by their family members. During the process of family planning, China has had an increasingly unbalanced sex ratio at birth in rural areas since 1975 (SSB, 1996: 72). In 1990 there were 35 million more males than females. Because life expectancy of females in China is considerably longer than that of males, the sex imbalance is greater in the reproductive age range. This means that there are many millions of males who will remain unmarried and without a family to support them in old age. So the number of Five Guarantee Households is likely to increase.

5.2. Migration: The "Floating Population".

With the development of a free market in food and the relaxation of administrative restrictions on population movement, people have begun to move in large numbers in search of economic opportunities. Some have managed to settle permanently and gain formal urban status, some are reflected in population statistics as "long-term migrants", and some - commonly called the "floating population" - are statistically invisible. A 1992 survey of both urban and rural areas found that in-migrants without residence status where they were living constituted 8.1 percent of the total sample, which would put the total informal migrant population at about 95 million in that year. Registration statistics of the public security department put the size of the floating population at 31 million in 1990 and 84 million in 1995.[4]

Whatever their exact numbers, the floating population of temporary migrants, most of them rural-urban, have been playing an increasingly important role in China's urbanization and population redistribution. They fill many jobs at the lower end of the earnings ladder and in a variety of sectors, including construction, manufacturing, transport and services. Migration is thus economically motivated. According to the 1 Percent National Population Survey in 1995, the main flow of migrants moves from the poorer central and western parts of the country to the more prosperous eastern region. They tend to be better educated and more literate not only than the local population of their point of origin, but also of the national population, as shown by Table 3.18. They also tend to be much younger, as revealed in Figure 3.11. All of the studies of migrant characteristics indicate that the sex ratio is heavily weighted toward men. The opportunity cost of migration for women, who bear most family responsibilities, is higher, and the relative income they can expect to earn in urban low-skill jobs is lower, as attested to by Figure 3.12.

[4] There are several important surveys on population mobility in China in the 1990s. Their estimates of the size of the floating population ranges from 80 million to 120 million. For a list of studies, see Cai Fang 1997.

Table 3.18. Educational Level of Migrants (%)

	Illiteracy	Primary school	Junior high school	Senior high school and above
Population aged 6 and over	20.9	41.2	28.6	9.2
Migrants of 1990 survey	8.3	23.0	35.7	33.1
Rural labour force in Shandong	13.0	33.7	40.1	13.2
Rural-urban migrants in Jinan	0.8	15.6	71.2	12.4

Source: Population Census Office of the State Council, Department of Population Statistics of SSB: China 1990 Population Census Data, Vol. 1 & Vol. 4, China Statistics Publishing House, 1993; Shandong Rural Sample Survey Team: Shandong Rural Statistics Yearbook . 1993, China Statistics Publishing House, 1993

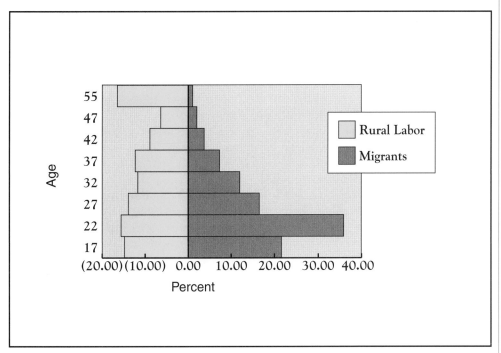

Figure 3.11. Age Comparison: Migrants vs. General Rural Labour
Source: Shandong Rural Sample Survey Team: Shandong Rural Statistics Yearbook .
1993, China Statistics Publishing House, 1993; Survey on Urban Labour In-migrants in
Jinan City, 1995.
Note: For rural labour, read age bars to the left from 0.00; for migrants, read age bars
to the right

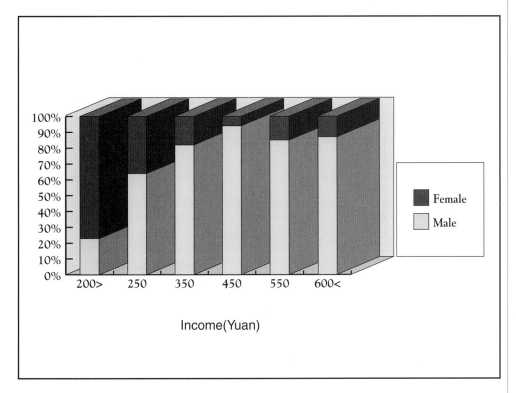

Figure 3.12. Gender Comparison of Migrant Income
Source: Jinan Sample Survey on Rural Labour Migrants

The new labour mobility has made big contributions to China's economic and social development. Both equity and economic efficiency are furthered by the freedom of people to move. Mobility has also raised the living standards of many of the migrants and their families, allowed rural incomes in poor and labour surplus areas to rise (or prevented their decline), and fed the growing demand for a flexible labour force generated by rapid urban economic growth. The flow of income remitted to the migrants' home communities in poorer areas, sometimes in the form of direct investment there, has been a significant source of fiscal resources in some poor communities. Migration has probably slowed the increase in the urban-rural income gap. Studies show that rural-urban migrants who return to their home villages tend to adopt many of the values and behaviour patterns of urban life, devote more attention to their children's education, and opt for lower fertility (Cai Fang, 1997).

Migration has also generated some problems and controversy, however. Urban migrant communities, which are less subject to the strict neighbourhood organisation of Chinese cities than permanent communities, have justly or unjustly been taxed with being breeding grounds of various social problems growing in Chinese cities, such as crime, prostitution and drug abuse. But some problems concern the welfare of the migrants themselves: for instance, there are reported cases of migrant workers, especially women, being mistreated. Moreover, migrants are excluded from obtaining various public services available to full status urban residents, such as schooling and health care. Such a huge influx of people into urban areas over such a short period of time is bound to put great strain on the urban infrastructure and the job market. Localities have tried to reduce the pressure by denying services to the migrants, but they inevitably produce sewage and garbage, use water, ride on buses, etc.

Migration contributes to the so-called "feminization of agriculture": in 1995, the estimated 150 million rural women doing farm work constituted over 60 per cent of the farm labour force (UNICEF 1995). Women are of course represented among the "floating population", where they tend to work in light industry or as live-in nannies; however, as we have seen, the most common pattern is for rural men to seek work in the towns while the women remain at home to bear the "triple burden" of farm work, child care and elder care.

5.3. Pension Reform.

Beginning in 1986, new state sector workers were to be hired on a contract basis rather than with lifetime tenure. A new social insurance system along with an unemployment insurance system were established to handle contract workers. These systems were to pool contributions from the various parties (enterprise, individual and state), with the local or provincial government setting a levy rate based on the estimated expenditure requirement for the pooled area, and then paying out the fund to enterprises according to their actual pension obligations. In 1992, further reform called for shifting all public employees to a contract basis. However, progress in accomplishing this has been uneven. Only about a quarter of the workforce were on contract at the end of 1994. Nevertheless, pension reform has proceeded and in 1996 was said to cover most state employees as well as 70-80 percent of urban collective workers and one-third of urban non-public enterprises (Ge, 1996). Almost 80 million employees had begun to contribute to pension funds as of 1996.

The main principles of the new pension system are (1) to average out the pension burden among enterprises with different numbers of retirees; and (2) to move from a "pay as you go" system to one of at least partial accumulation of pension funds. On both counts there have been major problems. Whereas insurance principles dictate the highest possible level of pooling of risk, in practice pooling has been widely variable, ranging from the locality to the province. In August 1997 the Minister of Labour revealed a plan approved by the State Council to unify the pension system at the national level.

While the fund pooling system may

The new labour mobility has made big contributions to China's economic and social development.

help some of the harder pressed enterprises with large retirement burdens, and taps a previously untapped source of funds - namely, employees - it leaves many unresolved problems. Employees in enterprises that cannot pay wages obviously cannot make pension contributions. Loss-making enterprises that default on their contributions are cut off from payments from the pooling fund. Current pension obligations are absorbing most or all available contributions, leaving little for building accumulations to graduate from "pay as you go" to a funded system. The new system as it exists now cannot cope with the long-term ageing problem. Individuals' contributions are not transferable, which impedes labour market flexibility. The social pooling system has encountered many serious operational problems and falls well short of representing a coherent, nation-wide, long-term strategy to provide a substitute for enterprise-based pensions.

New reform proposals in 1995 sought to deal with many of the above difficulties. They envision a multi-tiered system with the state providing a basic pension, an earnings-related supplement and optional occupational additions, and employees contributing to individual retirement accounts. Administration of the system would be shifted to specialised social insurance agencies, the system would be unified over different ownership sectors, benefits would be indexed and gradually reduced from 70-80 percent of the average wage to 60 percent (ESRC, 1995). However, the prospects for moving to higher levels of pooling were compromised by giving local governments the right to choose between competing reform schemes.

5.4. Urban Health Insurance. China's urban free health care system has encountered great financial difficulties in the reform era. Expenditures on medical care have grown rapidly due to the aging population and the rising cost of medical care. Total medical expenditures (in current prices) increased by 706 percent from 1978 to 1992, while the number of employees in state units grew by 147 percent. Thus, expenses per capita rose by 450 percent (see Figure 3.13.). During the period 1986 to 1990, the annual growth rate of public medical expenditure has been over 25 percent. Enterprise medical expenses have also grown rapidly. Many state and collective units have experienced a payment crisis for health care. Thus, the old system is no longer economically sustainable, which provides the main impulse for its reform.

The old urban health insurance system is no longer economically sustainable.

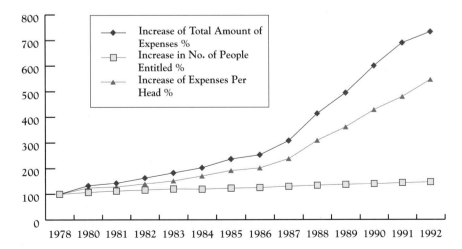

Figure 3.13.: Medical Spending of State Employees, 1978-1992
Source: Chinese Social Statistics, 1993.

The main trend in health insurance reform has been towards cost sharing by state, employees and work units. Most individuals entitled to public medical care now have to pay part of the costs of services provided by the government or enterprise. A number of provinces and cities have introduced risk pooling funds for serious diseases and a social risk pooling fund for retirees, and a several pilot studies from individual cities have been widely popularized in the effort to find a new financial basis for providing medical care to the urban population.

5.5. Unemployment Insurance.

China began establishing unemployment insurance in 1986. The benefits are generous. For the unemployed with more than five years' working history, benefits can last for two years, at 60-75 percent of the standard wage in the first year, and 50 percent in the second year. For the unemployed whose working history is less than five years, benefits last one year.

The numbers of urban unemployed receiving relief are shown in Figure 3.14. The number, while well below that of registered unemployed, has been rising faster than the latter (compare with Fig. 3.10.). Thus, in 1991 only 105 thousand out of 3.5 million registered unemployed received relief, whereas by 1996 the number had risen to 3.3 million out of some 6 million registered unemployed, or 55 percent.

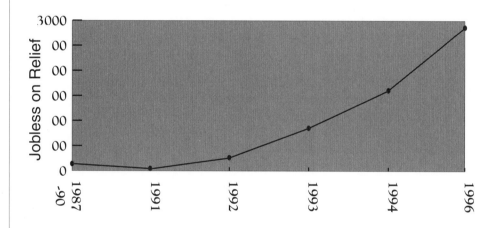

Figure 3.14. Urban Jobless on Relief, 1987-1996 (thousands)
Source: White and Shang, 1996; Li Boyong, Vice-Minister of Labour, speech at national conference on social insurance work, 15 August 1997.

In practice, there are two ways in which the unemployed are currently treated. Unemployment insurance and re-employment measures such as training have been a secondary approach. The main one has been to keep surplus workers formally linked to their enterprises, so the rate of open unemployment remains low. Official estimates of the total number of surplus workers in enterprises vary, from about 15 million (Ministry of Labour), to 20 million (Economic and Commercial Committee) to over 30 million (ACFTU) (Planning and Financial Bureau, MCA, 1996: 109).

Open unemployment thus represents only the tip of the iceberg of surplus urban labour. The Ministry of Labour in 1996 estimated that there will be about 3.6 million newly unemployed workers each year reaching a total of 21 million in the year of 2000. Of these, only half will be re-employed before running out of unemployment benefits (Planning and Financial

Bureau, MCA, 1996:108).

China's unemployment control mechanism and unemployment insurance face two short term problems. One is that the amount of open and potential unemployment is huge. Not only is the current unemployment insurance fund not up to meeting this potential demand, but also a large portion of the unemployed, especially unskilled and older workers, will not be able to find new jobs. These people have to survive either through unemployment benefits or social relief.

In an increasingly open labour market, the segmentation that separates migrant from resident workers will continue to break down (see sec. 5.2.). Although migrants often create new jobs in their host communities, they will increasingly come into competition with residents for the same jobs. Open urban unemployment has already brought pressure to drive rural migrant workers from their jobs and expel them from the cities in order to vacate job positions for the urban unemployed. This idea has in fact been partly practised by most municipalities which restrict job opportunities for migrants. This has taken the form of giving enterprises migrant worker quotas and imposing various fees on both enterprises and migrants, in order to raise both the cost to enterprises of hiring migrants and the cost to migrants of migrating. Such policies may cut down on urban employment of migrants at the cost of increasing rural poverty, since rural-urban migration has a significant positive impact on improvement of rural household income (Li Shi, 1997).

In the long run, as the volume of migration increases and the link between migrants and their places of origin weakens, unemployment among migrants is likely to become a more serious problem. Such a situation could lead to mounting social unrest, which suggests the need to pay more attention both to the welfare needs of migrant workers and to the huge urban-rural gap in social security coverage and benefits.

5.6. Re-employment programs. Formal re-employment programs

began in 1993-1994 when a large number of SOE workers were laid off. The number of re-employed workers in the two years of 1994 and 1995 accounted for almost 80 per cent of the total number during the entire period, 1986-95.[5] Re-employment policies include:

* Provision of labour brokerage services. Up to May 1997 these numbered 8,700 nationally. They serve not only the unemployed but also new entrants to the labour force and retired workers who are hunting for jobs. Some 70 million people found jobs during 1983-96 and most of them obtained assistance from the employment service organs (Cao Min, 1997).

* Training programs for acquisition of new skills. These are organised by labour departments, labour unions and women's federation offices or by industrial or sectoral administrative authorities (now called "corporations" or "companies"). The courses are also supported by enterprise contributions and local budgets.

* Subsidised credit, rent and other support for unemployed workers who elect to set up individual businesses.

* Subsidy schemes to promote hiring the unemployed. For example, in Tianjin, enterprises are entitled to a one time subsidy of 1000 yuan from the Labour Bureau for each unemployed worker hired (Personnel News 1997).

Policies of promoting employment of full status urban residents at the expense of rural migrants have been discussed in the previous section. Such urban biased employment policies hark back to the practices of the planned economy. Whenever the pressure of surplus labour built up in the cities, part of it would be sent back to the countryside. This happened several times in the 1950s-70s, but such attempts have been less successful since the mid-1980s, because there are no longer institutions in the countryside that can effectively restrain rural labour from migrating. Moreover, urban enterprises now have more autonomy than before, and they increasingly hire on

In an increasingly open labour market, the segmentation that separates migrant from resident workers will continue to break down.

[5] See Chapter IV, section 4, Table 4.5.

*China's social secu-
rity reforms still face
many thorny problems.*

the basis of market principles: for job applicants with similar qualifications they prefer to employ low wage rural migrants rather than absorb urban unemployed workers who expect to get their former wages, well above market-clearing levels.

To some degree, since the early 1990s state and collective enterprises, facing increasingly expensive urban labour in comparison with the low-priced capital they were privileged to obtain, responded by adopting capital-intensive technologies (Zhou Qiren 1997). Therefore, policies that cause enterprises to replace rural migrants with urban unemployed might reduce unemployment-related poverty in the short run, but will encourage more unemployment and poverty in both urban and rural areas in the long run.

Furthermore, the differential treatment of rural and urban labour has been only one type of discriminatory policy. Another type concerns property ownership, especially state and non-state enterprises. The ideological status and social security arrangements of state enterprises are superior to those of township and village enterprises, which in turn out-rank the private sector. There is an obvious contradiction between this status ranking of enterprises and the employment strategies China must follow: if state* enterprises are most favoured, they become the first choice for workers seeking jobs. However, state enterprises cannot absorb more employment and are even shedding labour. Thus, a large share of new additions to the labour force and the unemployed will have to find jobs in non-state enterprises or become self-employed, both of which mean suffering an inferior political status. This is no doubt one reason why a considerable portion of the unemployed would rather live on relief or partial wages and wait for re-assignment to other state enterprises, than be self-employed.

**5.7. Outstanding
Problems.** The above discussion makes clear that China's social security reforms still face many thorny problems. The financial base of the current social insurance system is inadequate. State and collective enterprises are still the main contributors to the current pooled insurance fund, but their performance has been unsatisfactory and has continued to worsen in recent years (SSB, 1996: 34). Their current social insurance burden is already very high, varying between 35 and 45 percent of the total wage bill. The current levy rate for pension insurance has been above 20 percent of the total wage bill on average. In some areas such as Shanghai, the levy rate is 28.5 percent of the wage bill (25.5 percent from enterprises and 3 percent from individuals). The levy rate for unemployment insurance is 1-1.5 percent of the wage bill. Health expenses are estimated at between 11 percent and 17 percent of wages.

The system faces a dilemma: On the one hand, there is little room left for increasing the levy rate; on the other, the requirements for pension, health and unemployment funds already exceeds available funds and will continue increasing. Urban employees very much want to retain the benefits they are currently enjoying, even if part of these benefits has already become only nominal (White and Shang, 1996: 53). This makes it very difficult to reform both the enterprise management and the social insurance systems simultaneously. The pressure exerted on the government by employees in loss-making enterprises is forcing local authorities to bear the responsibility for providing social security benefits to them and to transfer the cost to profit-making enterprises through a social pooling system. Such a policy is continuing to increase the burden on currently profitable enterprises, pushing some of them into the same vicious circle affecting state and old collective enterprises: from high contribution rates to high costs, from high costs to higher losses and thence to even higher contribution rates.

The longer-term problem of caring for an aging population will require some combination of (a) gradual raising of the retirement age and its unification for men and women; and (b) gradual reduction in China's generous pension benefits relative to wages, in line with international experience. The short-term problem of financing costs of the transition from the old to the new retirement system will require special measures to handle the pension costs of current retirees and of workers who retire shortly after the new system is in place. Such costs can be met through a combination of government borrowing , increased taxes, and perhaps a temporary surcharge on the retirement contributions of workers and enterprises (World Bank 1997).

Expansion of the financial base from the public to non-public sectors will face much resistance and be difficult to implement. If done locally, it will cause capital to flow to areas with lower labour costs, which will hinder its widespread adoption. Yet an environment of continued rapid growth should make a national system of social insurance with the broadest possible financial base, including individual and state contributions, feasible. Lying behind many of the outstanding problems facing social security reform today is China's great divide between urban and rural societies. As the spreading market erodes the wall separating these two great sectors, the feasibility of a segregated social security system for the privileged city dwellers crumbles with it. China will inevitably face the issue of how to provide some social security for its huge population, both urban and rural, from a limited but growing income.

⑥ China's Growing Environmental Challenge[1]

6.1. Major Environmental
Issues. The concept of sustainable human development focuses attention upon the rate of use of natural resources - renewable as well as non-renewable - both as sources of raw materials for production and as a sink for the absorption of waste products (pollution). Economic growth that uses up the available stocks of non-renewable resources without investing in development of renewable substitutes is not sustainable. The use of renewables at a faster rate than they are being regenerated is also non-sustainable. In some cases it also generates serious hidden costs to society (e.g., to health). A society may choose to postpone dealing with these issues, but it should do so with as full knowledge as possible of the present and future costs and benefits. Some environmental ills (e.g., air pollution) can be reversed quite quickly, while others e.g., loss of biodiversity or soil loss) can never be undone.

China has for some time faced a shortage of basic natural resources to serve its large population. It has only 28 percent of the average per capita world supply of fresh water. Its cultivated land constitutes only 7 percent of the world total, from which it must feed 21 percent of the world population. The high growth rates that China has achieved during the reform period have brought new attention to the issue of sustainability. Crucial as high speed economic growth has been in raising living standards and minimizing the social disruption accompanying transition to a market economy, it has also promoted further widespread and severe environmental degradation in both rural and urban areas.

Thus, wastes produced in the 1990s by urban industry are in general much higher than those produced in the 1980s. Solid waste generation in 1996 was about four times the 1981 level. The accumulated amount of urban industrial solid waste almost doubled to 6.5 billion tons, and it occupies 51,680 hectares of land. SO2 emissions from industrial sources have trended upward from 11.65 million tons in 1991 to 13.97 million tons in 1996. Air pollution in general shows a rising tendency during the past two decades. Acid rain is an increasingly serious problem. Many of the major pollutants in urban air exceed state environmental standards.

Crucial as high speed economic growth has been in raising living standards, it has also promoted further widespread and severe environmental degradation in both rural and urban areas.

---

[1] *This section relies upon Pan 1997.*

Deteriorating water quality has also attracted much attention. In February 1997, the Ministry of Water Conservancy announced the results of a survey on river pollution (Meng, 1997). This survey is the largest of its kind carried out in China, and covered almost all of the country's major water regions. It found severe and widespread pollution of rivers both large and small. Over 65 percent of the Yellow River, China's second longest, failed to meet the lowest national standard for domestic and recreational use. Many rivers in urban areas have actually become sewage channels. Over 90 percent of the water surface area in urban regions has been seriously polluted and 26 percent of all the major lakes suffer from eutrophication. Access to safe drinking water remains a major problem for large numbers of people.

Desertification in China

China suffers from desertification. A national survey team has recently completed its report on Desertification in China after a two-year study. The report reveals that desert areas total 2.622 million km2, accounting for 27.3% of China's total area. Most of the desert area is located in Northwest China, the northern part of North China and the western part of Northeast China. For the last 20 years, the rate of desertification has been as high as 2460 km2 per annum on average. China has paid particular attention to control of desertification. During the 8th five year plan (1991-1995) period, national desert prevention and control projects success-fully reversed desertification on some 4.287 million hectares of land. However, despite such local successes, the desert area in general is still spreading.

Source: CCGDP, 1997.

Although statistics on industrial waste water discharge appear to show a downward trend in recent years after a long period of increase in the 1980s, these figures do not cover the ever increasing discharge from household sources and from the generally dirty TVEs, which contribute half of China's total industrial output. Therefore official statistics of waste generation are an underestimate. An analysis of survey data concludes that the total amount of waste water discharge is more than twice as high as it was in the early 1980s, about 70-80% going without treatment (Meng, 1997).

In addition, China plays a significant role in shaping the global environment. It is the second biggest emitter of global greenhouse gases (after the United States), and produces over 10 percent of global ozone depleting substances (ODS). China has thus become increasingly aware of the need to address environmental problems from both a domestic and an international perspective.

The single most severe environmental problem currently facing China is water shortage and water pollution: more than 300 cities lack sufficient water and agriculture cannot get the irrigation water it needs. Green Revolution technologies require vast amounts of water, which is chronically short, especially in North China. The water table under Beijing fell from 5 meters below the surface in 1950 to 50 meters in 1994. Many people in western and northern areas of the country cannot get adequate supplies of drinking water. Large irrigation works and long distance water transfer have helped ease water shortage problems in some cities and areas, but reduction of water in source rivers in Northern China has precipitated water conflict between regions and users (CWYB, 1995). Such reduction also leads to serious ecological consequences. In Taiyuan city, Shanxi, the ground water level has declined from 1.99 m below surface in 1969 to 48 m below surface in 1993 (TDI, 1995). The diversion of Yellow River water has dried up the river flow in some 700 km of the lower reaches in recent years, the drought lasting 136 days in 1996 (NEPA, 1996). In Tianjin depletion of aquifers has allowed sea water to infiltrate underground reserves. Moreover, as we have seen, much of the existing water supply is seriously polluted.

The fee structure for industrial discharge of waste water is very low, and water use is virtually free for households. Although local experiments with increased water prices have had positive results, a public used to essentially free water from the government has been slow to accept the need for user fees to encourage conservation. Changing this situation, encouraging the recycling of industrial waste water, and finding other means of managing water use in a much more conservationist mode would appear to be the likeliest near-term responses to the growing water crisis.

China also faces a major problem of atmospheric pollution. Air pollution stems largely from the dependence on burning coal, which supplies over 75% of all commercial energy. Energy in adequate and sustainable supply is of course crucial to national development. China's energy sector, in addition to its dependence on coal, is burdened with an underdeveloped level of management and technology. Efficiency of energy use is low and waste is high. China needs to develop a comprehensive energy planning and management system suitable to sustainable development; to improve energy efficiency and promote conservation; to widely disseminate cleaner coal technologies as well as less polluting mining techniques; and to develop new and renewable energy sources, especially in off-grid areas where poverty is most widespread.

More than 1.2 billion tons of coal are burned each year (one ton per person). Twenty percent of energy is supplied by oil and natural gas, and the remaining 5 percent by hydropower. Nuclear, hydropower and oil are relatively clean energy sources but they are unlikely to provide a big share of China's energy consumption. As constrained by fossil reserves, coal will dominate the energy sector for the foreseeable future. This means that coal burning will continue to emit large amounts of CO_2, SO_2, particulate, and other gaseous wastes.

Some 35 percent of coal burned is consumed by power stations, and over 60 percent by households and industry, mainly in boilers for the generation of heat and steam that embody a very low energy efficiency and high energy use per unit GDP. This represents a serious loss to the national economy, as well as a threat to the environment. As a fraction of the world total, China's total commercial energy use accounted for 9.6 percent in 1994, but its CO_2 emissions from industrial processes constituted over 14 percent. In other words, China's energy production is far more polluting than the global average. Each metric ton (oil equivalent) of com-

China plays a significant role in shaping the global environment.

mercial energy produces 3.47 metric tons of CO_2, which is 50 percent higher than the world average.

With China's rapid industrialization, continued growth in coal combustion and greenhouse gas emissions "is virtually certain" (Sinton 1997). A study by the National Environmental Protection Agency (NEPA) and the State Planning Commission (SPC) indicated that, without policy changes, total primary energy demand would rise by the year 2020 to 3.3 billion tons of coal equivalent, of which two-thirds would be supplied by coal itself. Other scenarios, involving somewhat slower GDP growth and increased efficiency, result in slightly lower predictions for the increase in coal burning, but in all cases it at least doubles its 1995 levels (Ibid.) Thus, the searches for ways of controlling greenhouse gas emissions bill become increasingly important. China was one of the first countries to ratify the UN Framework Convention on Climate Change, and has established an inter-agency National Climate Change Coordination Group, responsible for formulating policies and programmes in this area. It has promoted research on greenhouse gas sources and strategies for reducing emissions, but the outlook is for them to increase in the near-to-medium-term future.

There are a number of relevant public policy issues. Promotion of greater efficiency of energy use calls for a rational structure of energy prices, for instance. In the case of coal, prices already reflect market supply and demand forces to a considerable extent, but - as in other countries - they do not include the high external costs of coal's impact on the environment. The lack of significant pollutant emissions fees provides no incentive for consumers to pay higher prices for leaner coal. Moreover, various reforms of the 1990s, such as the new tax code instituted in 1994, eliminated many previously existing financial incentives to invest in greater energy efficiency. The "extremely valuable" energy conservation service centers have lost their government funding. Preserving efficiency-promoting institutions and incentives and adapting them to work effectively in the

conditions of a market economy would appear to be an important environmental priority for China (Sinton, 1997).

Along with greenhouse gases, industrial expansion is very likely to increase the output of ozone depleting substances (ODS). In 1992, China, which is basically self-reliant in production of chloroflourocarbons (CFCs) and other ODS, prepared its Country Programme for phasing them out over the period 1993-2010. However, the incrementally rapid growth of industrial sectors outside of direct state control, such as township and village enterprises, will make it very difficult to bring about the shift to non ODS substitutes. Legal, educational and administrative efforts will have to accompany economic ones that address the incremental costs of substitute technologies.

Biological diversity will continue to come under threat from the loss of habitats to population growth, industrialization and development. With GEF support, China has prepared a National Biodiversity Action Plan to set priorities for protection of biodiversity, and has prepared a World Bank investment programme to strengthen the capability of the Ministry of Forestry to manage its system of nature reserves and wildlife resources. Preservation of biodiversity is an issue likely to grow in importance over the coming decades.

Wetland resources are increasingly threatened with drainage and reclamation. China has the world's second greatest national endowment of wetlands habitat. Not only are they important for domestic and migratory waterfowl, they also play a crucial role in maintaining local water tables, providing groundwater purification, and contributing to flood control and aquaculture. There is currently great pressure to drain wetlands for cultivation, especially in view of China's increasing loss of cultivated land to development. The resulting short term increases in output would almost certainly be surpassed by the more long-term adverse environmental impacts, including loss of habitat, flooding and water contamination. China is a signatory to the RAMSAR convention for protection of wetlands.

China was one of the first countries to ratify the UN Framework Convention on Climate Change.

6.2. TVEs and the Environment.

A good part of the success of China's transition has been due to the dynamic township and village industries. TVE gross output value has risen from 11.64% of China's gross industrial output in 1978 to 27.7% percent in 1996, considerably out-producing the state enterprises. Over the 8th 5-year plan period (1991-5), TVEs contributed 30% of the net increase of China's GNP, and 50% of the net increase in industrial value added. It is estimated that the total amount of value added from TVEs in 1996 amounted to 1770 billion yuan, accounting for 26% of China's GNP in 1996 (Jiang, 1997). TVEs now employ over 135 million people, making a major contribution to the absorption of China's large rural labour surplus and keeping many people from falling into poverty.

The rapid growth of TVEs has clearly contributed to sustainable human development for the rural population. As TVEs are in many cases collectives by ownership, part of their profits goes to their township and village, where it finances investments in rural education, health care and culture and permits a reduction in the levy on agricultural production, as well. By 1995, the total amount of capital assets accumulated by TVEs reached 910 billion yuan, accounting for 80 percent of the total asset value of the rural collectives. Furthermore, many TVEs promote farm production by investing in agricultural development directly (Jiang 1997). Finally, the development of TVEs stimulates the upgrading of rural infrastructure because they require better buildings, transport, and communications.

However, TVEs have also been perhaps the single biggest cause of the growing pollution associated with China's rapid economic growth, often with devastating consequences for the health of the population. There are many examples:

* Fangshang Village of Mencheng County, Hebei Province, set up 98 small paper mills, which discharged untreated waste water at a daily rate of 80,000 tons, contaminating both surface and ground water.

* In Fujian Province, there are as many as over 6000 small paper mills, generating over 70 million tons of waste water per annum and contaminating nearby rivers.

* The leaders of Lushui Township of Chalin county, Hunan Province set up 77 small ironworks within half a year. For none of them was an environmental impact assessment undertaken or official approval received from environmental authorities. With no treatment facilities, such small ironworks lead not only to waste of resources, but also to serious damage to the environment and human health.

* Heavy metal smelters using primitive technologies and involving elements such as mercury, lead, cadmium and arsenic are found in many parts of Guizhou, where they have caused poisoning and cancer in and around the affected areas (CEYB, 1995, 1996).

Because TVEs are relatively small in scale, dispersed in location, and often use obsolete technologies, their environmental impact is difficult to monitor. They individually have little financial or technological capacity for pollution control. Their scattered location makes it easy to avoid environmental assessment and government control. As a result, they tend to be considerably dirtier than urban industries. The dust removal in TVE fuel combustion is only one-fifth the urban rate; there is very little treatment of waste water from coking and paper making, and the ratio of solid waste to product is some 4.3 times that of urban industry. Because of stricter environmental control in urban areas, rural regions become havens for pollution, and TVE industrial sectors are largely dominated by heavy polluting industries, accounting for two-thirds of total TVE output value: construction materials (18.94%), textile (13.61%), machinery (7.75%), food processing (6.31%), plastics (4.42%), pharmaceuticals (4.0%), metal smelting (3.8%), paper making (2.47%), and coking (0.17%) (Wang et al, 1996). A recent survey on TVE industrial pollution sources indicates that TVE industries are responsible for a very high share of many key pollutants (Table 3.19.).

A good part of the success of China's transition has been due to the dynamic township and village industries.

However, TVEs have also been perhaps the single biggest cause of growing pollution.

Table 3.19. TVE Waste Generation in Comparison with Total Industrial Waste

	TVE[a]	% of Total Industrial Wastes
Air pollutants (mill ton.)		
SO2	5.49	28.2
Nox	n.a.	n.a.
Particulates	13.58	68.3
COD	6.70	46.5
Solid waste (bil ton.)	0.41	38.6

[a] Preliminary results from a national survey on sources of industrial pollution by TVEs. NEPA, 1997.

In general TVEs are more wasteful in resource use than large enterprises. For instance, the recovery rate of TVEs in mercury smelting is only 22 percent, compared to 82 percent in state owned enterprises; in lead smelting the rate for TVEs is 28 percent, compared to 57 percent in state factories. For each ton of mercury produced, state owned enterprises would consume 1025 tons of ore , while TVEs would require 3030 tons of ore. To obtain one ton of lead and zinc, 17.5 tons of mineral ore would be smelted by state owned enterprises, only half the figure for TVEs. Waste of resources is costly not only to TVEs but to society at large, and especially so for non-renewable mineral resources, which belong to both current and future generations.

TVEs often occupy arable land for production as well as for disposal of wastes. The total land area used by TVEs in 1992 amounted to over 63 million hectares, which was about 3% of the total arable land in China. At current rates of return for agricultural production, the opportunity cost could be well over 10 billion yuan per year (Wang et al 1996).

The use of low-cost and often dirty technologies are one reason that TVEs have been so competitive compared to state owned enterprises. The market, by which TVEs have thrived, by itself cannot capture as payable expenses the high external costs of the pollution they generate. Unless influenced by enlightened public policy, the market thus causes over-production of polluting industries. This problem has been less serious for state enterprises, which have been bound to observe administrative orders rather than market signals. That is why "institutionalization of China's environmental protection policies has taken place primarily within the state sector" (Jahiel, 1997). As state enterprise reform proceeds, and many smaller enterprises are privatized or otherwise pass from direct government control, the institutional channels for obtaining compliance with environmental laws and regulations will further weaken. The government will have to become adept at using economic incentives and disincentives to protect the environment.

6.3. From Administrative to Economic Controls. In the past, China's approach to environmental preservation had three principal characteristics: (1) it was an "end-of pipe" or "ex post" approach based on western models and on the principle that the polluter pays. (2) it was vertically organized with the National Environmental Protection Agency (NEPA) at the top and environmental protection bureaus within the various Ministries and localities; and (3) it relied on administrative controls, requiring many people for implementation. These characteristics designed to fit into a centrally planned economic system, have been challenged by the transformation of the economy into a much more market-driven one. Moreover, an end-of-pipe approach is now being recognized by the government as fundamentally inadequate to deal with China's most basic problem of resource scarcity.

Thus, attitudes are slowly changing in favor of a more price-oriented, ex ante approach to discourage pollution before it happens. At the same time, however, financial responsibility for environmental protection has also been shifted downward to provincial and municipal governments. This has tended to make the same regional and local authorities responsible for both promoting economic growth and also protecting the environment. In such a contest for scarce resources, the economic growth imperative is likely to dominate environmental concerns. Moreover, a nation-wide administrative reform in 1994 resulted in a significant weakening of environmental protection bureaus at the county and township level. (Jahiel, 1997).

Services such as conservation of soil and of biodiversity are under-valued or not valued at all by the market. Ignoring them, however, risks elimination of future development options through loss of resources. Furthermore, resource development may threaten the existence of unique ecosystems and/or endangered species, which are irreplaceable once gone. These kinds of value that are not reflected in the market have been acknowledged in China, and efforts have been made to reduce their loss. But in a transitional developing economy, more attention is apt to be paid to tangible than to intangible values, not only because the latter add less to immediate economic growth, but because they are difficult to quantify and value in money terms. Yet quantifying them would make it easier to incorporate them into the economic decision making process.

China has established a firm foundation for doing such economic evaluations of environmental impact. The law requires that all development projects undertake environmental impact assessments (EIA) and produce environmental impact statements (EIS). All industrial projects must have EIA and EIS if they are to get official

approval from planning authorities. In recent years, agricultural and TVE projects are also being brought into the fold. Standard methods of evaluating environmental costs tend to be complex, time consuming and expensive. The Asian Development Bank (ADB, 1995) is experimenting with the use of cruder but simpler methods of attaching economic values to environmental impact. The box below details some devastating experiences of pollution of the Huai River in 1994. If such rough estimates had been made of the pollution impact of waste water discharge into the Huai, either many paper mills and small tanneries would not have been established in the first place or discharge treatment plants would have been built.

At project level, China is close to incorporating environmental impact into economic decision making. Economic evaluation is likely to challenge the conventional wisdom of project appraisal and its role in human development, for it will reveal the degree to which damage to the environment and to human health offsets whatever benefit a project may bring.

6.4. Land, Food and the Environment. Due to topographic and climatic constraints, the proportion of land in China suitable for cultivation is very low, being about 10 percent. The scope for expansion of arable land is very limited. Official survey data show that there are some 14.7 million hectares of potentially cultivable land (Information Office, 1996), which comes to only 1.5 percent of total land area and 15 percent of existing arable land. Urban and industrial expansion, the construction of highways and other infrastructure, and rural housing and TVE development are among the major reasons for loss of farmland. In the mid-1980s, annual reduction of arable land exceeded one million ha. From 1991 to 1995, the total reduction amounted 3.29 million hectares. Newly reclaimed land does not come close to equaling the amount of farmland lost, and is generally of inferior quality to what is lost.

The quality of arable land also constitutes a constraint. Only 65 percent of existing arable land is flat; the rest is hilly

At project level, China is close to incorporating environmental impact into economic decision making.

Benefits of Environmental Protection Vs Costs of its Neglect

Benefits. In 1996, floods swept across Hebei Province, causing serious damage to the economy. But little damage could be observed in some 58 small watersheds where soil and water conservation projects had been completed. In Huailai County, grapes were introduced in the soil and water conservation projects. Local people established a winery and developed more than seventy products using grapes. In 1996, a pretax profit of over RMB 70 million yuan was realized. Such projects have helped eliminate poverty: the number of poor fell by more than 50% in the key project areas. For the past several years in China, several million poor people have risen above the poverty line as a result of conservation related development.

Costs of Delay. The Huai River has been the most important source of water for household consumption, industrial use and farmland irrigation for a large number of people living in the river basin. At the same time, it is also used as a waste disposal channel by industries, causing serious pollution. On May 8, 1994, farmers in Yinshang County, Anhui, brought river water in for irrigation. The polluted water contaminated 2870 ha. of fish ponds on its way to the paddy fields, causing direct losses of RMB 20.14 million yuan. Thousands of people were affected, hundreds were hospitalized for poisoning, diarrhea and skin afflictions. Costs ran to over 40 million yuan. In July of the same year, 200 million tons of waste water were released into the main river channel, as a result of which 70 km of the river were rendered unfit to drink, affecting over 1.5 million people in Anhui and Jiangsu Provinces. The direct monetary loss was estimated at 200 million yuan. This incident shocked the country and prompted the central government to step up pollution control policies.

to one or another degree (CAAS-ANR, 1995, p.67.) The second national soil survey showed that among total cultivated land, 34 percent suffers from soil erosion, 32 percent from drought, 5% from salinization, and 2% from desertification. In total, 63.5% of arable land is restricted by various factors fertility-limiting factors (CAAS-ANR, 1995, p.41).

Nevertheless, China's grain output has increased from 113 million tons in 1949 to 450 million tons in the 1990s. Per capita food consumption rose from 210 kg in 1949 to 380 kg in recent years. This achievement is mainly attributable to increases in yields. Grain yield per ha. has risen from only 1035 kg in 1949 to 4239 kg in 1995, a more than three-fold increase.

Current inputs, new high-yield varieties, and improved cropping patterns have all played important roles in this yield increase.

The pressure of human development on land will continue increasing, as illustrated in Table 3.21. In the past two decades, per capita food consumption has fluctuated between 340 and 389 kg. Any further increase must come from higher unit output. But diminishing returns to further chemical inputs will elevate production cost and widen environmental impact. Take fertilizer use as an example: the elasticity of grain output with respect to fertilizer input was 0.51 between 1979 and 1990, but only 0.15 between 1990 and 1995 (MOA, 1996b).

Table 3.20. Yield Implications of Growing Food Demand[a]

	Unit	Early 1990s	2000	2010	2030
Population	billions	1.2	1.3	1.4	1.6
Grain requirement	kg/capita	380	385	390	400
Total grain requirement	mill tons	450	500	550	640
Yield level	kg/ha	4500	5000	5500	6400
Yield increase	% per annum	na	2.1	0.96	0.76

[a]Assuming no change in cultivated land.
Sources: Information Office, 1996, OP, 1996b.

In 1949, virtually no chemical fertilizers were employed on agricultural land. From 1979 to 1995, fertilizer application has soared from 11 to 36 million tons. In terms of unit area application, China's fertilizer use in 1995 has reached 378 kg/ha., higher than that in Europe and 3.5 times as high as in the United States. Agricultural plastic film and pesticides all jump dramatically in the first half of 1990s (Table 3.22.).

Table 3.21. Consumption of Agrochemicals, 1990-1995 (unit: million t)

	1990	1991	1992	1993	1994	1995
Fertilizers	25.0	28.5	29.0	31.0	33.8	35.9
Agric. plastic films	0.48	0.64	0.78	0.70	0.89	0.92
Pesticides	0.74	0.76	0.76	0.85	0.98	1.09
Food output	446.24	435.29	442.66	456.49	445.10	466.62

Source: MOA, 1996a, 1996b, NEPA, 1996.

Agrochemical pollution has long been an acknowledged problem in developed countries. Its toxic effects have led to the banning of some biologically non-degradable pesticides such as DDT. As crops only utilize part of the chemical fertilizers applied, much of the unused nutrients run off into the water supply. In the United States, for instance, over half of water pollution concerns can be traced back to agriculture; chemical fertilizers account for 80 percent of the total nitrogen load and 50 percent of the phosphorus load in water bodies (Fang, 1988). As point sources have been brought under control in developed countries, efforts have been made to curb diffuse sources (Pan, 1994), with the result that fertilizer application has been on the decline.

In China, urban and industrial pollution has dominated the discussion of environmental pollution, but many serious pollution problems have been connected to the use of agrochemicals. Nutrients from agricultural land find their way into water bodies through leaching and runoff to become the principal source of eutrophication. According to latest environmental bulletin (NEPA, 1996, 1997), all kinds of inland lakes and reservoirs are assessed as being eutrophied to various extents, some quite serious. A case in point is Anhui's largest lake, Chao Lake, with a surface area of over 820 km2, which suffers from excessive loads of nitrogen and phosphorus. The intensive farming surrounding the lake has been identified as the cause of its pollution.

As nutrients enter the sea along with river runoff, they also pollute coastal areas of the ocean. Monitoring data on seawater quality suggest that inorganic nutrients, i.e. nitrogen and phosphorus, are primarily responsible for the deterioration of the ocean environment. Both nutrients have been detected to be higher than allowable levels in Yellow Sea and East China Sea (NEPA, 1997). These nutrients largely originate from the use of chemical fertilizers.

Pesticides, herbicides and fungicides play a very important role in crop protection, but there are a number of side effects, which offset their positive roles. First, they kill not only pests and weeds but also destroy natural the pests' natural enemies, such as birds and frogs. The drastic population reduction of beneficial species harms agricultural ecosystems, and thus stimulates the use of still more inputs to protect crops, in a never-ending vicious circle. Second, many pests develop resistance to pesticides and require increased levels of application and development of new pesticides. This further weakens the resilience of the ecosystem and pollutes the environment as the chemicals find their way into the water supply. Third, some toxic chemicals contaminate farm products such as vegetables and fruits and accumulate inside grains and aquatic products, human consumption of such products poses a direct threat to human health. Finally, the use of toxic chemicals threatens the health of farm workers who have to handle them. Thus, heavy reliance on chemical pesticides cannot be regarded as a feasible way to promote further agricultural development.

Plastic film has been widely employed in northern China and mountainous regions to provide cover for crops and thus increase soil moisture and temperature. While they are very helpful in raising yield in dry and cold areas, plastic films have caused "white pollution" because the remnants of film do not decompose in soil. Such pollution may not hurt water and product quality, but it hinders crop growth by preventing proper development of the root system and changing the physical characteristics of the soil.

It may be concluded that agrochemicals cannot be employed with ever-increasing intensity to promote agricultural production. Environmental pollution and ecological damage have become such a concern that the use of such chemicals has already been brought under control in many developed countries. Alternative means of crop protection and growth promotion, such as biological pest control, crop rotation, moisture retaining methods of soil preparation and organic fertilizers, should be extended and popularized.

China is in fact at the frontier of global knowledge about such sustainable practices. For instance, integrated pest management (IPM) techniques have been developed and extended quite widely since the late 1970s under the leadership of the Agriculture Ministry, with good results. Integrated Plant Nutrition Management (IPNM) techniques, designed to tailor the quantity, mix, timing and methods of plant nutrient applications to the requirements of specific localities and crops, have also been applied on a growing scale. Moreover, many traditional farming practices that are both highly productive and ecologically sound continue to be used in China.

In the late 1970s, fundamental principles of sustainable agriculture were summed up and made the basis of "Chinese ecological agriculture" (CEA), a school of thought that stressed a holistic, environment-friendly, and flexible approach to farming in specific eco-systems. Models and experimental sites of CEA have been developed for plain areas, river basins and mountainous areas. By late 1990 there were some 1100 CEA pilot units utilizing about 3.3 million ha. of land. Studies indicate that these have been quite successful in raising both yields and farmer income. Nevertheless, despite a 1991 national conference to promote ecological farming practices, very little extension of this approach has occurred beyond the experimental sites themselves.(UNDP 1997) What is most required is appropriate incentive structures and extension work to popularize methods that are known to work.

More broadly, various adjustments in policies affecting farming would contribute to a more sustainable agriculture. For instance, the elimination of urban grain subsidies to all but low-income residents would make available a substantial sum of money for re-direction toward agricultural research, development and extension of sustainable farming technologies, rural human resource development, and the building of infrastructure in poorer rural areas. Elimination of subsidies for chemical fertilizers and pesticides, together with stepped up farmer education and extension services and greater incentives for soil and water conservation (including more rational water pricing structures), would move China firmly in the direction of agricultural sustainability. A study prepared for the Ministry of Agriculture and UNDP concluded that phasing out grain delivery quotas and allowing the market to determine grain output would have a number of beneficial environmental effects (UNDP 1997).

There is widespread discussion of the property rights issue in connection with farm investment and land conservation. Secure ownership of land can give its owners a strong incentive to preserve its fertility and invest in its improvement. Conversely, the uncertain and attenuated use rights to land that Chinese farmers now hold, are thought to give them only weak incentives for conservation and improvement. Although after 1984 farmers were to be provided with 15-year leases to their land, in practice most village governments have intervened one or more times to adjust land holdings as village population changes, so as to preserve the original equality of land access.[2] There is much evidence for the general proposition that security of tenure promotes better treatment of the land. Some experiences in China also support this position. Partly for this reason, the government decided in 1993 that new contracts should give farmers guaranteed use of their land for 30 years and freeze land adjustments during that period, regardless of changes in village population.

However, there is also much evidence from around the world that legally secure land ownership rights do not necessarily prevent predatory use of land, especially when those rights are economically insecure, or when strong incentives are provided to use unsustainable methods of cultivation. The current system also has some very major achievements to its credit that should weigh heavily: (a) an extremely large increase in output and yields since it was established in the early 1980s; (b) avoidance of the growth of landlessness and of the abject poverty that often accompanies it; (c) provision of basic income and food security to the rural population; (d) accomplishment of gender equality in access to land for subsistence production. All of these are major human development concerns. There is evidence, moreover, that many - perhaps most - farmers prefer

Elimination of subsidies for chemical fertilizers and pesticides, together with stepped up farmer education and extension services and greater incentives for soil and water conservation (including more rational water pricing structures), would move China firmly in the direction of agricultural sustainability.

2 See Kung 1994 and Kung 1995.

Poverty is both a cause and a consequence of environmental degradation.

the existing tenure arrangements to longer term, inflexible tenure because they support the principle of equal per capita access and want to be able to exploit it if their own families grow.[3] Peer pressure and the insistence upon yield maintenance as a precondition for contract renewal appear to have limited the extent of predatory use. In short, land tenure is not merely a technical issue; it deeply affects the lives of China's rural majority.

Given the stakes involved, any change in land tenure arrangements should be very carefully considered, with full participation by those who would be most affected, the farmers themselves. The full range of issues, including productivity and investment, conservation, income distribution, income and food security, gender equality, and poverty alleviation, should be included in such a discussion.

6.5. Environment and Poverty.

Poverty is both a cause and a consequence of environmental degradation. A glance at the spatial distribution of poverty reveals that there is a concentration of poor population in both arid and semiarid parts of North China and in hilly and mountainous regions of the west, where economic activities are restricted by climate, poor soil and remoteness of thriving markets. Such fragile environments disadvantage people in their efforts to alleviate poverty and preserve the environment, and may set the goal of short-term subsistence at odds with that of environmental preservation - and thus of longer term survival.

For instance, in the arid Dingxi region of Gansu, deforestation forced the local population to tear up the sod to use as fuel, thus further reducing the already inadequate carrying capacity of the land and exacerbating the region's serious poverty. Such a vicious cycle can be observed in many parts of china, especially in places where the environment is fragile. To break the cycle, human development, particularly investment in enhancing the capabilities of the poor, is the key, and external sources of capital are a necessity to combat both poverty and environmental damage. With help from the national government and

from other internal and external sources, much progress has been made in Dingxi by an integrated development plan that includes planting the hills with drought-resistant shrubs that stem erosion and offer a livelihood to the local people.

6.6. China's Agenda 21.

The principal for dealing with environment and sustainable development is provided by China's Agenda 21: White Paper on China's Population, Environment and Development in the 21st Century, adopted by the State Council in 1994. This document made China the first industrializing country to promulgate a comprehensive national plan for sustainable development as mandated by the Agenda 21 statement adopted by the 1992 UN Conference on Environment and Development in Rio. China's Agenda 21 sets out the principles for achieving sustainable development in both the social and environmental spheres in the context of the Ninth Five-Year Plan (1996-2000) and of the longer-term Plan for 2010. Governments at all sub-national levels have been directed to devise means of carrying out the Agenda 21 Programme consistent with local conditions. However, many localities have yet to put environmental protection on their agendas, especially when it conflicts with short-run economic growth goals.

China has committed itself to achieving concrete environmental goals by the end of the century, including specific limits on industrial waste water discharge and specific treatment rates for waste water; limits on sulfur dioxide emissions; high treatment rates of industrial waste gas emissions; increased rates of utilization of industrial solid wastes; an increased afforestation effort; annual targets for control of land threatened with desertification; targets for the protection of cultivated land; and a goal of 7% of the nation's territory to be devoted to nature reserves.

To achieve these goals will require substantial capacity building at all levels of society. Much progress has been made in

---

[3] See Kung and Liu 1997 for the results of an opinion survey on this issue.

establishing a legal and institutional framework for environmental protection. A committee on environmental protection has been set up under the State Council, chaired by a State Councilor, to foster a coordinated approach to the problem. Over forty central ministries and agencies are members of the committee, including the State Planning, Economic and Trade, and Science and Technology Commissions, and the Ministries of Water Conservancy, Forestry and Agriculture, as well as NEPA. However, the line ministries still have principal responsibility in policy-making and this allows sectoral interests to find their way into the policy arena.

More needs to be done both in developing new laws and regulations and, especially, in achieving compliance with existing ones. Much of the current legal framework was developed to fit the context of a planned economic system and requires reorientation to the conditions of a market economy. Effective means are needed for ensuring compliance with environmental laws on the part of local governments that now flout the laws to engage in deforestation or polluting activities on behalf of local economic growth.

China needs to establish a comprehensive national system for measuring, monitoring and managing its natural resources, including the concomitant statistics, planning and information support systems.4 A "green" national accounts method should be developed so that the full costs of economic activity, including pollution costs and depreciation of natural capital, can be properly counted. A recent World Bank study estimates that pollution, alone, costs China about eight percent of its GDP each year. If a green national accounts system were in place now, China's recent GDP growth rate would have to be deflated by a substantial percentage to approximate the growth of net national welfare.

An important subset of this issue is the pricing of natural resources. Such prices have historically been very low in China, constituting a subsidy for depletion and pollution. Economic liberalization has brought some increase in resource prices

and thus greater economic incentives for conservation and efficient use. However, there are still important structural barriers to rational allocation of natural resources. Last but certainly not least, increasing public education about the importance of environmental protection is a national priority. The current lack of public awareness, including among some decision makers, weakens support for national protection policies and impedes the movement of the national Agenda 21 from paper to practice.

If environmental protection is to be integrated into longterm planning, then basic decisions about the structure and pattern of development should take environmental factors into consideration. Important public policy choices and investment allocation decisions, such as those regarding housing and settlement patterns and transport strategies - for instance, whether to encourage development of an automobile industry or invest in urban and suburban rail systems - have a fundamental environmental significance that needs to be recognized explicitly in the decision making process.

Beyond that, as China's Agenda 21 acknowledges, specific industries must put sustainability in a high position on their agendas. Vigorous promotion of waste water treatment and other methods of combating water pollution, adoption of cleaner coal burning technologies and of renewable energy sources, control of methane emissions, promotion of sustainable agriculture, financing of environmental capital investment, encouragement of conservation and recycling of water and other natural resources, and public education about the importance of environmental protection are all necessary elements in the national program. Increasing public awareness of environmental issues, encouraging the increasingly popular consumption of "green" products produced in an environmentally benign manner, and promoting public participation in environmental decision-making are all important methods of supporting the evolution of a pro-environment social norm. ¡

A recent World Bank study estimates that pollution, alone, costs China about eight percent of its GDP each year.

CHAPTER IV

Poverty and its Alleviation[1]

The challenge before China was to preserve the considerable progress in human development achieved by the previous system while moving to solve the great problems it had left behind.

 ## Main Trends in the Reduction of Poverty

One of the great success stories of China's reforms - in contrast to that of many other transition economies - has been its remarkable record of reducing the incidence of poverty, especially in the early years of the reform period. Possibly never before in recorded history had such a large number of absolutely poor people been raised above a minimum acceptable absolute income in such a short time. Paradoxically, the exodus from poverty slowed to a halt in the mid-1980s, just when China was setting up a poverty alleviation program, and it remained stalled through the rest of the decade. Progress has resumed in the 1990s, albeit more slowly, as the country approaches the end-of-century target date for its commitment basically to eliminate absolute poverty.

This great success was achieved through the economic reform which brought rapid growth to the Chinese economy, especially in the agricultural sector. An early reform policy was to raise procure-

ment prices for major farm products by 20 percent in 1979 alone, with the premium for above-quota deliveries increased from 30 to 50 percent in the case of grain procurement. There were continuous increases in procurement prices until 1985, though more moderate. At the same time, the government reduced both the types and quantities of farm products subject to compulsory procurement quotas and farmers were allowed to sell an increasing proportion of their output on the free market, which also increased the average price they received.

As for the new institutional arrangements in agriculture, there are two especially important points to note. First, land was distributed to village members on an essentially equal per capita basis. Everyone got his or her share of farmland. To this day, the distribution of land in rural China - that most important of all rural productive

---

[1] *Parts of this section make extensive use of Zhu Ling 1997.*

> The Great Exodus. China's per capita income was quite low before the start of the economic reform in late 1978. There was no official "poverty line" at the time, but poverty was believed to be pervasive. According to the State Statistics Bureau (SSB), 250 million rural people, or 30.7 percent of the rural population, were living in poverty in 1978.
>
> A World Bank study comes very close to this figure, estimating that 260 million people in rural areas were living in poverty at that time. By 1985, the number of rural people with incomes below a poverty line of 200 yuan (in 1985 prices) had come down to 125 million, or 14.8 percent of the rural total, implying an annual reduction of 18 million on average. The World Bank estimates show even greater progress up to 1984, when the estimated number of poor reached 89 million.
>
> Thus, between 125 and 171 million people had escaped abject poverty in a short six years.

and security assets - is exceptionally even (Brenner 1997). The phenomenon of landlessness, which is associated with abject poverty and inequality in much of the developing world, is virtually absent in China, which is a fact that seldom receives the attention it deserves.

The second point concerns incentives. The initial reform involved a variety of experiments trying to link payments more closely with actual efforts made by individual farmers within the commune system, while maintaining the latter. The now well-known Household Responsibility System (HRS) was initiated by farmers and basic level cadres and quickly spread throughout the countryside. The government permitted HRS to be adopted in poor areas at the beginning, and then endorsed its spread everywhere else. What HRS did was provide the immediate link between effort and reward that had been missing in the collective system, as well as greater freedom for farmers to choose and manage their resources and products in accordance with the needs of the market.

Stimulated by the new institutional arrangements and by better prices, as well as supported by increased supplies of mod-

ern inputs, agricultural production increased at a remarkable speed during the 1978-84 period. The annual growth rate of real agricultural GDP reached 6.69 percent for the period from 1977/79 to 1983/85, compared with only 2.22 percent in the previous 13 years (1964/66 to 1977/79). Rapid general economic growth in Chinese agriculture brought large increases in per capita income in the rural areas across the country and, because poverty had been so pervasive, this general growth effectively eradicated much of it.

As growth in agriculture slowed down in the mid-1980s, so did the decline in the incidence of poverty. Recognizing this situation, the Chinese government formally assumed responsibility for lifting the remaining 125 million people out of poverty. Poverty alleviation (PA) strategy was incorporated into the Eighth 5 Year Plan (1986-90), and the Leading Group for Economic Development of Poor Areas was established under the State Council. Similar government bodies were established at provincial, prefecture/city, and county levels. Poverty alleviation through specific anti-poverty efforts became a regular job for the government starting in 1986.

Nature, Location and Incidence of Poverty

Rural Poverty. The government adopted the regional development approach as its PA strategy. Poor counties were identified by the state and provincial governments according to a rural per capita income threshold, which was set higher for minority nationality autonomous counties and old revolutionary base areas. Financial support from various government sources, as well as other public support, was mainly channeled into these government-designated poor counties, leaving poverty alleviation in other counties to general economic growth.

In 1986, there were three "poverty lines" used in state designation of poor counties: 1) 150 yuan of rural per capita income in 1985, as the general standard; 2) 200 yuan as the standard for minority nationality autonomous counties; and 3) 300 yuan applied to counties which had been old revolutionary base areas. The Leading Group formally designated 258 poor counties in 1986, among which 83 counties were in the first category, and 82 and 93 in the second and third categories, respectively. The total figure increased to 273 by 1990, and the total number of counties receiving state poverty alleviation funds reached 331, if other special funds of similar nature are counted. At the same time, there were also 351 province-designated poor counties that received PA funds from provincial sources.

There has been ongoing discussion of the official rural poverty line, both in China and abroad, focusing on such issues as its relation to a minimum food intake and its treatment of changes in cost of living. Estimates of the incidence of poverty in rural China have been derived from different data sets or through the use of different approaches.[1] Moreover, many policy considerations were involved in the process of defining the official poverty line; the line finally set was the result of a series of compromises between the central government and local administrations (Zhu and Jiang 1996).

Also, the poverty line is observed differentially throughout the country. For instance, it was set at an income of 500 yuan (about 1/4 of the national average rural income) in 1994, and 592 poor counties were designated as the main targets of the national program for poverty alleviation during the years until the century's end. However, in poor provinces such as Yunnan Province in the Southwest, the poverty line was in practice set much lower, with PA assistance confined to those counties with per capita incomes below 300 yuan. On the other hand, some governments of more well off areas have used poverty lines above the official one. Thus, the identification of the poor depends in practice on available resources, local commitment and the local cost of living.

Table 4.1 presents official and World Bank estimates of the incidence of rural poverty in China for various years from 1978 to 1996. Although there is some difference in precise numbers, the trends are similar. After a very sharp fall for several years at the beginning of the period, the rate of reduction in poverty then slowed down considerably from the mid-1980s to the early 90s, or even rose somewhat, before resuming its decline.

However, there are important questions about the way the poverty threshold is established and updated over time. For instance, the World Bank has also estimated the amount of rural poverty in China using a universal standard of $1 a day in 1985 PPP dollars, instead of China's own rural poverty line, which is equivalent to about PPP$0.60. By the $1 standard, China had 350 million poor in 1993 (shown in the right-hand column of the World Bank estimates in Table 4.1.), almost 30 percent of the rural population.

---

[1] See, e.g., World Bank 1992; Riskin 1993; Khan 1996.

Table 4.1. Some Alternative Estimates of Rural Poverty Incidence, 1978-1996 (millions)

| Year | World Bank Estimates | | | | Official Estimates | |
| | Population (mills) below: | | % Rural Pop in poverty | %Pop <$1 a day | Poverty Incidence (mills) | % Rural Pop in poverty |
	Pov. line	+10%				
1978	260	306	33		250	32
1980	218	272	27			
1981	194	255	24			
1983	123	163	15			
1985	96	131	12		125	15
1988	86	113	10	(32)*		
1990	97	121	12		85	10
1992						
1993			8	29	80	9
1994			7	27		
1996	70**		7**		58	5

* 1987 figure   ** 1995 figure

Sources: World Bank estimates: World Bank, 1992; World Bank 1996; Piazza 1997; State Statistical Bureau 1993; Official Estimates: Beijing Review, Feb. 27, 1995 and information provided by Leading Group for Economic Development of Poor Areas.

Another estimate corrects for the apparent understatement of cost of living increases in the official figure. Using survey data, it estimates the rural poverty rate in 1995 at between 17.4 and 28.6 percent of the rural population - much higher than the official estimates - and also finds the decline in rural poverty between 1988 and 1995 to have been more modest than the trend in the official figures.[2] Evidently, there are still important methodological issues that must be sorted out before consensus is reached on the estimate of poverty incidence and its trend in rural China. In particular, it seems too early to conclude that rural absolute poverty has been marginalized to a very small percentage of the population.

Urban Poverty. Unlike in most of the developing world, poverty in China has been largely a rural phenomenon. That is in part because of past strict prohibition of population movements, which kept the urban population to an unnaturally small fraction, virtually all of whom had public sector jobs. Furthermore, a pronounced urban bias in past development strategies channelled most of the benefits of economic growth to the towns and cities. Urban inhabitants enjoyed stable social welfare conditions and extensive government sub-

[2] See Khan 1997.

sidies of their basic needs such as food, clothing, shelter, and transportation. Even today there are virtually no formal urban residents with incomes below the rural poverty line (migrants are not counted in the urban population).

Thus, urban and rural societies in China are in many respects different worlds with different cost structures and different social and economic expectations. For some time, the Chinese government has estimated an urban poverty line, therefore, which is substantially above the rural one in real terms.

In 1997, China set a poverty line for urban residents at a per capita annual income of 1,700 yuan (the per capita annual income of an average urban households was 4,839 yuan in 1996). This is about three times as high as the rural poverty line - greater than the difference in cost of liv-

ing between town and countryside. Virtually no full status urban residents (i.e., excluding migrants) have incomes below the rural poverty threshold. Thus, the poverty line for towns and cities reflects a higher standard of expectations regarding a minimally decent level of living. By this standard, the number of urban poor totalled 11.76 million in 1996, according to the government (Xinhua News Agency 1997). This is the first time that nation-wide statistics on urban poverty have been published by the media. However, SSB has for several years defined one, derived with a methodology similar to that used for estimating the rural poverty threshold. It is based upon a nutrition standard set at a daily intake of 2160 kcal and a food basket consisting of components suggested by the Chinese Nutrition Association (Li Shi 1996). Some estimates of urban poverty are shown in Table 4.2.

Table 4.2. Urban Poverty Estimates

Years	Poverty Line (yuan)	Head-count Index (%)	Number of poor (mills)	Survey Estimates: Headcount Index (%)
1989	672			6.7*
1990	696			
1991	752	5.8	14.2	
1992	837	4.5	11.3	
1993	993	5.1	13.3	
1994	1 300	5.7	15.3	
1995	1 547	4.4	12.4	8.0

Sources: Ren Caifang 1996; Li Shi 1997; Survey Estimates: Khan 1997.
* 1988.

Once again, there is a wide range of estimates of poverty incidence. Those based upon SSB definitions and cost of living adjustments show a moderate rate of urban poverty that fluctuates through the 1990s. If 1996's figure (see above text) is

taken into account, the trend is downward for the last three years. The Survey Estimates, however, indicate both higher urban poverty rates and an increase in the rate between 1988 and 1995. None of these estimates, of course, includes the migrant population, among whom one would guess the poverty rate is higher than that for formal urban residents. In view of the increasing problem of layoffs from state enterprises and a rising unemployment rate, it is difficult to put much credence in a falling trend in urban poverty.

Location of the Poor. With changes in the causes of poverty over time have come changes in its location. In the 1970s, some households were poor because of institutions and policies that greatly limited their production incentives and kept them from investing in activities appropriate to their local conditions. The general release of incentives and diversification of rural activities that resulted from the adoption of the household responsibility system brought about a rapid and widespread increase in rural production and incomes and a corresponding escape from poverty of tens of millions of households. By the mid-1980s the rural poor may have been concentrated in remote and ecologically disadvantaged areas that were outside the reach of the general changes in rural China as a whole. Moreover, growth of average rural income slowed sharply from the mid-1980s to the early 1990s (see below), which limited the impact that general growth could have on the incomes of the poor.

At the same time, new factors began to enter the picture. One was the decentralization of the fiscal system, which reduced its redistributive nature and thus impacted heavily on poor localities, where families found themselves faced with increasing personal costs of education and medical care (see Chapter III). Another was the rapid increase in labour mobility as large numbers of rural workers traveled to towns and cities. Still another was the decline in collective modes of income distribution as the market grew in importance, which made possible the appearance of both rich and poor individuals in both poor and rich areas. A result of these trends was the development of a significant amount of urban poverty.

With respect to poverty alleviation policy, the changes in and variegation of kinds and causes of poverty suggest the desirability of broadening the current focus

on a limited number of poor rural counties. Although poor people are concentrated in these counties and may live in conditions there that are especially difficult and intractable, they are not the only poor people in China. The State Statistical Bureau estimates that one-third of the rural poor live outside of officially designated poor counties, while some outside studies suggest that this proportion may be as large as half.

Between 1988 and 1995, the proportion of rural poor to the total number of poor in China has fallen, according to one estimate, from about 93 percent to 90 percent (Khan 1997). This was due not only to the falling rural poverty rate and (according to this estimate) rising urban one, but also to the rise in the urban share of the population.

Characteristics of the Poor. Table 4.3. shows some selected characteristics, other than location, that distinguish poor from non-poor households in the countryside. Poor households are relatively lacking in labour, having only 89 percent the number of working age members of non-poor households. The human capital endowments are substantially smaller and the illiteracy rate higher among the poor. They are more concentrated in farming, in terms of both occupation and source of income, and have less representation among wage earners. They are also more likely to be in poor health or injured (not shown).[3]

The poor are almost three times as likely to be a member of an ethnic minority. They have significantly less land, especially irrigated land (given twice the weight of unirrigated land in Table 4.3.). Non-poor households have 54 percent more productive assets per capita, and 1.8 times more housing assets than poor households. Surprisingly, the tax rate (net of subsidies) seems to be quite regressive in rural China, extracting a much larger share of the incomes of the poor than of the non-poor.

The State Statistical Bureau estimates that one-third of the rural poor live outside of officially designated poor counties.

---

3 Poor health is a significant factor in rural poverty, both as cause and result. See Yin Dakui 1994.

Table 4.3. Selected Characteristics of the Rural Poor and Non-Poor, 1995

	Poor	Non-Poor
Labour Endowment (% of Household)		
Members Between 15 and 60	64.3	72.0
Educational Attainment (% of Members)		
Middle Prof./Tech./Vocational School	0.8	1.6
Upper Middle School	5.1	7.7
1-3 Years Elementary School	15.1	12.0
Illiterate or Semi-Literate	19.9	13.4
Average Years of Education Per Member	4.2	5.3
Occupational Category (% of Labour Force)		
Farm Labour	86.5	70.5
Worker	1.5	1.7
Temporary/Short-Term Contract Worker	3.6	4.2
Worker in Non-Farm Individual Enterprise	0.7	3.6
Ethnic Minority (% of All Members)	14.7	5.5
Land Per Person (Unirrigated Mu equivalent)	1.9	2.4
Productive Assets Per Capita (Yuan)	447.4	687.7
Housing Asset Per Capita (Yuan)	1470.7	4111.2
Per Capita Debt (Yuan)	95.2	157.8
Sources of Income (% Total Income)		
Wages, Pensions etc.	4.8	24.4
Net Income from Farming	65.9	44.1
Net Taxes & Fees to State & Collectives		
(% of Total Income)	3.9	0.1

Source: Khan, 1997. "Poor" refers to the category of "extreme poor" in this study.

Table 4.4. displays some interesting characteristics that distinguish urban poor from non-poor households. A lower labour endowment and substantially less human capital characterize the poor. Thus, they are only one-fourth as likely as the non-poor to have higher education and twice as likely to have failed to finish elementary school. They are much more heavily concentrated in the private/individual sector, indicating the complex nature of private activity as a recourse for the poor as well as a channel for acquiring wealth.

Table 4.4. Selected Characteristics of the Urban Poor and Non-Poor

	Poor	Non-Poor
Labour Endowment (% of Members)		
Members Between 15 and 60	66.1	73.9
Educational Attainment (% of Members)		
College or Professional School	4.8	16.9
Middle Prof./Tech./Vocational School	5.7	13.1
Elementary School	22.6	14.6
Below Elementary School	16.6	8.0
Occupational Category (% of Labour Force)		
Owner of Private/Individual Enterprise	6.73	1.3
Professional/Technical Worker	6.07	21.3
Office Worker	17.6	19.2
Skilled Worker	20.0	20.8
Unskilled Worker	29.3	16.3
Ethnic Minority (%of All Members)	7.4	4.3
Per Capita Assets and Liabilities (Yuan)		
Productive Fixed Assets	67.4	154.1
Financial Assets	927.5	3980.0
Housing Asset	2408.8	5366.7
Other Assets	157.4	583.4
Debt	225.4	263.4
Sources of Income (% of Total Income)		
Cash Wages	69.6	61.0
Income of Retirees	11.4	11.7
Receipt from Enterprises	4.8	0.5
Income from Property	0.3	1.3

Source: Khan 1997. "Poor" refers to "extreme poor" category in this study.

On the other hand, their occupational characteristics are revealing. While the poor are much less likely to be professional or technical workers than the nonpoor, the two groups' representation among skilled workers and office workers is very similar. And both groups have a similar degree of dependence upon wage income or retirement pensions. These similarities probably reflect the degree to which laid-off state sector workers are joining the ranks of the urban poor. SSB reports that 70.2 percent of poor urban households are headed by state or collective workers, and another 16.7 percent are households whose principal earners are retired.[4] Many of these are workers who have been laid off without pay or with minimum subsistence allowances from their enterprises. At the end of 1995, 41 thousand enterprises were bankrupt, semi-bankrupt or had partially or completely stopped production. They had about 6.65 million employees, 4.79 million of whom received no payment or reduced payment. 1.63 pensioners rely on these enterprises, 0.7 million of whom were not receiving their pension on time or in full (Fan, 1996). Such workers are not entitled to unemployment insurance, since they are not considered to be unemployed. The retired workers among them often cannot get their pensions, in full or in part, because of their enterprises' lack of funds. Moreover, the Civil Affairs Bureau may decline to help such people on the grounds that such aid is the enterprises' responsibility.[5]

As in the countryside, the poor in the cities are more likely to be members of an ethnic minority, and they hold far less wealth of all kinds. They have less than half the productive fixed assets and housing assets, by value, and less than one-quarter the financial assets.

---

[4] China Daily, August 16, 1997.

[5] Ibid.

③ Poverty Alleviation Policy

A regional approach was taken both to defining the poverty problem and attacking it.

Before the mid-1980s poverty alleviation (PA) was treated as a function of macroeconomic reform and general growth. The Leading Group for Economic Development of Poor Areas was established under the State Council in 1986, and corresponding leading groups and executive poor area development offices (PADO) were then set up under its aegis at various levels down to the county. A regional approach was taken both to defining the poverty problem and attacking it. As we have seen, poor counties were designated by the central and provincial governments according to a rural per capita income threshold, and financial and other support was channelled to these designated counties. Poor counties that are selected by the central government receive central PA support, while provincial aid goes to provincially-designated counties. There is no co-ordinated program aimed at poverty elsewhere.

Since the mid-1980s, the government has emphasised economic capacity building in poor areas rather than provision of relief. This approach has included investment in basic infrastructure improvements, such as water, electricity and roads, as well as provision of support for livestock breeding, processing industries and other economic enterprises that enhance the poor area's capacities for development and accumulation. [Gao Hongbin, "Introduction", Poverty alleviation in China, Beijing, UNDP, 1997].

In January 1994, the State Council announced a National 8-7 Poverty Reduction Plan intended to remove the remaining estimated 80 million rural poor from poverty over an eight year period ending in the year 2000. This Plan set the rural poverty line at 320 yuan (in 1993 prices) and aimed to raise per capita income to at least 500 yuan (1990 prices) for the great majority of rural poor. A new list of poor 592 poor counties was drawn up. All central PA aid must be restricted to these counties.

Total funding for poverty alleviation came to RMB 3.2 billion in 1985 and around 4 billion in 1989. It grew to RMB 4.6 billion in 1990, 9.8 billion in 1995, 10.8 billion in 1996 and 15 billion in 1997 (about US$1.8 billion). Central government regulations require provincial governments to allocate at least 30 percent of the central allocation. Thus, some 20 billion yuan (US$2.4 billion) were spent on poverty alleviation programmes in 1997. This amount is slated to increase further before the year 2000.[1] Most of the funds are directed to economic and infrastructure projects that are designed to give poor areas the means of developing their economies and overcoming poverty. Water, roads and natural resource development have received particular attention.

PA efforts go through three official channels. The bulk of financial aid is provided in the form of low interest loans by the Agricultural Development Bank (ADB), which was spun off from the Agricultural Bank of China (ABC) in 1994 to be a policy bank. Seventy to eighty per cent of these loans are to be used for crop-growing, animal husbandry and related processing and marketing activities. Most of these funds go to the specific production-oriented projects. Next, there are funds from the State Planning Commission, which finances a "food for work" (FFW) program to pay residents of poor areas in kind and cash for working on roads, water supply and other infrastructure development projects. Finally, the Ministry of Finance provides a small amount of PA money, which is used mostly for training (see Figure 4.1.).

1 Office of the Leading Group (1989); interview with Leading Group, June 24, 1996; and Gao Hongbin, 1997.

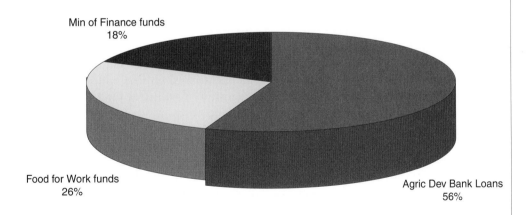

Figure 4.1.: Source of Poverty Alleviation Funds, mid-1990s

Besides the official PA programs, China has carried out social mobilization on a broad scale so that poverty issues have increasingly become public concerns. Each line ministry has been allocated additional resources for specific programs in a few chronically poor counties. The Ministry of Agriculture, for instance, carries out a food security program (wenbao gongcheng) in remote areas involving extension of hybrid maize growing technologies; while the Ministry of Water Conservancy conducts special projects in the most arid parts of the Loess Plateau in the northwest for solving the problems of water shortage; and the Ministry of Forestry Science Committee and the Chinese Academy of Sciences set up the projects in the karst topographic areas with the same purpose. Local provincial, prefectural and county governments have taken similar actions. A number of developed provinces and cities have established "twins" relationships with poor area counterparts and help them with economic cooperation projects, administrative and managerial assistance, etc.

Moreover, throughout China individuals are donating funds in support of social development programmes in poor areas, to establish village schools, to supply scholarships for the children of poor families, and to assist mothers of poor families to develop small businesses. Some of these programmes - in particular, Project Hope, sponsored by the China Youth Development Foundation - have become very well known and popular in urban China.

Finally, while China's poverty alleviation programs rely overwhelmingly on domestic resources, various international organizations, including the World Bank and UNDP, and the development agencies of industrialised countries are playing an active role in the anti-poverty campaign in China through the provision of resources and new ideas and concepts to assist poor areas. In response to the World Summit for Social Development in March 1995, UNDP Beijing has established an inter-agency Task Force on Poverty Alleviation and launched a series of initiatives, including workshops, discussion papers and compendia of experience. In cooperation with the State Council Poor Area Development Office, UNDP has initiated a training programme for cadres in poor areas that has trained several thousand government staff and enterprise managers in such areas.[2]

3.1. The "Food for Work" Program.

In contrast to past practice of providing relief to the poor, PA policy introduced through the current reforms has placed special emphasis on tapping existing potential to bring about economic development in poor areas. This is accomplished in part through public works (yigong daizhen, meaning 'to offer jobs instead of relief').

The Food for Work (FFW) program began at the end of 1984. It has had some special characteristics:

* Central government investments originally took the form of 'in-kind' financing. The in-kind goods supplied were sur-

PA policy introduced through the current reforms has placed special emphasis on tapping existing potential to bring about economic development in poor areas.

plus items produced during the central planning period. More recently, especially since 1996, as the economy has turned increasingly toward market relations, state investment has become monetized.

* Regulations stipulate that the in-kind goods allocated by the central government must be distributed as wages. Local governments are supposed to raise supplementary funds of an equal or greater amount to pay for project materials and cover other expenses. In practice, however, with few exceptions, provinces and counties have not been able to supply matching funds. Therefore, funds from other channels (such as from the line ministries) have been used.

* Local governments have mobilized rural residents to furnish part of their labour free of charge or at reduced wages. FFW projects have made use mainly of simple labour-intensive technologies. Normally, the works have been carried out during slack periods in the farming cycle, thereby providing some additional income to local participants.

* Between 1985 and 1990 the FFW projects focused on road building and construction of facilities for the supply of drinking water. Since 1991 the scope has been extended to farmland and water conservation, afforestation, and the renovation of rural post offices, supply and marketing cooperatives, health care stations for women and children, and old schoolhouses. The results of a study of the FFW program suggest that it has helped improve regional infrastructure and social services (see accompanying box) and directly provided short-term job opportunities and additional incomes to many poor rural residents (Zhu and Jiang 1996).

A distinguishing feature of the FFW program has been the nature of the targeting mechanism employed. Some researchers have recommended self-targeting, whereby the wages offered for work are so low that only the poor will apply (Ravallion 1990, Braun, Teklu and Webb 1991). However,

[2] Gao Hongbin 1997.

Major Achievements of Food for Work Program, 1985-95

Public roads: 214, 000 kilometres
Public roads connecting: 1,500 townships and 10,000 administrative villages
Bridges built: 20, 000
Clean drinking water facilities for: 40,900,000 people and 33,000,000 animals
Source: State Planning Commission and Office of the Leading Group of the State Council for Economic Development of Poor Areas.

this kind of targeting mechanism has not been adopted. The government chooses FFW project sites and avenues of investment, and the targeting mechanism differs from that of public works projects in other developing countries in several ways:

* The FFW program does not directly target the poorest segments of the population. The primary purpose is rather to improve infrastructure and social services in poor regions, consistent with the regional focus of China's PA approach, and to create conditions for regional economic growth. Thus, the long-term goal of economic growth has taken precedence over the short-term one of maximizing job opportunities and supplementary income of the poor. Likewise, efficiency has been pursued throughout the implementation of the projects by seeking a maximum rate of success in project investments. These priorities mean that the poorest villages and the poorest people do not necessarily benefit the most.

* Within the poor regions, the projects are focused on village communities, that is, administrative villages, and not on rural households or individuals. During the implementation of the project, the village communities are responsible for the mobilization of the labour force. Because of the nature of infrastructure projects, project benefits spread well beyond the poor themselves.

The rise in the number of FFW projects has led to a rapid expansion in the matching funds needed at the local level. In turn, this has eaten away at local financial resources. To fill the gap, more and more goods and materials allotted by the central government for payments to the farmers working on the projects have been converted either into hard currency, or directly into needed goods by local governments in the project areas. This has been occurring regularly despite repeated warnings by the central government, and has resulted in a reduction in wages paid to farmers, thereby weakening the project focus on poverty alleviation. For the same reason, county and township governments have resorted to raising the number of obligatory workdays (in essence, a corvee). This not only undermines the program's acceptability in the countryside, but may make the condition of the poor even worse by keeping them from gainful employment during project implementation.

3.2. Poverty Alleviation Credit Programs. Until 1984, the central government appropriated funds to support investment in poor areas mainly through the state budget. In that year, consistent with the ongoing reforms in the state finance system, a new approach was adopted of using credit institutions to provide funds. The objective was to push governments and institutions in poor areas to use funds more efficiently.

The first priority of the specially subsidised credit program (zhuan tie dai) has been to achieve food security for the poor (LSCEDPA 1986). Thus, about 1 billion yuan of credits were earmarked to a Ministry of Agriculture project to popularise a hybrid maize growing technique (He 1994). This project boosted maize yields by at least 100 kilograms per mu (1,500 kilograms per hectare) and effectively eased food shortages among 15 million inhabitants of mountain areas (Yang 1993).

The central government has set two standards to gauge the success of the credit programs. One is the food security line, and the other is the level of loan repayment.

Food security in a poor county is considered to be achieved if over 90 per cent of the poor households do not experience food shortage problems during a normal harvest year. For this calculation, households receiving permanent relief or relief because they are eligible for the 'five guarantees' (food, clothing, housing, health care, and burial expenses for the elderly or education for the young) are not counted as having a food shortage problem (Guo 1995). In 1990, per capita food grain availability of 300 kilograms was considered the food security line, and 58.3 per cent of the 331 poor counties receiving state assistance had achieved food security up to 1992 (OSCEDPA 1993).

Special subsidised credits were issued by the Agriculture Bank of China (ABC), more recently by its policy loan spin-off, the Agricultural Development Bank (ADB), but the funds are provided annually by the central bank, that is, the People's Bank. Repayments are supposed to be made to the People's Bank. The support of the central bank has apparently strengthened the liquidity of poor areas and thereby helped local economies. Previously, many ABC branches in poor counties had only meagre funds available for lending, and issued less than 20 million yuan in credits annually. The PA credit programs have raised available funds at these branches by 40 per cent (Li and Li 1992). According to estimates of ABC general headquarters, the credit programs have covered more than 10,000 middle and large-scale projects, from which poor areas containing more than 100 million people have benefited (He 1994). Such statistics are generally confined to production and construction results, and do not directly report the impact on the poor population itself.

In terms of loan repayments, the situation is not as good as was initially expected by the central government. Since 1991,

the recovery rate for the special subsidised loans issued by the ABC has been below 57 per cent. The loan recovery rate for other credit programs, in particular the credits for county-owned enterprises, has been worse. Moreover, some of the repayments are being made using new loans.

Major reasons for repayment problems include the following:

(1)   Because of the direct intervention of local governments, banks cannot independently select the projects to be financed. This has led to a number of credit failures.

(2)   The state protects enterprises and individuals in the planned economy, which has allowed borrowers to evade their obligations under loan contracts. The legal system for enforcing contracts remains weak. Many borrowers continue to violate their contracts.

(3)   Weak financial accounting systems: a large number of transactions in rural areas have not yet been entered into the accounts of financing institutions. This has created huge difficulties in the supervision of credit by banks.

(4)   Borrowers may not be capable of repaying some loans since the credit terms for the loans may be shorter than the time required for returns on capital investments.

A major problem of the loan programs is that in many localities the poor have lost access to the subsidised credits, although the programs were specifically aimed at providing 'credits to assist the poor' (fu pin dai kuan). The lack of access is an inevitable outcome of the way the credits are distributed and the loans used. The credits are distributed in a 'top down' manner via the administrative hierarchy. At the central level, the Poverty Alleviation Office of the State Council and the general headquarters of the Agriculture Bank together draft a plan for the distribution of the funds among the various provinces according to the size of the poor population in each province. The corresponding institutions at the provincial level

A major problem of the loan programs is that in many localities the poor have lost access to the subsidised credits.

allocate the funds among the poor counties designated by the state. The distribution process in each county involves not only discussions among the county branch of the ABC, the Finance Bureau and the Poverty Alleviation Office, but also a project approval procedure which relies on the submission of project proposals at the township level (People's Bank of China and Agriculture Bank of China 1986). Although, since 1995 the credits for poverty alleviation and for comprehensive agricultural development projects have been the responsibility of the Agriculture Development Bank, set up in November 1994, the method of fund allocation remains the same.

Interest rates on poverty alleviation credits are at least 20 per cent lower than normal rates and have often been much lower. The credit periods are usually one to three years, but can run up to five years. The repayments are due in full at the end of the period. During the second half of 1993, the official annual interest rate for capital construction credits for a term of one to three years was fixed at 12.4 per cent, while the interest rate for poverty alleviation credits for the same term was 2.88 per cent. This latter rate was adjusted in 1995 to 4.7 per cent. Over the same period, the officially published inflation rate was around 15 per cent. Thus, poverty alleviation credits bore a high negative real interest rate. For this reason, the demand for PA credits always far outstrips supply.

The specially subsidised credits were originally intended to be distributed mainly to poor households. In 1986-87, household credits represented 60 per cent of all the specially subsidised loans (GHABC 1987). But local decision makers have argued that it is more efficient to offer credits to economic entities, which can then solve food shortage problems and raise the incomes of poor households. This idea has been accepted by the central government. Poor farm households have no opportunity to state their views, for they no longer possess any direct access to the credit programs.

In fact, enterprises and local government institutions prefer to employ the specially subsidised loans to implement their own projects at locations where the natural environment and economic conditions are relatively more favourable. Thus, the credits have tended to be used in comparatively rich areas near residential centres, public roads and factories in poor counties. Poor households have not usually been direct project beneficiaries (Wu 1994). Rather, the beneficiaries have been the entities that organised the projects and the non-poor and 'average poor' households that have participated directly in them.

Moreover, the focus of the use of the credits has shifted from the agricultural sector to the non-agricultural sector. In 1986-87, loans to the agricultural sector represented about 55 per cent of all specially subsidised credits (Agriculture Bank of China 1988). By 1993, however, this share had declined to less than 40 per cent (OSCEDPA 1994). The strategy of accelerating non-agricultural development should certainly not be criticized if a poor county has no agricultural resource potential. However, a thoroughgoing policy and economic analysis of the changes in priorities for the use of credits ought to be undertaken.

In poor areas, many local governments run budget deficits and depend on subsidies from the central government, a system rendered perilous by the fiscal decentralisation, which weakened the center's capacity to redistribute resources. Often, township and county governments are unable to pay their employees on time. Urban populations in poor counties, including the children of government and enterprise workers, have few job opportunities because the non-agricultural economy is not well developed. Thus, to improve their financial situation and guarantee the support of government employees, local governments in poor counties have a strong incentive to establish non-agricultural TVEs. However, non-agricultural rural development can be very costly. Many of those who have established enterprises are not experienced entrepreneurs, but government officials. They have little business experience and very little of their own capital, and start their businesses mainly using bank loans. If the enterprises are successful, they become an achievement of the local

Poor households have not usually been direct project beneficiaries.

government leadership and an additional source of local tax revenue. If they fail, however, the losses are borne by the banks and bank depositors.

Under the demand pressure of the local governments, the county branches of the ABC have also strongly favoured the development of TVEs. However, the banks have a clear interest in the security of their credits, and this often leads to conflicts between the banks and local governments over project selection. Even if proposed projects are quite risky, the banks must often reach compromises with local governments in the face of pressure from officials and the lobbying of borrower groups.

The central government is also supportive of development of industries in poor counties that have achieved food security (LSCEDPA 1989). This approach is probably dictated by the fact that healthy local financing systems foster social stability and also tend to lighten the financial burdens of the central government. The fundamental purpose of the central government in its anti-poverty initiatives has been to reduce regional differences and guarantee basic needs of low-income groups in order to enhance national cohesion and strengthen social stability. Thus, given the current social structure, there is some basis for the existence of credit programs, which benefit not only the poor, but also local governments and the non-poor in poor areas.

The poor usually are not in a position to make use of formal financial markets. In the implementation process of the PA credit programs, they benefit if at all from trickle-down or spread effects; when the programs are completed, most poor farmers are still left needing relief intervention in the market economy. The poorest cannot borrow because they are considered bad risks. The average poor depend mainly on informal financial services which do not require collateral or other guarantees. Therefore, the poor who most need credit service are often excluded from it, and it is necessary to address this problem through improvements in institutional arrangements of the rural credit system (Zhu, Jiang and von Braun, 1997). One such improvement is the use of micro-credits based on

the Grameen Bank model, an approach to which the government, in cooperation with several international organizations, has been devoting increasing attention.

3.3. Some Outstanding Issues of the Rural PA Programme.

Firm conclusions cannot be drawn yet about the relation between rural poverty reduction and the PA efforts of the 8-7 Plan. Statistics on the number of poor come from independent sample survey-based estimates by the State Statistical Bureau and do not indicate the degree of correspondence between PA project locations and poverty reduction. China's PA offices, which collect a wealth of data about the investment and production results of their projects, have very little information about their impact upon the incomes and general well-being of the targeted poor households. Moreover, the incidence of poverty is greatly affected by broader developments in the economy, quite independent of the PA program (see sec. 6 below).

While provincially-designated poor counties have anti-poverty programmes, China has not yet established specific programmes to help rural poor who live in areas that have not been designated poor at any level. Poverty relief for this segment of the poor population is largely left to general economic growth rather than to specific PA efforts. Among both rural and urban poor there are vulnerable groups that have been beneficiaries of relief programs since the 1950s, such as the disabled, orphans, the childless aged and the families of revolutionary martyrs. Moreover, victims of natural disasters are eligible for short-term relief. The Ministry of the Civil Affairs and its local bureaus have responsibility for these relief functions. Also, rural villages, as their means permit, care for target groups for traditional relief intervention, a social care system inherited from the People's Communes. There were about 31.5 million rural relief recipients in 1995, who received an average of 18 yuan apiece that year, while about 4.3 million urban recipients got 19 yuan per person per month in the same year (SSB 1996). These amounts are obviously very small.

Market-oriented reforms have begun

The fundamental purpose of the central government in its anti-poverty initiatives has been to reduce regional differences and guarantee basic needs of low-income groups in order to enhance national cohesion and strengthen social stability.

to produce the kind of poverty that is associated with the normal workings of a market system. As population mobility and market competition increase, individualised poverty, based on low demand, bankruptcy or personal misfortune can occur in rural as well as urban areas. There is as yet no unified program for dealing with it.

Poverty in China, as elsewhere, is multi-faceted in respects other than just location. It is apt to involve poor education, poor health, undernutrition, unsanitary living conditions, lack of potable water, and high infant and maternal mortality rates, as well as low quality, loss and/or degradation of land, water, air and other natural resources, geographic isolation, etc. Often, several of these conditions exist at once, and they are mutually reinforcing.

Because of these close links between human resource problems and economic underdevelopment, there is a need to integrate social sector objectives closely in PA program planning. Investment in human resources should complement investment in tangible capital. The PA program however tends to be project and production oriented. Whereas projects targeted at improving local health and education conditions are sometimes included, they have usually been left to the social sector organs. And there have been some structural obstacles to co-ordination. The Leading Group and its executive office have in the past not had direct control of PA funds. Instead, these funds have been allocated by the ministries, the State Planning Commission, the Ministry of Finance, and the ADB, according to the kind of funds concerned. Many of these agencies have their own ideas and agendas and, understandably, want to keep control of their resources and make their own allocation decisions. Production-oriented development projects and longer-term infrastructure projects are formulated separately, submitted through different channels and approved by different agencies. Similarly, ADB loans and "food for work" funds are also handled separately. The Leading Groups at each level, with limited budgets of their own and meeting only once or twice a year, have acted essentially as advisory bodies. This

programme structure complicates the achievement of a comprehensive approach to poverty reduction.[3]

In addition to their human resources, other important assets of poor areas, such as land, infrastructure, and technology, have been neglected in recent years. State investment in agriculture and land improvement has in general been only a small fraction of total state capital construction investment (2.6% in 1994). The fiscally strapped poor areas have very limited ability to engage in such investment. The agricultural research system has given little attention to new technologies suited to such areas. As is true of health and education programs, PA efforts also have been affected by the decentralisation of the fiscal system, which has made it much less redistributive and thus left poor localities less able to finance their PA programs and projects. As discussed above, these localities have often tried to develop township and village enterprises (TVEs) to provide jobs and local revenues, but the success of this highly dynamic sector - it now produces half of China's industrial output, generates over half of township tax revenue, and provides 120 million rural jobs - has been geographically uneven, and TVEs have not done well in poor areas. There, scarce resources devoted to TVE development often would have been better spent on infrastructure, loans to farm households or basic education (Rozelle et al., 1995).

In September-October 1996, a special working conference on poverty alleviation was convened in Beijing by the Party Central Committee and the State Council. It was the highest level meeting on the poverty issue ever held in China. A number of important decisions emerged from the meeting, including a substantial increase in government financial resources to be committed to the anti-poverty mission: an additional 1.5 billion yuan per year in central government allocations for economic development in poor areas and an additional 3 billion yuan per year of government loans for anti-poverty purposes.

Market-oriented reforms have begun to produce the kind of poverty that is associated with the normal workings of a market system.

---

[3] A reorganization of China's PA program took place in late 1996 with the intent of responding so some of these issues and of strengthening the powers of the Leading Group and the central PA Office.

Also, it was decided to make the top Party and government leader at each level, from the province to the county, principally responsible for the implementation and success of the anti-poverty programme - a decision that underlined the seriousness of the government's intentions regarding fulfilment of the National 8-7 Plan goals. Moreover, because estimates from the field indicated that some 55-70 percent of poverty alleviation funds were not reaching poor households, but were being shunted by the administering counties into other uses, a State Council decision issued in October 1996 directed that PA programmes must henceforth target the poorest households.

One way of reaching poor households directly is through the microfinance approach, made famous by the Grameen Bank model in Bangladesh. Microfinance has thus been getting increasing attention in China. United Nations system organizations have been collaborating with their Chinese counterparts in support of microfinance projects to promote a variety of social objectives for many years, but have only recently begun to emphasize them specifically as poverty alleviation tools.

3.4. Alleviation of Urban Poverty.

Institutions And Resources. No specific group has been designated at the national level to deal with urban poverty issues. The Ministry of Labour is responsible for providing assistance to unemployed and retired workers, the Ministry of Civil Affairs takes handles target groups for traditional relief, and the Ministry of Personnel is in charge of helping low income groups associated with public undertakings. Municipalities have played the leading role in reaching the poor with resources and employment intermediation.

There are no data available on the total resources committed in urban antipoverty programs throughout China. It is reported that in 1997, 4.2 billion yuan are needed in relief funds to keep the 11.76 million urban poor above the poverty line (Xinhua News Agency, 1997).[4]

Relief Intervention. Since the new urban poor overwhelmingly consist of unemployed workers, the first response of the government was relief intervention and acceleration of social security reform with a focus on replacing the former enterprise-based safety net with state-based pension, unemployment insurance and health care systems, consistent with the operation of a market economy. Since the social security reforms are still incomplete (see Chapter III), relief intervention has played the major role in assisting the urban poor. However, because of a shortage of public funds, donations made by enterprises, Labour Unions, the Women Federation and individuals initially composed the main basis of relief actions. Such donations obviously cannot meet the urgent needs of the urban poor for very long (Table 4.5.). By 1997, some 165 cities have institutionalized safety net systems for their urban poor based on resources from two channels: local government finance and enterprise funds (Workers Daily 1997).

Relief support for the urban unemployed comes in part from these new municipal relief systems and in part from the new unemployment insurance systems still in formation. There are many difficulties. First, in the absence of a national social security law, it is easy for both enterprises and local fiscal authorities to fail to deliver their shares to the funds. Second, the funds are often not effectively managed, and leakage and misappropriation have become serious problems. Third, a considerable number of cities in poor fiscal condition have not been able to set up relief systems. For example, unlike burgeoning Shanghai, which could cover all of its unemployed workers under its unemployment security programs, city governments in the Northeast, where the traditional state-owned heavy industries are concentrated and where both enterprises and governments run large deficits, cannot do so. Therefore, China is quite far from reaching the goal that the government has proposed for the year 2000, of establishing a system to ensure minimum living standards of the urban population in more than 600 cities.

---

[4] See section 2 of this chapter for discussion of the urban poverty line and estimates of urban poverty incidence.

Table 4.5. Unemployment Relief and Re-employment Programs for State Sector Workers, 1986-95

	1986-95	1994	1995
The number of the unemployed workers receiving relief (million people)	6	1.96	2.61
The number of the re-employed workers (million people)	3	0.99	1.38

Source: Ministry of Labour 1997 Outline of Social Security Reforms, April, 1997, Beijing.

The other major strand of the approach to urban poverty is re-employ- ment and job training programs. These are dealt with in Chapter III, sec. 5.

Poverty and General Development Strategy

If PA programs have had uncertain effects on the poverty rate, development approaches and policies of a more general kind have been highly relevant to it. These include price policies toward agriculture and natural resources, fiscal decentraliza- tion, and investment allocation decisions. The effect of these broader policies on rural poverty is probably much greater than that of specific PA policies themselves. For instance, the early 1980s decline in poverty was aided by a sharp rise in farm procure- ment prices paid by the government. Agriculture's terms of trade with industry increased by 50 per cent between 1978 and 1985, whereas from then until 1993 they rose hardly at all. Agricultural output per capita and agriculture's terms of trade together account for 90 per cent of the variation in rural per capita income over the 1978-94 period.[5] Thus, decelerating rural growth plus stagnant terms of trade led real farm incomes - which had more than doubled between 1978 and 1985 - to stagnate from then until 1991, when mod- est growth began again.

With the super harvest of 1984 the government turned its attention to the urban economy, and development strategy changed in significant ways. The result was a shift in the direction of resource flows away from agriculture, the rural economy, and interior China and toward industry, the urban economy and coastal areas. A major goal of the new strategy was the attraction of foreign direct investment to coastal cities with developed infrastructure, and the expansion of exports. Both of these goals were attained brilliantly. However, the negative side of this change in strategy was a decline in attention to agriculture. For instance, investment in agriculture fell from the late 1970s to the early 1980s and then remained flat, both absolutely and as a percentage of total capital construction investment. And we have already seen that rural incomes also remained flat for the second half of the 1980s, despite continued rapid increase in per capita GNP (see Figure 4.2.).

[5] Khan 1996.

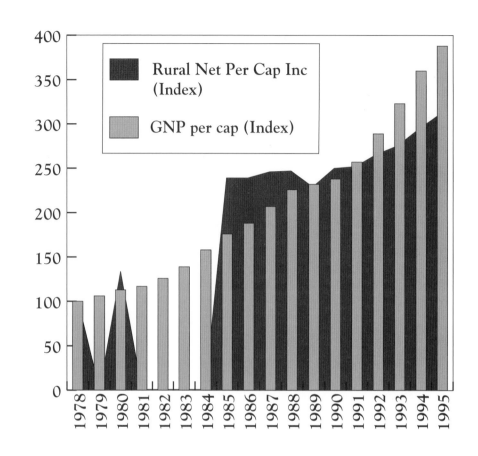

Figure 4.2. GNP and Rural Income Per Capita, Indexes, 1978-1995

Looking at Figure 4.2., it is clear that the years of most rapid reduction in poverty - 1978 to 1984 - were years in which rural incomes were growing fast, even faster than per capita GNP; whereas the years in which rural income stagnated - 1985 to 1991 - were also years in which poverty reduction halted although GNP continued to grow. Resumed progress in lowering the poverty rate began in 1992, which is when rural income growth also resumed. However, a lower growth rate of rural income (well below that of GNP per capita) and a continued rise in inequality of distribution (see Chapter III) have acted together to bring down the rate of poverty reduction relative to the spectacular rates of the early 1980s. Since most poor people live in the countryside, rapid and widely shared rural income growth has been the most effective route to poverty reduction. Conversely, with slow or no rural income growth and increasing inequality in rural distribution, poverty reduction has been hard to achieve.

In contrast to rural income, investment in state enterprises grew by almost eleven times (in current yuan) between 1983 and 1994 (see Fig. 4.3.). Indeed, as Yang and Hao (1996) point out, not only did investment in state units increasingly dwarf agricultural investment, but the government price subsidies to the urban population alone were several times the level of agricultural investment. The increase in investment in state enterprises in 1985 was three times the total amount of PA spending in that year. In 1985 investment in state units was 33 times PA spending; by 1994 it had grown to 67 times PA spending and a shift of only 1.5 per cent of it toward poverty reduction would have doubled the amount of PA resources.

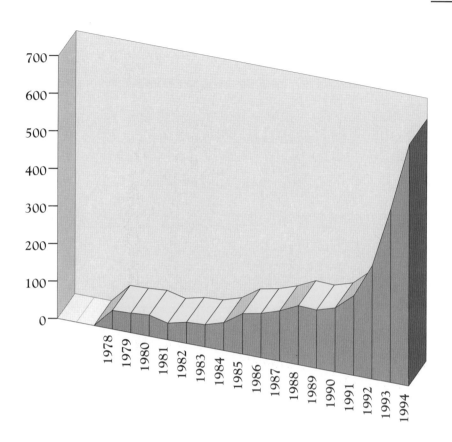

Figure 4.3.: Investment in State Units, 1978-1994

In sum, the lag in growth of rural income, the shift in resources to coastal industries and the sharp increase in inequality all resulted in a slow-down in poverty reduction despite continued economic growth from the mid-1980s to the early 90s. Both the rise in inequality and the persistence of poverty despite increasing direct poverty alleviation efforts, are unintended consequences of broader economic polices that, in themselves, have been extremely successful. This suggests that, as in the case of environmental concerns, "poverty impact assessments" ought to accompany policy formation about a wide range of issues, so that steps can be taken to deal with the potential negative impacts of such policies on the poor and near-poor.

CHAPTER V

Conclusion: Promoting Human Development for the New Millennium

 Introduction

With the beginning of the new millennium a scant two years away, China can be justly proud of the extraordinary gains in human development it has achieved in a relatively short period of history, and against great obstacles. This first national Human Development Report has tried to summarize those gains as comprehensively as possible, while also identifying the outstanding challenges that remain to be overcome. The skill, inventiveness and perseverance of the Chinese people, which have been mobilized so successfully thus far on behalf of the objective of human development, will be required in full measure to confront problems, both old and new, that stand in the way of furthering this objective in the years ahead.

This final chapter seeks to highlight several broad themes, running through the body of the report, that concern the compatibility of China's transition to a market economy with its goal of furthering human development. In part this is a national learning experience, and China like every nation faces unique circumstances that it must come to understand and learn how to cope with on its own. In part, however, knowledge of international experience and, indeed, of China's own valuable past experiences, can be helpful in formulating effective approaches and avoiding the need to "re-invent the wheel" in all circumstances. For instance, the historical experiences of other market economies have yielded many insights about the things that markets do particularly well, and those they do poorly or not at all.

The recommendations set out below by and large are not highly specific. Rather, they put forward broad strategies and approaches that would have the effect of bringing social and economic development in various areas into closer alignment with human development objectives. A common suggestion is to treat these objectives not as ancillary considerations to be addressed after economic development policy has been worked out, but to bring them into the heart of development policy formation itself. While there are many international examples of economic and human development taking divergent paths, it also seems clear from world experience that the most successful development in the long run is that in which human development is fully integrated.

Economic Growth, Human Development and The Environment

China is increasingly linked to the global market economy and is itself becoming a market economy. During most of the reform period, China has benefited from international economic expansion associated with the globalization process stimulated by newly opening markets and by rapid technological change, especially in communications, which has permitted greater capital mobility.

However, both the global economy, more tightly integrated than ever before, and China's own transition economy, are subject to the normal fluctuations of a market regime. For example, indications of excess capacity and lower profit expectations could trigger a reduction in investment along a broad scale that would reverse the high growth environment of recent years. When that happens, remaining transitional problems will be much more painful and difficult to solve. Therefore, it is important that China aggressively attack these problems, such as completion of state enterprise reform, building a comprehensive social insurance system, refurbishing the fiscal system, finding ways to gain compliance with environmental laws, restructuring resource prices in the interest of conservation, etc., while the favorable growth environment is available.

Continued economic growth is an important pre-condition for smooth accomplishment of the rest of the transition. Yet growth has come at a high environmental cost, as witness the World Bank's finding that pollution costs China about 8 percent of GDP per year in damage to life, health and property. Any reasonable estimate of the growth of "net national welfare" would have to subtract this costly damage (as well as the depletion of natural resources) from the GDP growth rate. Obviously, environmental damage has caused net national welfare to grow much slower than GDP.

Economic growth, like fire, can yield both bad and good results, and the challenge for policy is to shape growth so as to minimize the bad and maximize the good.

The deterioration in China's air and water quality during the reform period signals the need to increase attention to the environment in the coming years. More effort and resources will have to be put into development of cleaner energy sources. Both government regulation and market incentives should be brought into play, as China moves from concentration on cleaning up pollution after it occurs to minimizing it in the first place. In this respect, planning of industrial structure should give high priority to environmental considerations. For instance, in planning for development of the transport sector, China might consider putting more emphasis on emulating the Japanese example of building high-speed light rail systems for mass transit, as opposed to encouraging rapid expansion of private automobile consumption.

The endemic water shortages of north China will demand much attention. Conservation will have to play a much greater role than at present, and market incentives as well as regulations should be aimed at encouraging the treatment of fresh water as a scarce and precious natural resource. In agriculture, a major user of fresh water resources, emphasis should be given to popularizing sustainable practices that stress more economical application of irrigation water and soil treatments for water-retention. At stake is not only the overall balance of supply and demand for this resource, but also the country's long-run food security.

Besides shortage, the water supply suffers from widespread pollution and contamination. China should step up efforts to ensure that industrial and municipal waste

Economic growth, like fire, can yield both bad and good results, and the challenge for policy is to shape growth so as to minimize the bad and maximize the good.

water is treated to appropriate standards before release into the environment. In the countryside, more emphasis needs to be placed on alternatives to the use of farm chemicals. Many parts of the world have cut back on the use of pesticides, as their propensity to produce vicious cycles of increasingly heavy doses to fight increasingly resistant pests has come to be understood. China, whose rural water supply has been subject to considerable contamination - including eutrophication from nutrient runoff and toxic contamination from pesticides - should take greater advantage of its world renowned expertise in sustainable and ecological agriculture, to popularize farming techniques that are highly productive and also preserve the environment instead of damaging it.

③ Dealing with Growing Inequality

While a certain amount of increased inequality was inevitable within certain domains - e.g., within the urban population - indications are that some kinds of income inequality have increased faster than was necessary and desirable. Inequality has also been widened by persistent local and regional barriers to resource (including labour) mobility, and inadvertently boosted by some government policies, such as those connected with the coastal development strategy, pricing and procurement policies toward agriculture, the tax structure and the nature of urban housing reform. In the interest of equity as well as social stability, such policies should be re-examined with a view to bringing them into conformity with the goal of equitable income distribution. For instance, the structure of rural public finance should be reshaped to remove the excessive net tax burden from the bottom deciles of the population and shift it upward through the income distribution in accordance with the widely observed "ability to pay" principle. The same general objective can be furthered by increased public spending on education, health care and nutrition in the poorer areas.

The last point puts the focus on growing regional inequalities, especially that between the developed coastal regions and the underdeveloped southwest and northwest interior. These inequalities have been exacerbated by the decay of the former revenue-sharing system that helped the central government contribute to education, health and infrastructure development of the poor interior provinces. Fiscal decentralization, which has greatly weakened that function, has thereby left poorer localities hard-pressed to provide for the basic social spending needs of their regions, and this situation threatens to contribute to further polarization.

To ameliorate this situation, the national government should stem and reverse the long-term trend toward reduction in its share of GDP. While it is appropriate for the government to withdraw from direct involvement in production and investment activities of enterprises, it needs substantially to increase its role in those areas that a market economy cannot handle well, such as provision of public goods and of goods with substantial "external economies" such as health and education. Greater government investment in the people of the poorer interior regions of the country, and especially in improving their educational opportunities and health care, is required to prevent current inequalities from congealing into permanent polarization. The fact that HDI ranks of several western provinces are lower than their per capita GDP rankings suggests opportunities for the government to move forcefully to reduce the special drag that poor education, nutrition and health care create for economic development.

Continuing the Mission of Eliminating Poverty

China faces a major challenge in building on its past successes in reducing absolute poverty and meeting its target of basically eliminating absolute poverty by the year 2000. China deserves much credit for its willingness to make such a radical commitment, and for taking serious steps to accomplish it. At the same time, as income inequality has increased and the economy has moved toward greater reliance on the market, the nature of poverty alleviation is becoming more complex.

In seeking ways to strengthen the poverty alleviation effort, it is important to ensure that the poverty threshold accurately reflects the minimum socially acceptable standard of living, and that it remains constant in real terms over time. There is some evidence that its annual adjustment for inflation has not fully reflected the cost of living increases of the poor population, and that the poverty line therefore has represented a declining real income. The methodology of estimating and updating poverty lines for urban and rural populations should be checked and adjusted where necessary to assure accuracy and consistency.

In addition, while maintaining its commitment to help the remaining poor in remote, ecologically disadvantaged regions, China needs to give more attention to poverty outside of the designated poor counties, where there is insufficient organized government response at present. This effort should be integrated with the project of building a comprehensive social insurance system that will cover people's retirement and health needs as well as unemployment insurance.

China's poverty alleviation effort now involves the whole of society, with localities and enterprises "twinning" with poor area counterparts in an effort to help the latter develop and escape from poverty. The mobilization of the entire society to fight poverty in various ways is admirable. It also calls for special efforts at coordination and ensuring coherence of the anti-poverty effort. Such efforts at coordination should be strengthened even for official poverty alleviation programmes. The multi-dimensional nature of much poverty requires intervention on several fronts - production, finance and credit, infrastructure, health, nutrition, and education - if more than short-term success is to be achieved and if recidivism is to be avoided. While continuing to lay emphasis on development and opening up, China's poverty alleviation effort should give greater attention to the multi-faceted nature of poverty, including the health, education and nutrition needs of the poor population, and should develop the capacity to implement comprehensive programmes for poverty reduction based upon the totality of local needs.

Economic development, rising incomes, rising educational levels and a very high labour force participation rate have all helped to achieve very low fertility rates in Chinese cities. In the countryside, on the other hand, the move to family farming has somewhat strengthened the economic functions of the family, which puts upward pressure on the fertility rate. International experience has shown that socioeconomic development is the most potent and reliable force for reducing fertility. Measures that increase the opportunity cost of children in the countryside - in particular, measures that improve women's level of education and skill, and increase their economic opportunities - will predictably lower the birth rate. For this, not only should the access to education of women and girls be protected and expanded in poorer rural areas, but also labour-intensive economic development programs are needed to absorb the surplus labour of such areas and provide income-earning opportunities. In addition, China should begin to supplement the traditional rural

China's poverty alleviation effort now involves the whole of society.

system of old age security, which places sole reliance on family resources and thus strengthens the need for male children, with a system that supplements private savings with public social security resources. By means of such policies, the goal of keeping fertility rates low and decreasing can be achieved while minimizing the undesirable side effects, such as unbalanced sex ratios, of an administrative approach to population control.

⑤ Carrying Through The Two Health Care Revolutions

China has proved in the past that a high level of basic, preventive health care coverage can be provided at very reasonable costs.

China's principal tasks in the health care field are twofold. First, to strive to even up the health status of the population by successfully bringing the "first health care revolution" to those substantial areas that have not yet achieved it. The victory enjoyed by most Chinese over infectious and parasitological diseases should be brought to all. China has proved in the past that a high level of basic, preventive health care coverage can be provided at very reasonable costs, in part because it is a labour-intensive enterprise and China has an abundance of low-cost labour. The eleven major diseases associated with poverty that, in 1990, accounted for almost a quarter of China's disease burden, can be targeted for public health intervention at a quite reasonable cost (World Bank 1997). In particular, the goal of bridging the gap between the low infant and maternal mortality rates of the cities and prosperous rural regions, on the one hand, and the much higher ones of poorer rural areas, on the other, should be vigorously pursued.

Accomplishing this first task will require strengthening the public health orientation and emphasis on prevention of China's health care system. This in turn requires increased public funding for health and reduced emphasis on fee-for-service payments that have caused resources to be redirected from public health priorities to fee-collecting activities. The re-establishment of cooperative health insurance coverage for the rural population should be encouraged, so that no rural women will have to go without delivery and pre- and postnatal care for lack of ability to pay.

The second principal health care task involves the newly prominent causes of mortality among the majority of Chinese who have successfully gone through the "first health care revolution". These include cardiovascular disease and cancers, both of which are connected with life style issues, such as smoking and diet, and environmental causes, including air and water pollution. Health considerations thus need to play a prominent role in social policy formation for issues as broad-ranging as industrial location and provincial finances (some of which benefit from tobacco revenues). In addition, China faces stern new challenges in combating sexually transmitted diseases, whose prevalence has been increasing, and, in particular, in stemming the spread of HIV/AIDS. Narcotics addiction is another growing problem for which effective solutions need to be found.

⑥ Education

Preparing for the 21st Century. Improving China's education is a sine qua non for escaping poverty and competing in the modern world. While the average educational attainment of the Chinese people has continued to advance, more could and should be done to improve both the quantity and quality of education. It is essential to achieve the target of universal compulsory nine-year schooling. School enrollment rates in poor areas need to be raised and the right to education in particular of girls in poorer rural areas needs protection and encouragement.

The outstanding problem of inadequate resources devoted to education should be addressed forthrightly, in part by moving vigorously to obtain compliance with the government target of raising educational spending to 4 percent of GNP by the end of the century. China should also take steps to remove the excessive financial burden of schooling on families in poor areas, which is partly responsible for their lower enrollment rates. Although Project Hope and Project Spring Bud are playing an important role in mobilizing Chinese citizens to contribute to the educational needs of poor children, such voluntary efforts do not substitute for public funding sufficient to provide good quality education for all children.

Here, as in other areas of human development, success depends upon reversing the decentralization of the fiscal system and strengthening the government's ability to address social welfare needs left unaddressed by the market. The argument that because of government fiscal stringency the bulk of new spending on education must come from higher tuition fees and student loans illustrates the danger of examining each human development component in isolation. Such a solution inappropriately takes the current budget constraint as a given instead of strongly advocating its correction. Greater reliance on fee-for-service schooling would be bound to make education increasingly a vehicle for perpetuating and magnifying social and regional inequalities. China's educational system, at the primary and secondary levels, at least, should rely overwhelmingly on public funding, and the current fiscal obstacles constitute a serious impediment to human development and deserve urgent attention.

Although China has been putting increasing emphasis on developing technical and vocational education, in an effort to alleviate labour market problems by producing more qualified workers, there is a danger in over-emphasizing such specialized approaches and in giving insufficient attention to the importance of good general education in coping with the demands of the modern world. Market economies in a time of rapidly changing technologies and tastes require workers who can learn new techniques and adapt to new conditions quickly. These attributes tend to be the products of good general education, especially learning to think independently and critically and to solve problems creatively, rather than of narrower technical education.

China should also take steps to remove the excessive financial burden of schooling on families in poor areas, which is partly responsible for their lower enrollment rates.

Promoting Full Equality for Women

Continued progress of China's women toward full equality of rights and opportunities with men is important for its own sake. It is also an essential ingredient in achieving several other important goals. These include controlling population size, which depends very much on improving the lives and status of women; eliminating absolute poverty, for which investment in women's human capital development and provision of micro finance to groups of village women have proven to be effective methods; and developing sustainable farming practices in agriculture, a sector increasingly controlled by women. Special efforts are called for to eliminate the greater burden of illiteracy still suffered by women. Only with full equality can the great talents of China's women be fully developed and utilized.

The unbalanced sex ratio at birth, which signals the widespread inequality of treatment of girls in rural China, should be tackled not solely by administrative and legal means, but most importantly by finding social answers to the material need for more children, and especially sons, that now exists in rural society. This means providing alternatives to children as sources of old age security and as income earners. Enhanced education and income earning opportunities for women, which raise the opportunity cost of having children, and the establishment of a social security system covering the rural population, are the two most powerful potential responses to sex discrimination in the countryside. Beyond that, the active encouragement of women's participation in leadership roles throughout society, including at the highest levels of the economic and political systems, would provide role models encouraging girls and young women to aspire to full lives outside the immediate family.

China has rightly paid much attention to labour market problems of women in the transition environment, when market pressures and discriminatory attitudes have led some enterprises to lay off or refuse to hire women workers. Since maternity and child care responsibilities of women are undertaken on behalf of society as a whole, China should move toward socializing these costs just as is being done for retirement and other social welfare obligations of enterprises. The 1992 Law on Protection of Women's Rights should be strictly enforced to prevent the still widespread practice of discriminating against women in hiring and firing.

Women's life expectancy at birth is now formally put at 73 years. The difference in retirement ages for women and men, which prevents women from achieving senior positions and the higher incomes and pensions that go with them, should be phased out. If a relatively low retirement age is thought justifiable in China's labour surplus economy, it should be applied equally to men and women. Appropriate exceptions designed to retain the wisdom and judgment of older workers should also apply equally to both sexes. Women should also be assured equal rights to housing, and be treated with absolute equality in implementing the housing reform.

⑧ Building a Modern Social Insurance System

Nothing is more important to China's successful transition to a market economy than completion of a national social insurance programme to cope with unemployment, retirement, and health care needs of the urban population. Economic logic suggests the desirability of a unified national system with the broadest possible financial base. The government has recently decided upon just such a system for handling pensions, and now needs to act decisively to overcome the confusion caused by the coexistence of competing systems and move toward unification of at least the main components of the system, even if local variation is permitted for ancillary components. A reformed pension system should have a substantial social insurance base administered by the government, as well as a mix of supplementary components combining mandatory and voluntary individual accounts. It is highly desirable that China try to complete such a system while still in a high growth phase, when demands on the system are smaller and higher growth dividends are available for its support. Successful establishment of a social insurance system will depend upon (a) improvement of China's revenue-raising ability to capture a higher share of GDP, commensurate with international experience, and (b) completing reform of the financial system and capital markets, which is necessary for the management of individual accounts.

The means of dealing with the longer-term problem of the aging population will have to include some combination of (a) gradual raising of the retirement age;

(b) unification of the retirement age of men and women; (c) gradual reduction in China's generous pension benefits relative to wages. Transition costs of pension reform will require special measures to handle the pension costs of current retirees and of workers who retire shortly after the new system is in place. Such costs can be met through a combination of government borrowing, increased taxes, and perhaps a temporary surcharge on the retirement contributions of workers and enterprises.

Unemployment, which is contributing to problems of urban poverty, is going to be a regular part of China's market economy, as it is of all market economies. There is a need for a modern system of labour statistics, including those for unemployment, so as to be able to monitor labour market conditions more accurately. Employment and unemployment statistics, using standard sampling techniques, should be comprehensive and encompass all members of the labour force, including migrant workers and workers in all ownership sectors.

Solution of the social insurance problem inevitably raises the question of the social and administrative divide that still separates urban from rural China. The prospects for successful implementation of pension reform are increased by the low coverage rate of the social insurance system in China, compared to some other developing countries. Yet, as labour market development erodes the distinctions between permanent and migrant workers, China should start planning for the incorporation into the social insurance network of the millions of migrant workers who will be permanent fixtures in the urban scene and who will be competing with - and working next to - "full status" urban workers. Similarly, the tens of millions of township and village enterprise workers, outside the formal state sector, should have access to effective social insurance.

Unemployment, which is contributing to problems of urban poverty, is going to be a regular part of China's market economy, as it is of all market economies.

Facing the Future

The economic difficulties experienced by various neighbors of China in late 1997 are a reminder of various truths: that markets fall as well as rise, that integration with the world market brings risks as well as rewards, that the market expects transparency in national financial systems and will eventually punish unsound economic decisions, however well hidden they might have been. From a longer-term perspective, however, the newly industrializing Asian countries did many things right, starting with investment in their own people. As China faces an uncertain future global economic climate, it too should put full confidence in its strongest asset - its own people - and aim to improve their level of well-being, health and knowledge, as well as their ability to participate in solving the problems facing them as individuals and as citizens. Not only is this desirable in itself as an end of policy making, it is also the best way to ensure robust economic and social progress into the new millennium.

The tasks facing China are complex. On the one hand, reform has to be completed, factor market institutions built up and perfected, barriers to free and competitive markets eliminated, openness and transparency enhanced. On the other hand, even while markets are being established, their inherent limitations should be grasped, and a full understanding developed of the many substantive areas that are under-served by markets or outside their domain, where the government can and should act vigorously on behalf of human development objectives. Such areas include:

* meeting the education, health, and nutrition needs of the population, concentrating on those parts of the rural population that are particularly under-served

* continuing progress toward the elimination of absolute poverty

* formulation of effective policies to ameliorate excessive income inequality

* discouragement of discrimination that compromises the equal status of women and girls in society

* protection of the natural environment

* investment in infrastructure, such as mass transit and waste water treatment facilities

* promotion of sustainable agricultural technologies that can feed the population while conserving China's precious soil and water resources over the long run

* establishment and adequate funding of social insurance and social security institutions

* enhancement of the independence and transparency of the emerging new legal system.

Such an agenda, of which the above points are only a part, is obviously large in scope, complex and challenging. Moreover, its many features are both interconnected and linked to broader economic development strategies. For instance, construction of effective public transport systems is an essential means of fighting pollution and improving the natural environment, as well as a means of promoting labour mobility and reducing labour costs. And erecting an adequate social security system will enhance the status of women, encourage lower fertility and work to correct demographic imbalance.

Implementation of such a human development agenda will require perfecting a different role for government than that of the past. Human development is not a peripheral concern to be considered after decisions have been made on "purely economic" grounds. While eschewing micromanagement of the economy, the government, with full participation from the people at large, can undertake to formulate and implement broad strategies toward such crucial areas as energy policy, agriculture, transport structure, human habitat develop-

ment, etc., that take environmental and other human development objectives fully into account. Effective implementation of the above agenda will also require that government substantially increase its relative financial weight in the economy.

The human development agenda facing China at the dawn of the new century is indeed challenging. Yet, both the record of China's achievements to date and its extraordinary endowment of human resources provide firm hope that these challenges can be met and overcome. If so, the new century will witness not only the continued emergence of a new economic power in the world, but, more importantly, a model of human development showing how modernization can promote the interests and well-being of people and the health of the planet. ¡

Master Bibliography of the China National Human Development Report

Adelman, I. and C.T. Morris. 1973. Economic Growth and Social Equity in Developing Countries. Stanford: Stanford University Press.

Agriculture Bank of China. 1988. "Improving Rural Financial Services to Support Economic Development of Poor Areas." Beijing: Agriculture Bank of China.

Ahmad, Ehtisham, Jean Dreze, John Hills, and Amartya Sen, eds. 1991. Social Security in Developing Countries. Oxford: Clarendon Press.

ACWF (All China Women's Federation), Urban and Rural Department, ed. 1995a. Urban Women's Employment and Development. Beijing: China Women's Publishing House.

_____1995b. Essay on Rural Women's Participation Development. Beijing: China Women's Publishing House.

ADB (Asian Development Bank). 1995. Economic Evaluation of Environmental Impacts. Manila: Asian Development Bank.

Barr, Nicholas, ed. 1994. Labour Markets and Social Policy in Central and Eastern Europe: The Transition and Beyond. New York: Oxford University Press.

Bernstein, Thomas P. 1993. "China: Change In A Marxist--Leninist State." In J.W. Morley, ed. Driven By Growth: Political Change In the Asia--Pacific Region. New York: M.E.Sharpe, Inc.

Bloom, Gerald, Tang Shenglan, and Gu Xingyuan. 1995. "Financing Rural Health Services in China in the Context of Economic Reform." Journal of International Development 7(3): 423-441.

Braun, J. von, T. Teklu and P. Webb. 1991. "Labour-intensive Public Works for Food Security: Experience in Africa." Working Papers on Food Subsidies, No. 6. Washington, DC: International Food Policy Research Institute.

Brenner, Mark. 1997. "The Distribution of Land in Rural China." Paper read at Workshop on Income Distribution in China, July 4-6, at Beijing, China.

Brown, Lester. 1995. Who Will Feed China? Wake Up Call For A Small Planet? Washington: Worldwatch Institute.

Cai Fang. 1997. "China's Population: Structure, Dynamics and Impact on Economic Development: Background Paper for the China National Human Development Report," photocopy, Beijing: UNDP.

Cao Min. 1997. "Ministry Works Hard to Solve Job Problem." China Daily. 8 May. Beijing.

Carter, Colin, Funing Zhong, and Fang Cai. 1996. China's Ongoing Agricultural Reform. San Francisco: The 1990 Institute.

CCCPC (Central Committee of the Communist Party of China) and the State Council. 1996a. Decision on Expediting the Solution of the Food and Clothing Problems of Rural Poor.

_____1996b. Decision on Doing a Good Job in Reducing the Burdens of Farmers.

_____1997. Decision on Health Reform and De5velopment.

Chan, Cecilia L. 1993. The Myth of Neighbourhood Mutual Help: The Contemporary Chinese Community-Based Welfare System in Guangzhou. Hong Kong: Hong Kong University Press.

Chan, Cecilia L.W. and Nelson W.S. Chow. 1992. More Welfare After Economic Reform? Welfare Development in the People's Republic of China. Hong Kong: Hong Kong University Press.

Chan, Kam Wing. "Migration Controls and Urban Society in Post-Mao China." Working paper No. 95-2, Seattle Population Research Center. University of Washington, Bettelle.

Chen Chunming. 1996. "Nutrition Problems of the Poor." Tribune of Economic Development. No.7. Beijing.

Chen Chunming, and Shao Zongming. 1990. Food Nutrition and Health Status in China's Seven Provinces. China Academy of Preventive Medicine and China Statistics Bureau. Beijing: China Statistics Press.

Chen Demei. 1997. "Boom and Bust: Labour Migrants Returned Hometown to Start Enterprises." Chinese Peasantry. Vol. 3.

Chen Junsheng. 1994. "Fight with Absolute Poverty." Development and Common Wealth. 17 October. Beijing.

Chen, Liangjin, ed. 1994. Chinese Social Work Encyclopaedia. Beijing: Chinese Social Press.

Chen Muhua and Hua Fuzhou. 1996-97. Oral reports on the "Theory & Skill-Achievement & Contribution" movement and the "Women's Poverty-Alleviation Action" (Shuangxue Shuangbi; Jinguo Fupin Huodong) presented at the ACWF annual conference in January.

Chen Shaohua and M. Ravallion. 1995. Data in Transition: Assessing Rural Living Standards in Southern China. Washington, DC: Policy Research Department, World Bank.

Chen Yonghui. 1996. "Goddess Mazu Cries." (Mazu You Lei) China Women's News (Zhongguo Funu Bao). 15 January, p. 1.

Cheng, Kai Ming. 1995. "Education, Decentralization and Regional Disparity in China." In Social change and educational development, edited by G.A.P a. L.W. On. Hong Kong: Centre of Asian Studies, The University of Hong Kong.

CCICED (China Council for International Cooperation on Environment and Development). 1994. "Strategic Energy Alternatives for China." Report of the working group on energy strategies and technologies. Beijing.

CEYB (China Environmental Yearbook Editorial Committee). 1995. China Environmental Yearbook 1995. Beijing: China Environmental Yearbook Press.

_____1996. China Environmental Yearbook 1996. Beijing: China Environmental Yearbook Press.

China Network for Training and Research in Health Economics and Financing. 1994. Financing and Organization for the Health Services in Poor Rural Areas in China. Research Report (Part One).

China Population Information Research Center, ed. 1994. "Population and Development in China: Figures and Facts." Population in Contemporary China, Vol. 3. (Special issue for International Conference of Population and Development).

China Population: National (in Chinese). 1989. Beijing: Chinese Finance and Economy Press.

China Research Centre on Aging (CRCOA). 1994. Proceedings of the Conference on the Support Systems for China's Elderly. Beijing.

CA (China's Agenda 21 Preparatory Group). 1994. China Agenda 21: China's White Paper on Population, Natural Resources and the Environment. Beijing.

CCGDP (China's Coordinating Group on Desertification Prevention). 1997. "Report on Desertification in China." People's Daily. 12 May.

CEMS (China's Environmental Management System Drafting Group). 1991. China's Environmental Management System. Beijing: China Environmental Science Press.

CWYB (China Water Conservancy Yearbook Editorial Committee). 1992. China Water Conservancy Yearbook 1992. Beijing: Water Conservancy & Electricity Press.

_____1995. China Water Conservancy Yearbook 1995. Beijing: Water Conservancy & Electricity Press.

China Women's News. 1995a. "Human Traffickers Stopped." (Maimai renkou zhe jie) 24 April, p. 1.

_____1995b. "Rural Women Finally Can Keep Their Land When Divorced." 4 December, p. 1.

CAAS-ANR (Chinese Academy of Agricultural Sciences - Institute of Natural Resource Zoning for Agriculture). 1995. China's Arable Land. Beijing: China's Agricultural Science & Technology Press.

CASS (Chinese Academy of Social Science), Institute of Economics. 1995. 1995 Household Income Survey. Beijing.

CASS, Institute of Population Studies. 1988. "China 1986 Internal Migration Sampling Survey Data." Editorial Department of China Population Sciences.

_____1992. 10 Province Sample Survey on Household Economy and Fertility in China.

CSD (UN Commission on Sustainable Development). 1996. Indicators of Sustainable Development Framework and Methodologies. New York: United Nations.

ICC (Committee on International Cooperation). 1994. Compilation of Documents on International Cooperation Committee. Beijing: China Environment Science Press.

_____1995. Compilation of Documents on International Cooperation Committee, Volume II. Beijing: China Environment Science Press.

Cui Buo. 1995. "An Important Source of Human Labor: Young Rural Out-migrate Laborers." Beijing: China Youth Daily. 2 April.

Cui Fengyuan and Cheng Shen. 1997. "A New Study of the Research Methods on Women's Status: Gender Equality Development Index." Collection of Women's Studies. Beijing: ACWF Institute of Women's Studies.

Contemporary Chinese Women (Dangdai Zhongguo Funu). 1994. Beijing: Contemporary China Publishing House.

Dasgupta, P. and K. Maler. 1994. Poverty, Institutions, and the Environmental-Resource Base, Washington, DC: World Bank.

Daxing County Women's Federation, and People's University Beijing and Women's Studies Center. 1996. "A Comparative Study on Two Hundred Households of Daxing County." Recent Development of Women's Studies (Funu Lilun Yanjiu Dongtai). Beijing: Association of Women's Studies.

DPES, SSB (Department of Population and Employment Statistics, State Statistics Bureau), and DOPW, MOL (Department of Overall Planning and Wages, Ministry of Labor), eds. 1995. China Labour Statistical Yearbook 1995. Beijing: China Statistical Publishing House.

Dreze, J., and A. Sen. 1989. Hunger and Public Action. Oxford: Clarendon Press.

Duoji Cairang. 1995. Theory and Practice of Chinese Social Security System Reforms in a New Era (Xinshiqi Zhongguo Shehui Baozhang Tizhi Gaige de Lilun yu Shijian). Beijing: Party College of the Central Committee of the CCP Press.

Eckaus, R.S., S. Lahiri, and Z.X. Wu. 1994. "Trial Solutions to a Model for the Projection of Future CO2 Emissions in China." Unpublished research report. MIT and Qinghua University.

ESRC (Economic Structural Reform Commission). 1995. Social Security System Reforms. Beijing: Chinese Reform Press (in Chinese).

Esping-Andersen, Gosta and Walter Korpi. 1984. "Social policies as class politics in post-war capitalism: Scandinavia, Austria and Germany." In John H. Goldthorpe (ed.). Order and Conflict in Contemporary Capitalism. Oxford: Oxford University Press.

Esping-Andersen, Gosta. 1990. The Three Worlds of Welfare Capitalism. Cambridge: Polity Press.

_____ ed. 1996. Welfare States in Transition National Adaptations in Global Economics. London: SAGE Publications.

Fan, Ping. 1996. "China's Urban Low Income Group--a Sociological Investigation on Urban Poor Employees." Chinese Social Science. Vol. 4: 64-77.

Fan, Shenggen. 1996. "Why Projections on China's Future Food Supply and Demand Differ?" Paper prepared for international conference titled "Food and Agriculture in China: Perspectives and Policies." Beijing.

Fan Xiaoyu. 1996. "Problems, Policies, and Basic Characteristics of China's Rural Labour Employment." (Dangqian Woguo Nongcun Laodongli Jiuye de Wenti Ji Duice; Dangqian Woguo Nongcun Laodongli Jiuye de Jiben Tezheng) Unpublished report by the Rural Survey Team of the State Statistical Bureau.

Fang, Zhiyun. 1988. Handbook on Water Resources and Conservation. Nanjing, China: Hehai University Press.

Fei, Ranis, and Kuo. 1979. Growth with Equity: The Taiwan Case. New York: Oxford University Press.

Feng Yuan. 1997. Women in Contemporary China: Background Paper for the China National Human Development Report", photocopy, Beijing, UNDP..

Ge Keyou. 1996. Diet and Nutrition of Chinese in 1990s (National Nutrition Survey of 1992). China Academy of Preventive Medicine, Nutrition and Food Hygiene Institute. Beijing: People's Health Publishing House.

Ge, Man. 1995. "China's Social Insurance: Reflections on Predicaments and Directions." In White, Gordon and Shang Xiaoyuan (1996a), Issues and Answers: Reforming the Chinese Social Security System. Brighton, UK: Institute of Development Studies.

GHABC (General Headquarters of the Agriculture Bank of China). 1987. "The Report with Regard to Improvement of Utilization of Subsidized Credits Specific for Poverty Alleviation." 16 October. Beijing: General Headquarters of the Agriculture Bank of China.

General Team of the Urban Social Economic Survey, SSB, ed. 1994. Survey Materials of Income and Expenditure of Chinese Urban Households. Beijing: China Statistical Publishing Press.

GEF (Global Environment Facility). 1996. GEF Operational Strategy. Washington DC.

Grindle, Merilee S. and John W. Thomas. 1991. Public Choices and Policy Change: The Political Economy of Reform in Developing Countries. Baltimore and London: Johns Hopkins University Press.

Gu Xingyuan and Gerald Bloom. 1995. "Health Sector Reform in Poor Rural China." Policy briefing, Issue 4 (July). Institute of Development Studies, Sussex.

Gu Xingyuan, Gerald Bloom, Tang Shenglan, Zhu Yingya, Zhou Shouqi, and Chen Xingbao. 1993. "Financing Health Care in Rural China: Preliminary Report of a Nationwide Study." Social Science Medicine 36(4): 385-391.

Gu Xingyuan and Tang Shenglan. 1995. "Reform of the Chinese Health Care Financing System." Health Policy. 32:181-191.

Guangdong Women's Federation. 1995. Survey on Women's Social Status In Guangdong. Beijing: China Women's Publishing House.

Guo Jinping, ed. 1995. Zhongguo shehui baozhang zhidu zonglan (A Comprehensive Book on the Social Security System in China). Beijing: China Democracy and Legal System Publishing House.

Hay, D. A., and D. J. Morris. 1994. Economic Reform and State-Owned Enterprises in China, 1979-87. Oxford: Clarendon Press.

Hayward, M. And W. Wang. 1993. "Retirement in Shanghai." Research on Aging. 15 (1): 332.

He Linxiang. 1994. "To Promote the Realization of the National Anti-poverty Plan for the Years of 1994-2000." Development and Common Wealth, No. 5. Beijing.

He Qian and Huang Li. 1994. "Good and Bad of the Rural Out-migrate Laborer Boom." Sichuan Worker's Daily. 1 March.

Hu Shanlian. 1997a. China Health Sectoral Report: Problems and Prospects; Study on Social Sector Issues in Asian Transition Economics. Asian Development Bank (in press).

_____ 1997b. "Health and Nutrition: Background Paper for the China National Human Development Report", Shanghai: Shanghai Medical University, photocopy.

_____ 1997c. "New Horizon of Health Care Reform in China: Informing and Reforming." ICHSRI newsletter (1).

Huang Jian. 1995. "Occupation Change and Class Division of Peasants in Jie'an Village in Southern Jiangsu." Strategy and Management, Vol. 2. China Society for Strategy and Management Research.

Hussain, Athar. 1991. "Social Security in China: A Historical Perspective." In Ahmad, Ehtisham and Dreze, eds., op. cit.

Institute of Development, Rural Research Center of the State Council of PRC. 1987. A Choice for Modernization. Beijing: Publishing House of Economic Science.

IRD (Institute for Rural Development), CASS (Chinese Academy of Social Sciences) and SSB (General Team of the State Statistical Bureau for the Rural Socioeconomic Survey). 1996. '95 Rural Socioeconomic Development Report of China. Beijing: Social Science Publisher of China.

IFAD (International Fund for Agricultural Development). 1995. The Status of Rural Women in China. Rome.

ILO (International Labour Organization). 1994. "People's Republic of China , Employment Policies for Transition to a Market Economy." Bangkok: ILO/EASMAT, Regional Office for Asia and the Pacific.

International Monetary Fund. 1997. "PRC: Recent Economic Developments."

Jiang, Chunyun. 1997. Speech at National Conference on Township and Village Enterprises. People's Daily. (May 9).

Jiang Liu, Lu Xueyi and Shan Tianlun, eds. 1997. China in 1996-1997: Analysis and Forecast of Social Situation. Beijing: China Social Sciences Publishing House.

Jiang Xia. 1997. "Soil Erosion: Comprehensive Control." People's Daily. 13 May.

Jiang, Zemin. 1995. "Appropriately Dealing with Several Important Relations in the Construction of Socialist Modernization." Documents of the CPC's Fifth Plenary Meeting of the Fourteenth Central Committee. Beijing: People's Press.

_____ 1996. Speech at the Conference of the Central Committee of the Chinese Communist Party on Poverty Reduction Programs, 23 September. Beijing.

Jing, Jianming. 1994. Green Crisis: Proceedings on Degradation of Typical

Ecological Zones and Their Rehabilitation and Initialization. Beijing: China Environment Press.

Johnson, Gale. 1993. "Effects of Institutions and Policies on Rural Population Growth with Application to China." Prepared for presentation at International Conference on China's Rural Reform and Development in the 1990s. Beijing. December 3-7, 1993.

Khan, Azizur Rahman. 1996. "The Impact of Recent Macroeconomic And Sectoral Changes on the Poor And Women in China." Study prepared for the East Asia Multidisciplinary Advisory Team of the International Labour Organization, University of California, Riverside.

_____1997a. "Distribution of Income in China: Evolution of Inequality, 1988-1995." Paper read at Workshop on Income Distribution in China, at Beijing.

_____1997b. "Poverty in China in the Period of Globalization: New Evidence on Trend and Pattern." Paper read at Workshop on Income Distribution in China, August 4-6, at Beijing.

Khan, A. R., and C. Riskin. 1997. "Income and Inequality in China, 1988 to 1995." Unpublished manuscript.

Krieg, Renate and Monika Schadler, eds. 1994. Social Security in the People's Republic of China. Hamburg: Institute for Asienkunde.

Kung, J.K. 1994. "Egalitarianism, Subsistence Provision, and Work Incentives in China's Agricultural Collectives." World Development 22 (2).

_____1995. "Equal Entitlement Versus Tenure Security Under a Regime of Collective Property Rights: Peasants' Preference for Institutions in Post-reform Chinese Agriculture." Journal of Comparative Economics 21 (2).

Kung, J.K., and Shouying Liu. 1997. Farmers' preferences regarding ownership and land tenure in post-Mao China: unexpected evidence from eight counties. The China Journal (38).

Kunte, A. 1996. "Estimating a Nation's Wealth: Methodology and Preliminary Results." Information paper.

Kuznets, S. 1955. "Economic Growth and Income Inequality." American Economic Review, Vol. 45, p. 1-28.

Lardy, Nicholas R. 1978. Economic growth and income distribution in the People's Republic of China. Cambridge and New York: Cambridge University Press.

LSCEDPA (Leading Group of the State Council for Economic Development in Poor Areas). 1986. The Summary of the 3rd Plenary Meeting, 20 September. Beijing.

_____1989a. Document Compiled on Economic Development of Poor Areas. Beijing: People's Publishing House.

_____1989b. Outlines of Economic Development in China's Poor Areas. Beijing: Agricultural Publishing House.

_____1989c. Summary of the 7th Plenary Meeting, 1 February. Beijing.

_____1993. "A Profile of Economic Development and Poverty Alleviation." 15 September. Beijing.

_____1994. "An Analysis Report on the 1993 Statistics of Poor Counties." 23 September. Beijing.

Lee, Chingboon, 1994. "China in Transition: Reforming the Urban Social Security System--Issues and Options." Mimeo.

Lee, Wing On and Li Zibiao. 1995. "Education, Development and Regional Disparities in Guangzhou." In Social change and educational development, edited by G. A. Postiglione, and Lee Wing On. Hong Kong: Centre of Asian Studies, The University of Hong Kong.

Leung, Joe C.B. 1995a. "From Subsistence to 'Xiao Kang': Social Development in the People's Republic of China." Social Development Issues 17(2/3): 104-114.

_____1995b. "The political economy of unemployment and unemployment insurance in the People's Republic of China." International Social Work. 38 (2): 139-149.

Li Fan and Han Xiaoyuan. 1994. "Age and Educational Structure of the Rural Labour Out-migrants." China Rural Economy.

Li Jianguang and Li Guo. 1992. "Utilization of the Funds for Poverty Alleviation and Economic Development." Beijing.

Li Peng. 1995. "Note on the Ninth Five-Year Plan and Long Term Targets in 2010 for National Economic and Social Development." People's Daily. 6 October.

Li Shi. 1996. Changes in Poverty Reduction in China. Beijing. (forthcoming)

_____, 1997a. "Impact of Rural-Urban Labour Migration on Income

Distribution", photocopy, Beijing.

_____, 1997b. "Provincial Human Development Index in China: Background Paper for the China National Human Development Report", Beijing, photocopy.

Li Shi and B. Gustafsson. 1996. "The Structure of Chinese Poverty at End 1980s." Social Sciences of China, No. 6, Beijing.

Li Yining. 1996. Theories on Transition And Development. Beijing: Tongxin Publishing House.

Li Zhibao, "Education: Background Paper for the China National Human Development Report", Beijing, unpublished, 1997.

Liang Qiaozhuan. 1996. Report from the Guangdong Women's Federation (on employment) presented at an ACWF Conference, November.

Lin, Justin Yifu. 1992. "Rural Reforms and Agricultural Growth in China." American Economic Review. Vol. 82, No. 1, March.

_____1994. A Research on the Growth Potential of Per Unit Area Yield of the Major Food Grain Production and the Growth Perspectives. Project report.

Lin, Justin Yifu, Cai Fang, and Li Zhou. 1997. "Social Consequences of Economic Reform in China: An Analysis of Regional Disparity in the Transition Period." Beijing: UNDP.

Liu Danhua and Chai Haishan. 1996. "Equality and Women Workers' Rights." Paper for International Labour Standards Seminar, Beijing, 21-24 May.

Liu Guoxin, Liu Shao, and He Yaomin. 1994. Historical Chronicles of the People's Republic of China, 1977-94. Vol. 4, pp. 891, 905. Nanning: Guangxi People's Press.

Liu, Jiang, ed. 1996. "China Social Situation Analysis and Projection, 1995-1996." In SSB 1996a. China Statistical Yearbook 1996.

Liu Xiaojing. 1996. "Is There Nothing the Law Can Do?" (Falu nan dao jiu guan buliao?) China Women's News. 11 January, p. 1.

Liu, Y., S.L. Hu, W. Fu, and W.C. Hsiao. 1996. "Is Community Financing Necessary and Feasible for Rural China?" Health Policy (38):155-171.

Liu, Yongliang. 1995. "The Negative Growth of Shanghai Citizen Population and the Family Planning Management." China's Population Almanac 1995. Beijing: Economic Management Publishing House.

Liu, Zemin. 1994. Social Security in a Market Economy. Beijing: Chinese Material Press (in Chinese).

Logan, John R. and Yanjie Bian. 1993. "Inequalities In Access To Community Resources In A Chinese City." Social Forces 72(2):555-576.

Lu Lei, Hao Hongsheng and Gao Ling. 1994. "Table of Provincial Life-expectancy in China in 1990." Population Studies. May. (In Chinese).

Macridis, Roy C. 1983. Contemporary Political Ideologies (second edition). Boston: Little, Brown & Co.

Maternal Health Care Society of China Preventive Medical, ed. 1995. "Women's Health and Development." (abstract) Beijing.

Meng Xianfan. 1995. Chinese Women in the Tide of Reform. Beijing: China Social Sciences Publishing House.

Meng Xianzhong, "Human Development Policies and Practice of China: A Critical Approach: Background Paper for the China National Human Development Report", photocopy, 1997.

Meng, Xianjiang. 1997. "Water Resources Seriously Polluted." Economic Daily. 15 February.

Migrant Peasant-Workers Project Group. 1995. "The Situation with Regard to Migrant Peasant-Workers in the Pearl River Delta." Social Sciences in China (4). Beijing: Social Sciences in China.

Min Qi. 1996. "Reform of the Public Medical Care System and Labour Insurance Medical Care System in China." In White, Gordon and Shang Xiaoyuan, eds. 1996a. Issues and Answers: Reforming the Chinese Social Security System. Brighton, UK: Institute of Development Studies.

MOA (Ministry of Agriculture). 1996a. China's Development Report on Agriculture. Beijing: China Agriculture Press.

_____1996b. Statistical Data on China's Agriculture. Beijing: China Agriculture Press.

MOA (Ministry of Agriculture), Rural Economic Research Center. 1996a. Rural Labour Force Mobility Research Newsletter.

_____1996b. "A Study on Rural Labour Mobility: Out-migrants and the

Place of Origin." Paper for the International Seminar on Rural Labour Mobility in China, 1996.

MCA (Ministry of Civil Affairs), Planning and Financial Bureau, ed. 1994. China Civil Affairs Statistical Yearbook 1994. Beijing.

MCA, Research Institute for Social Welfare And Social Development. 1996. "Necessity of Establishing Security System for Guaranteeing Minimum Living Standard of Urban Residents." Economic Research Reference. No. 37. Beijing: Chinese Society Press.

MOH (Ministry of Health). 1993. Report of National Health Survey of 1993. Beijing.

_____1995. Digest of Health Statistics of China (1985-1995). Beijing.

_____1996. Review and Evaluation Report on the Third 85% Coverage Target for Expanded Programme of Immunization. Beijing.

_____1997. "Building a Socialist Health Care System with Chinese Characteristics." Collection of Documents of the National Health Conference. Beijing: People's Health Publishing House.

MOL (Ministry of Labor). 1995. The Establishment and Improvement of Chinese Social Security System. Beijing: Economic Press.

_____1996. "Opportunity and Ability: Employment and Mobility of Rural Labour Force in China." Paper for the International Seminar on Mobility of Rural Labour Force in China.

NEPA (National Environmental Protection Agency). 1994. Compilation on Environmental Statistical Data in China. Beijing: China Environment Press.

_____1996. China Environmental Bulletin 1996. Beijing.

_____1997. China Environmental Bulletin 1997. Beijing.

National People's Congress of the People's Republic of China. 1995. The Education Law of the People's Republic of China. Beijing: State Education Commission. (March).

Pampel, Fred C. and John B. Williamson, eds. 1992. Age, Class, Politics, and the Welfare State. Cambridge: Cambridge University Press.

Pan Jiahua, 1994. "Comparative Effectiveness of Discharge and Input Control for Reducing Nitrate Pollution." Environment Management. Vol. 18 (1): 33-42.

Pan Jiahua, 1997. "Environmental Challenges to China's Human Development: Background Paper for the China National Human Development Report", Beijing, photocopy.

Pan Shengzhou. 1993. "A Research on the Mobility of Rural Labour Force." The Management World, Vol. 3.

Panayotou, T. 1993. Green Markets (Number 7 in the ICEG Sector Studies Series). San Francisco: Institute for Contemporary Studies.

Peking University Project Group. 1995. "The Current Situation of Migrant Workers in Dongguan." Strategy and Management, Vol. 2. China Society for Strategy and Management Research.

People's Bank of China and Agriculture Bank of China. 1986. "The Temporary Regulations on the Management of the Specially Subsidized Credits to Poor Areas." 7 November. Beijing.

People's Political Consultative Newspaper (Renmin ZhengXie Bao). 1997. "Report about Laid-off Women Workers." 7 March, p. 2.

Pepper, Suzanne. 1990. China's Education Reform in the 1980s. Berkeley and Los Angeles: University of California Press.

Perroux, Francois. 1983. A New Concept of Development. Paris: UNESCO.

Personnel News. 1997. "Tianjin Offers Subsidies to the Enterprises for Recruiting the Unemployed." 8 May. Beijing.

Piazza, Alan and Liang, Echo H. 1997. "The State of Poverty in China: Its Causes and Remedies." Paper Presented to Workshop on Unanticipated Consequences of Reform in China, Harvard University, June 1997. Washington, DC

Qiu Dongfang. 1997. "Retirement Benefits Should Be Equal, Unequal Housing Allocation Unacceptable." (Tuixiu daiyu yao nannuping-deng, nannu fenfang bu pingdeng,bu xing.) China Women's News. 6 March, p. 2.

Ravallion, M. 1990. "Reaching the Poor through Rural Public Employment." World Bank Discussion Papers, No. 94.

_____1994. Poverty Comparisons. Singapore: Harwood Academic Publishers.

Ravallion, M., Chen Shaohua and J. Jalan. 1996. Dynamics of Poverty in Rural China. Beijing: World Bank Resident Mission.

Ren Caifang, and Chen Xiaojie. 1996. "Size, Situation and trend of Poverty in Urban China." Research Reference, Beijing (65).

Ren Fen, ed. 1989. The History of Chinese Women's Movement. North Publishing House for Women and Children.

Research Team for Designing a Comprehensive Plan for Chinese Economic System Reforms. 1993. "Separation of Social Security Functions from Enterprises." Economic Studies. Vol. 11.

Riskin, Carl. 1993. "Income Distribution and Poverty in Rural China." In K. Griffin and Zhao Renwei, eds. The Distribution of Income in China. London: Macmillan.

_____1996. "Social Development, Quality of Life, and the Environment", in China's Economic Future: Challenges To U.S. Policy. Study Papers submitted to the Joint Economic Committee, Congress of the United States, Washington, DC

Rural Women Know All Monthly, ed. 1996. Development and Strategy of Rural Women. Beijing: China Women's Publishing House.

Schmaleness, R., T.M. Stoker, and R.A. Judson. 1995. "World Energy Consumption and Carbon Dioxide Emission: 1950-2050." Unpublished report. MIT Sloan School of Management.

Serageldin, I. 1996. "Sustainability and the Wealth of Nations : First Steps in an Ongoing Journey." Draft paper.

Sha Lian Xiang, ed. 1995. Women's Role Development and Role Conflict in China. Beijing: Nationalities Publishing House.

Shandong Rural Sample Survey Team. 1993. Shandong Rural Statistics Yearbook 1993. China Statistics Publishing House.

Shang Xiaoyuan. 1997. "Towards a Sustainable Human Development: Institutional Change of the Chinese Social Security System in the Transition to a Market Economy: Background Paper for the China National Human Development Report." Institute for Development Studies, University of Sussex, photocopy.

SEPA (Shanghai Environmental Protection Agency). 1995. Encyclopedia of Legal Documents on Environmental Protection. Shanghai: Shanghai Science & Technology Literature Press.

Shi, L. 1993. "Health Care in China: A Rural-Urban Comparison After the Socio-Economic Reforms." Bulletin of the World Health Organization. 71 (6): 723-736.

Shi Shusi. 1995. "A Way Out for the Rural: How Wide the Urban Door Should Open?" Worker's Daily, Jan. 7, 1995.

Shi, Xianmin. 1993. "The Structural Differentiation and Double Dualistic Social Structures in China's Social Transition." Chinese Social Science Quarterly. Autumn, 55-65.

Shu Xiao. 1997. "Opinion Survey on Environmental Preservation." Nanfang Weekend. (May 9).

Sinton, Jonathan E., David G. Firdley, and James Dorian. 1997. "China's Energy Future: The Role of Energy in Sustaining Growth." In China's Economic Future: Challenges to U.S. Policy, edited by J. E. C. U.S. Congress. Washington, DC: U.S. Government Printing House.

Skocpol, Theda. 1995. Protecting Soldiers and Mothers the Political Origins of Social Policy in the United States. London: Belknap Press.

Song Defu. 1996. "Promoting China's Human Resource Development." People's Daily. Beijing. (11 November)

State Council. 1994a. China Agenda for the 21st Century. Beijing: Ecological Science Publishing House.

_____1994b. National Planning on Poverty Alleviation for the Years of 1994-2000. Beijing.

_____1994c. Outline for Reform and Development of Education in China. Beijing: Educational Science Press.

_____1995a. The Ninth Five-year National Plan for Socioeconomic Development. Beijing.

_____1995b. The Program for the Development of Chinese Women (1995-2000), English edition. Beijing: ACWF. August.

_____1996. The Resolution on Acceleration of Solving the Problems of Shortage of Food And Clothes for the Rural Poor. 23 October. Beijing.

State Council Leading Group on Economic Development of Poor Areas. 1989. Outlines (sic!) of Economic Development in China's Poor Areas. Beijing: Agricultural Publishing House.

State Council Working Commission on Women and Children's Issues. 1996. State Report on Children's Development in the Mid-90's. August.

SEdC (State Education Commission). 1996a. The Ninth Five-year Plan for Educational Development and the Long range Programme Toward the Year 2010. Beijing: State Education Commission. May.

_____1996b. National Report on the Development and Reform of China's Education 1994-1996. Beijing: State Education Commission. October.

_____1997. "The Statistics Bulletin on National Education Development 1996." China Education Daily. Beijing. 14 April.

SEdC Finance Department. 1997. The Annual Report of China's Education Funds 1996. Beijing: Higher Education Press. March.

SEdC Planning Department. 1997. The Concise Statistics of China's Education Development. Beijing: State Education Commission. January.

SSB (State Statistical Bureau). 1987. China Statistical Yearbook. Beijing: China Statistical Publishing House.

_____1990. Research Report on the Poverty Standard for Rural China. Beijing: China Statistical Publishing House.

_____1993a. 1990 Population Census Data. Beijing: China Statistical Publishing House.

_____1993b. Zhongguo Tongji Zhaiyao (Statistical Abstract of China). Beijing: China Statistical Publishing House.

_____1995a. 1995 Statistical Yearbook of China. Beijing: China Statistical Publishing House.

_____1995b. Series of Province Statistical Yearbooks. Beijing: China Statistical Publishing House.

_____1995c. Women and Men in China, Facts and Figures 1995. Beijing: China Statistical Publishing House.

_____1996a. China Statistical Yearbook 1996. Beijing: China Statistical Publishing House.

_____1996b. China Regional Economy: A Profile of 17 Years of Reform and Opening-Up. Beijing: China Statistical Publishing House.

_____1996c. Statistics on Chinese Women (1949-1989). Beijing: China Statistical Publishing House.

_____1997a. China Statistical Year Book (1985-1996). Beijing: China Statistics Publishing House.

_____1997b. Zhongguo Tongji Zhaiyao 1997 (Statistical Abstract of China 1997). Beijing: China Statistical Publishers.

Tang Hongqian. 1995. Forest Land, Ownership of Trees and Social Forestry. Chengdu: Chengdu Science & Technology Press.

Tang Jun. 1994. "Theoretical Reflections on Urban Community Services." Social Sciences in China. Spring: 77-83.

_____1996. "Determination of the Minimum Living Security Line in Urban China." In White and Shang. 1997a.

Tao Chunfang and Jiang Yongping, eds. 1993. A Survey of Chinese Women's Social Status. Beijing: China Women's Publishing House.

Tao Chunfang and Xiao Yang, ed. Research on Women's Reproductive Health In China. Beijing: New World Press.

TDI (Tianjin Design Institute, Ministry of Water Conservation and Electricity). 1995. "Economy and Water Resources." A report on the Yellow River Diversion to Shanxi Province.

Tianjin Normal University. 1993. Chinese Women and Development. Zhengzhou: People's Publishing House of Henan.

Tian Xueyuan. 1997. "Population Studies for Decision-Making in China." Newsletter of the Chinese Academy of Social Sciences. 20 May.

Tsui, Kai Yuen. 1991. "China's Regional Inequality, 1952-1985." Journal of Comparative Economics 15: 1-21.

UNICEF. 1995. Children and women of China: A situation analysis (draft). Beijing: UNICEF.

_____1997. Children's Status in the World in 1997. Oxford University Press.

UNDP (United Nations Development Programme). 1995. Human Development Report 1995. New York: Oxford University Press.

_____1996a. Human Development Report 1996. New York: Oxford University Press.

_____1996b. UNDP Initiative for Sustainable Energy. New York.

_____1997. "Promotion of Sustainable Agriculture and Rural Development in China: Elements for a Policy Framework and a National Agenda 21 Action Programme."

UNDP-Hungary. 1996. National Human Development Report.

UNDP-Russian Federation. 1995. National Human Development Report.

UNDP-Ukraine. 1996. National Human Development Report.

UNDP-Uzbekistan. 1996. National Human Development Report.

Wang Baoqing. 1996. The Overall Process of China 21st Century Agenda, Population, Resources and Environment in China Vol. 1.

Wang Fuling, ed. 1995. A Collection of Essays About the Development of Chinese Minority Women. Beijing: China Broadcast and Television Publishing House.

Wang Jianming. 1997. "The Study on Environmental Economic Policy for TVEs' Control." Draft, Interim report, NEPA, a study financed by World Bank, Beijing.

Wang Longde. 1996. "With Countryside as the Focus, Strive to Realize the Objectives of the Women and Children's Development Compendium." (Yu Nongcun Wei Zhongdian, Wei Quanmian Shixian Funu Ertong Fazhan Gangyao Mubiao Er Nuli) Unpublished report presented at the National Women and Children Work Conference sponsored by the Ministry of Public Health, November.

Wang Shaoxian and Virginia Cheng Li, ed. 1994. The Voice of Rural Women in Yunnan Appraise the Needs of Reproductive Health. Beijing: Publishing House of Beijing Medical University and Union Medical University.

Wang Xiaofang, Wang Hongguang, Wang Xuezhi. 1996. "There Is A Great Potential in China's Food Grain Production Growth." Paper for international conference, "Food and Agriculture in China: Perspectives and Policies." Beijing.

Wang Yuqing. 1994. China's Action Plan for Biodiversity Conservation. Beijing: China Environmental Science Press.

Wang Zhe. 1994. "New Thinking in Poverty Alleviation." Guangming Daily. 31 March.

White, Gordon and Shang Xiaoyuan, eds. 1996. Issues and Answers: Reforming the Chinese Social Security System. Brighton, UK: Institute of Development Studies.

_____1997. Reforms in Chinese Social Assistance and Community Services in Comparative Perspective. Brighton,UK: Institute of Development Studies.

Williamson, J. 1965. "Regional Inequality and the Process of National Development." Economic Development and Culture Change. Vol. 13, p. 25.

Wong, Christine, C. Heady, and L. West. 1997. Financing Local Development in the People's Republic of China. Oxford and New York: Oxford University Press.

Workers Daily. 1997. "The Funds for Guaranteeing Minimum Living Standard Would Not Substantially Increase." 24 May. Beijing.

Working Commission on the Affairs of Women and Children. 1996. State Report on Children's Development in the mid-90s (Jiushi niandai zhongqi zhongguo ertong fazhan baogao). Beijing.

World Bank. 1983. China, socialist economic development. 3 vols. Vol. III. Washington, DC: World Bank.

_____1984. China: The Health Sector. Washington, DC: World Bank.

_____1992. China: Strategies for Reducing Poverty in the 1990s. Washington, DC: World Bank.

_____1993a. World Development Report - Investment in Health 1993.

_____1993b. World Development Report 1993. Washington DC.

_____1995. "China Regional Disparities." Report No. 14496-CHA, Country Operations Division, China and Mongolia Department, East Asia and Pacific Regional Office.

_____1996a. Development Report 1996 - From Plan to Market. New York: Oxford University Press.

_____1996b. Poverty in China: What do the numbers say? Washington, DC: World Bank.

_____1996c. Poverty Reduction and World Bank: Progress and Challenges in the 1990s.

_____1997a. Financing Health Care: Issues and Options for China. Washington, DC: World Bank.

_____1997b. Old Age Security: Pension Reform in China. Washington, DC: World Bank.

_____1997c. World Bank Atlas. Washington DC.

_____1997d. 1997 World Development Indicators. Washington DC.

World Commission on Environment and Development. 1987. Our Common Future. New York: Oxford University Press.

Wu Guodong. 1994. "Research Report on Credit Policies for Poverty Alleviation." Paper presented at the International Workshop on the Anti-poverty Strategies of China, 4-7 December, Beijing.

Wu Jianzhong. 1997. "Deforestation in Yunnan." Nanfang Weekend. 23 May.

Xian Zude and Sheng Laiyun. 1996. The Measurement And Decomposition of Rural Poverty of China. Beijing. (forthcoming)

Xiao Jing. 1995. "Country Folks Go to Cities for Development, Urban Citizens Should Take It Easy." China Youth Daily. 18 May.

Xinhua News Agency. 1997. "Number of Urban Poor on Decline, Data

Shows." China Daily. 3 May. Beijing.

Xiong Yumei, ed. 1992. A Decade of Women's Studies in China (1981-1990). Beijing: China Women's Publishing House.

Xu, W. 1995. "Introductory Essay: Flourishing Health Work in China." Social Science and Medicine. 41(8): 1043-1045.

Yang, Dali. 1990. "Patterns of China's Regional Development Strategy." China Quarterly. June: 230-57.

Yang, Dennis Tao , and Hao Zhou. 1996. "Rural-Urban Disparity and Sectoral Labour Allocation in China." Research Papers in Asian/Pacific Studies of Duke University.

Yang Jianchun. 1997. "Size, Direction and Structure of China's Population Migration -- An Analysis on the Data from the 1% National Population Sample Survey." Research References, Vol. 2.

Yang, Tuan, Yang Tiren and Tang Jun. 1996. An Alternative for China's Social Security System (Zhongguo Shehui Baozhang Tizhide Zai Xuanze). Beijing: Central Broadcasting University Press.

Yang Zhong. 1993. "The Policies of the Chinese Government for Rural Poverty Alleviation and Food Security." Paper prepared for the International Policy Workshop on Employment for Poverty Alleviation and Food Security, Airlie House, Virginia, 11-14 October.

Yao, J. 1995. "The Developing Models of Social-Work Education in China." International Social Work. 38(1): 27-38.

Yao, Xin-wu and Yin Hua. 1994. Basic Data of China's Population. Beijing: China Population Publishing House.

Yi, Lin. 1994. "Social Security Reform in China Reviewed." Benefits and Compensation International. 23(10): 18-25, June.

Yin Dakui. 1994. "Improving Health Care for the People in Poor Areas." Development And Common Wealth. (5) Beijing.

Zhang Chunli. 1997. "Wang Guangmei and The Xingfu Project." People's Political Consultative Newspaper (Renmin ZhengXie Bao). Beijing: CCPCC. 14 February.

Zhang Maolin. 1996. "The Spatial Characteristics of Resource Ecology of China's Poverty-stricken Population and the Development-oriented Poverty-relieving Population Migration." Population and Economics, Vol. 4.

Zhang Ping, ed. 1995. Current Situation of Chinese Women. Beijing: Red Flag Press.

_____1996. Income Distribution in China During the Transition Period. Beijing. (forthcoming)

Zhang Tianlu, ed. 1993. The Evolution of Minority Ethnic Population in China. Beijing: Ocean Publishing House.

Zhang Xiaohui, Zhao Changbao, and Chen Liangbiao. 1995. An Authentic Picture of 1994 Transregional Flow of Rural Labour Force in China, No.6.

Zhang Zhong Xiang. 1996. "Macroeconomic Effects of CO2 Emission Limits: A Computable General Equilibrium Analysis for China." A paper presented at the Seventh Annual Conference of the European Association of Environmental and Resource Economists: Lisbon.

Zhao Dianchen, ed. 1992. Studies on Rural Women's Status in Yunnan. Kunming: People's Publishing House of Yunnan.

Zhao Jie, ed. 1995. Women Centered Reproductive Health. Beijing: China Social Sciences Publishing House.

Zhen, Bingliang. 1996. "A Study of China's Community Service Policy." In White and Shang. 1997. (in Chinese).

Zheng Xiaoying, ed. 1995. The Development and Problems of Women Population in China. Beijing: Peking University Press.

Zhou Binbin. 1991. "Poverty Issues in the Period of People's Communes." Economic Development Forums, No. 3. Beijing.

Zhou Qiren. 1997. "Economic Transition, Structural Adjustment And Urban Employment." (mimeo) March, Beijing.

Zhou, Xueguang. 1993. "Unorganized Interests And Collective Action In Communist China." American Sociological Review. 58: Feb:54-73.

Zhu Chuzhu and Jiang Zhenghua. 1991. Women Population in China. Zhengzhou: People's Publishing House of Henan

Zhu Jianfang. 1995. "Why, If Women Hold Up Half the Sky, Is There Such a Wage Gap?" (Weisha, Tong Ju Ban Bian Tian, Zheng Qian Cha Lao Yuan.) China Market Economic News. Beijing. 9 December.

Zhu, Jiazhen and Zhang Sia, eds. 1995. The Comprehensive Book of Chinese Social Insurance Work. Beijing: Chinese Statistical Press (in Chinese).

Zhu Kaixuan. 1997. "Speech at the National Education Conference." China Education Daily. Beijing. 21 January.

Zhu Ling. 1994. "Ensure the Farmers' Nutrition and Food in Poor Areas." Economy Research (2):52-59.

_____1995. "A Healthy Policy Bank of Germany." Financial Research. No. 9. Beijing.

_____1996. "Actions for Poverty Reduction in the Transition Period of China." Proceedings of the Joint World Congress of the International Federation of Social Workers and the International Association of Schools of Social Work, Hong Kong, 24-27 July.

_____ 1997. "Poverty and Poverty Alleviation in China: Background Paper for the China National Human Development Report", Beijing, UNDP, photocopy, 1997.

Zhu Ling and Jiang Zhongyi. 1994. Public works and Poverty Alleviation. Shanghai: Shanghai Joint Publishing House, People's Publishing House of Shanghai.

_____1996. Public Works and Poverty Alleviation in Rural China. New York: Nova Science Publishers.

Zhu Ling, Jiang Zhongyi and Joachim von Braun. 1997. Credit Systems for the Rural Poor in China. New York: Nova Science Publishers. (Forthcoming)

Zhu, Qingfang and Sheng Zhaoxing, eds. 1993. Social Security Index System. Beijing: Chinese Social Science Press (in Chinese).

Zhu, Yong and Pan Yi. 1995. Change in Social Welfare: Chinese Social Security Problems. Beijing: Party College of the Central Committee of the CCP Press (in Chinese).

Statistical Appendix[i]

[i] Table 1–8, concerning the Human Development Index and its components, were prepared by Li Shi

Table 1. Human Development Index by Province in 1990 (adjusted by regional price indices)

Province	Life expectancy index		Education index	GDP index	Human development index (HDI) value	HDI rank	GDP rank
Shanghai	0.84	0.80	0.949	0.862	1	1	
Tianjin	0.80	0.80	0.799	0.798	2	2	
Beijing	0.81	0.82	0.596	0.742	3	3	
Liaoning	0.76	0.78	0.556	0.698	4	4	
Guangdong	0.80	0.75	0.409	0.652	5	7	
Jiangsu	0.79	0.70	0.431	0.638	6	5	
Zhejiang	0.79	0.69	0.400	0.628	7	9	
Shandong	0.77	0.68	0.421	0.625	8	6	
Heilongjiang	0.72	0.75	0.401	0.624	9	8	
Jilin	0.72	0.76	0.346	0.609	10	11	
Shanxi	0.74	0.75	0.324	0.607	11	14	
Hebei	0.78	0.69	0.320	0.598	12	15	
Xinjiang	0.67	0.72	0.395	0.593	13	10	
Fujian	0.76	0.68	0.331	0.688	14	13	
Hainan	0.79	0.70	0.262	0.582	15	20	
Hubei	0.71	0.68	0.343	0.578	16	12	
InnerMongo	0.70	0.70	0.316	0.571	17	17	
Henan	0.75	0.67	0.246	0.558	18	24	
Shaanxi	0.72	0.67	0.253	0.550	19	22	
Guangxi	0.74	0.72	0.189	0.548	20	29	
Hunan	0.70	0.72	0.219	0.547	21	27	
Ningxia	0.72	0.62	0.289	0.543	22	18	
Anhui	0.75	0.60	0.251	0.533	23	23	
Sichuan	0.70	0.68	0.217	0.532	24	28	
Jiangxi	0.70	0.67	0.224	0.529	25	26	
Gansu	0.71	0.57	0.235	0.505	26	25	
Qinghai	0.61	0.56	0.319	0.498	27	16	
Yunnan	0.65	0.58	0.258	0.496	28	21	
Guizhou	0.67	0.58	0.159	0.470	29	30	
Tibet	0.58	0.32	0.266	0.388	30	19	

Sources: (1) Lu Lei, Hao Hongsheng and Gao Ling "Table of Provincial Life-expectancy in China in 1990", Population Studies (in Chinese), May 1994. (2) SSB, China Regional Economy: A Profile of 17 Years of Reform and Opening-Up, China Statistical Press, 1996. (3)1990 Population Census, China Statistical Press , 1993.

Notes: (1) Provincial price indices used for adjustment of GDP per capita are those of retail prices.

Table 2. Human Development Index by Province in 1995

Province rank	HDI rank	GDP rank	Life expectancy index	Education index	GDP index	HDI value
Shanghai	1	1	0.84	0.85	0.969	0.885
Beijing	2	2	0.81	0.86	0.960	0.876
Tianjin	3	3	0.80	0.83	0.954	0.859
Guangdong	4	4	0.80	0.79	0.850	0.814
Zhejiang	5	5	0.79	0.75	0.814	0.785
Jiangsu	6	6	0.79	0.77	0.724	0.760
Liaoning	7	8	0.76	0.80	0.708	0.756
Fujian	8	7	0.76	0.72	0.709	0.729
Shandong	9	9	0.77	0.74	0.604	0.704
Heilongjiang	10	10	0.72	0.78	0.526	0.676
Hainan	11	11	0.79	0.75	0.488	0.674
Hebei	12	12	0.78	0.77	0.464	0.670
Jilin	13	13	0.72	0.80	0.451	0.659
Shanxi	14	17	0.74	0.79	0.352	0.627
Xinjiang	15	14	0.67	0.75	0.438	0.619
Henan	16	16	0.75	0.74	0.358	0.618
Hubei	17	15	0.71	0.73	0.388	0.609
Guangxi	18	18	0.74	0.75	0.332	0.605
Anhui	19	19	0.75	0.72	0.328	0.600
Hunan	20	23	0.71	0.75	0.320	0.592
Sichuan	21	24	0.70	0.74	0.308	0.582
InnerMongo	22	25	0.70	0.74	0.296	0.578
Jiangxi	23	20	0.70	0.73	0.327	0.577
Ningxia	24	22	0.72	0.67	0.323	0.571
Shaanxi	25	27	0.72	0.73	0.259	0.570
Yunnan	26	26	0.65	0.64	0.289	0.526
Gansu	27	29	0.71	0.62	0.216	0.514
Qinghai	28	21	0.61	0.57	0.326	0.503
Guizhou	29	30	0.67	0.64	0.172	0.494
Tibet	30	28	0.58	0.36	0.226	0.391

Sources: (1) Lu Lei, Hao Hongsheng and Gao Ling "Table of Provincial Life-expectancy in China in 1990", Population Studies (in Chinese), May 1994. (2) SSB, China Regional Economy: A Profile of 17 Years of Reform and Opening-Up, China Statistical Press, 1996. (3) National 1% Population Survey 1995, China Statistical Press , 1997. (4) China Education Commission, Statistical Yearbook of China Education 1995, Press of People's Education, 1996. (5) China Population Yearbook 1996.

Notes: (1) GDP per capita is in 1990 prices. (2) Provincial price indices used for adjustment of GDP per capita are those of retail prices. (3) Life expectancy index is based on figures of provincial life expectancy in 1990.

Table 3. Change in Human Development Index between 1990 and 1995, by Province (percentage points)

Province	Human development index (HDI)	Education index	GDP index
Shanghai	2.2	4.7	2.0
Beijing	13.3	3.7	36.3
Tianjin	6.1	2.9	15.4
Guangdong	16.2	4.5	44.1
Zhejiang	15.8	5.9	41.4
Jiangsu	12.3	7.5	29.3
Liaoning	5.8	2.1	15.2
Fujian	14.1	4.4	37.9
Shandong	7.9	5.5	18.2
Heilongjiang	5.3	3.3	12.5
Hainan	9.3	5.2	22.6
Hebei	7.2	7.2	14.4
Jilin	5.0	4.6	10.5
Shanxi	2.1	3.4	2.8
Xinjiang	2.6	3.4	4.3
Henan	6.0	6.8	11.2
Hubei	3.1	4.7	4.5
Guangxi	5.7	2.7	14.3
Anhui	6.6	12.2	7.7
Hunan	4.4	3.1	10.2
Sichuan	5.0	5.8	9.1
Jiangxi	4.8	6.1	8.3
InnerMongo	0.7	4.2	-2.0
Ningxia	2.8	4.8	3.5
Shaanxi	2.0	5.5	0.6
Yunnan	3.1	6.1	3.0
Gansu	0.9	4.6	-1.9
Qinghai	0.5	0.8	0.7
Guizhou	2.4	5.8	1.4
Tibet	0.3	4.7	-4.0

Sources: (1) Lu Lei, Hao Hongsheng and Gao Ling "Table of Provincial Life-expectancy in China in 1990", Population Studies (in Chinese), May 1994. (2) SSB, China Regional Economy: A Profile of 17 Years of Reform and Opening-Up, China Statistical Press, 1996. (3) National 1% Population Survey 1995, China Statistical Press , 1997. (4) China Education Commission, Statistical Yearbook of China Education 1995, Press of People's Education, 1996.

Notes: (1) GDP per capita is in 1990 prices. (2) Provincial price indices used for adjustment of GDP per capita are those of retail prices. (3) Life expectancy index is based on figures for provincial life expectancy in 1990.

Table 4. Profile of Human Development by Province, 1990 (adjusted by regional price indices)

Province	Life expectancy at birth (years)	Adult literacy rate (%)	Combined 1,2,3-level gross enrolment ratio (%)	Adjusted Real GDP per capita (PPP$)	Adjusted real GDP per capita (PPP$) (with price index)
Beijing	73.6	89.2	67.8	3027.48	3027.48
Tianjin	72.7	88.4	63.0	4023.11	4023.11
Hebei	71.7	78.4	51.3	1669	1669
Shanxi	69.5	87.1	51.7	1689.32	1689.32
InnerMongo	66.9	78.9	51.7	1650.3	1650.3
Liaoning	70.8	88.8	55.1	2829.52	2829.52
Jilin	68.4	86.2	54.7	1797.52	1797.52
Heilongjiang	68.2	85.6	53.9	2068.85	2068.85
Shanghai	75.2	86.7	66.7	5921.4	5176.62
Jiangsu	72.2	77.7	53.2	2215.87	2215.87
Zhejiang	72.4	77.5	53.0	2061.67	2061.67
Anhui	69.8	66.5	47.3	1333.06	1333.06
Fujian	70.2	77.0	49.8	1722.25	1722.25
Jiangxi	66.7	76.1	48.1	1199.81	1199.81
Shandong	71.2	77.6	50.0	2166.72	2166.72
Henan	70.2	77.4	47.5	1309.39	1309.39
Hubei	67.5	77.5	50.0	1781.72	1781.72
Hunan	67.3	83.1	49.6	1172.78	1172.78
Guangdong	73.0	84.7	54.5	2107.9	2107.9
Guangxi	69.2	84.3	46.9	1026.8	1026.8
Hainan	72.2	79.5	49.9	1387.64	1387.64
Sichuan	67.1	78.6	46.3	1164.31	1164.31
Guizhou	65.1	64.3	46.3	878.21	878.21
Yunnan	63.9	64.4	45.3	1366.69	1366.69
Tibet	59.8	31.7	32.3	1403.8	1403.8
Shaanxi	68.4	75.0	51.8	1342.28	1342.28
Gansu	67.6	60.8	49.3	1252.03	1252.03
Qinghai	61.8	61.4	45.5	1665.07	1665.07
Ningxia	68.3	67.5	50.9	1517.64	1517.64
Xinjiang	65.0	81.6	51.7	2039.16	2039.16

Sources: (1) Lu Lei, Hao Hongsheng and Gao Ling "Table of Provincial Life-expectancy in China in 1990", Population Studies (in Chinese), May 1994. (2) SSB, China Regional Economy: A Profile of 17 Years of Reform and Opening-Up, China Statistical Press, 1996. (3) 1990 Population Cencus, China Statistical Press , 1993.

Notes: (1) Provincial price indices used for adjustment of GDP per capita are those of retail prices.

Table 5. Profile of Human Development by Province, 1995

Province	Adjusted real GDP per capita (PPP$ in 1990 prices)	Life expectancy at birth (years) in 1990	Adult literacy rate (%)	Combined 1-, 2- ,3- level gross enrolment ratio (%)	Real GDP per capita (PPP$ in 1990 prices)
Shanghai	4846.6	75.2	91.5	71.2	10901.1
Beijing	4799.7	73.6	92.1	73.1	7750.1
Tianjin	4772.6	72.7	90.7	67.2	6437.6
Guangdong	4731.9	73.0	88.6	60.1	5149.6
Zhejiang	4720.2	72.4	83.0	59.7	4932.4
Jiangsu	4402.9	72.2	85.4	60.2	4402.9
Liaoning	4305.2	70.8	90.7	57.5	4305.2
Fujian	4312.9	70.2	79.4	58.0	4312.9
Shandong	3684.6	71.2	82.4	57.0	3684.6
Heilongjiang	3227.1	68.2	89.2	56.7	3227.1
Hainan	2999.8	72.2	85.4	53.9	2999.8
Hebei	2853.9	71.8	86.7	56.5	2853.9
Jilin	2776.1	68.4	90.7	59.6	2776.1
Shanxi	2189.8	69.6	90.6	54.9	2189.8
Xinjiang	2702.2	65.0	86.6	52.0	2702.2
Henan	2228.3	70.2	84.1	54.5	2228.3
Hubei	2404.9	67.5	82.9	53.0	2404.9
Guangxi	2071.5	69.2	86.5	50.6	2071.5
Anhui	2047.8	69.8	80.6	55.7	2047.8
Hunan	2003.3	67.3	84.7	55.6	2003.3
Sichuan	1930.9	67.1	83.2	54.7	1930.9
Jiangxi	1926.4	66.7	81.4	55.8	1926.4
InnerMongo	1856.4	66.9	83.4	55.2	1856.4
Ningxia	2021.1	68.3	73.6	53.1	2021.1
Shaanxi	1636.1	68.4	81.7	55.1	1636.1
Yunnan	1813.7	63.9	70.6	51.4	1813.7
Gansu	1381.7	67.6	66.0	52.7	1381.7
Qinghai	2034.6	61.8	62.6	45.7	2034.6
Guizhou	1121.6	65.1	70.5	51.1	1121.6
Tibet	1442.5	59.8	38.5	32.9	1442.5

Sources: (1) Lu Lei, Hao Hongsheng and Gao Ling "Table of Provincial Life-expectancy in China in 1990", Population Studies (in Chinese), May 1994. (2) SSB, China Regional Economy: A Profile of 17 Years of Reform and Opening-Up, China Statistical Press, 1996. (3) National 1% Population Survey 1995, China Statistical Press , 1997. (4) China Education Commission, Statistical Yearbook of China Education 1995, Press of People's Education, 1996. (5) China Population Yearbook 1996.

Notes: (1) GDP per capita is in 1990 prices. (2) Provincial price indices used for adjustment of GDP per capita are those of retail prices. (3) Life expectancy index is based on figures of provincial life expectancy in 1990.

Table 6. Trends in Human Development by Province, 1982-90

Province	Life expectancy at birth (years)		Adult literacy rate (%)		Combined first-, second- and third -level gross enrolment ratio (%)		Real GDP per capita (PPP$)		Adjusted real GDP per capita (PPP$) (by province prices)	
	1982	1990	1982	1990	1982	1990	1982	1990	1982	1990
Beijing	71.9	73.6	85.0	89.2	60.5	67.8	2896.8	3478.7	2579.5	3027.5
Tianjin	70.9	72.7	82.8	88.4	57.3	63.0	2529.6	3907.1	2325.0	4023.1
Hebei	70.5	71.7	70.5	78.4	47.4	51.3	805.8	1580.7	728.6	1669.0
Shanxi	67.6	69.5	75.6	87.1	49.0	51.7	936.7	1648.7	861.7	1689.3
InnerMongo	66.7	66.9	68.9	78.9	46.4	51.7	816.0	1594.8	733.2	1650.3
Liaoning	70.7	70.8	83.4	88.8	51.6	55.1	1502.8	2911.1	1364.9	2829.5
Jilin	68.9	68.4	78.2	86.2	51.5	54.7	914.6	1883.9	811.5	1797.5
Heilongjiang	68.2	68.2	77.8	85.6	52.5	53.9	1295.4	2188.2	1147.4	2068.8
Shanghai	72.9	75.2	80.3	86.7	60.2	66.7	4890.9	6376.9	4466.6	5921.4
Jiangsu	69.5	72.2	65.4	77.7	46.8	53.2	1096.5	2269.1	1005.0	2215.8
Zhejiang	69.5	72.4	68.8	77.5	45.6	53.0	1014.9	2289.6	898.1	2061.6
Anhui	69.3	69.8	53.8	66.5	40.0	47.3	637.5	1275.4	593.0	1333.1
Fujian	68.5	70.2	62.8	77.0	45.0	49.8	778.6	1929.3	667.2	1722.3
Jiangxi	66.0	66.7	67.9	76.1	44.2	48.1	685.1	1217.1	606.3	1199.8
Shandong	70.2	71.2	63.2	77.6	45.2	50.0	902.7	1958.4	842.1	2166.7
Henan	69.7	70.2	63.0	77.4	43.9	47.5	600.1	1177.2	552.6	1309.4
Hubei	65.6	67.5	68.9	77.5	48.1	50.0	860.2	1678.9	793.5	1781.7
Hunan	65.4	67.3	76.1	83.1	44.5	49.6	731.0	1325.0	625.3	1172.8
Guangdong	71.3	73.0	77.1	84.7	43.4	54.5	1045.5	2584.2	836.4	2107.9
Guangxi	70.1	69.2	75.0	84.3	42.6	46.9	601.8	1150.2	513.9	1026.8
Hainan	-	72.2	.	79.5	.	49.9	867.0	1714.5	706.0	1387.6
Sichuan	64.0	67.1	68.0	78.6	40.3	46.3	647.7	1192.3	545.7	1164.3
Guizhou	61.4	65.1	52.1	64.3	38.7	46.3	472.6	874.0	410.6	878.2
Yunnan	60.7	63.9	50.7	64.4	40.3	45.3	576.3	1320.7	524.9	1366.7
Tibet	63.9	59.8	26.8	31.7	33.6	32.3	924.8	1376.8	856.3	1403.8
Shaanxi	64.8	68.4	66.8	75.0	48.7	51.8	661.3	1342.3	597.4	1342.3
Gansu	65.8	67.6	51.9	60.8	41.9	49.3	668.1	1185.8	619.2	1252.0
Qinghai	60.8	61.8	53.2	61.4	41.1	45.5	872.1	1681.1	794.3	1665.1
Ningxia	65.5	68.3	57.0	67.5	42.9	50.9	797.3	1503.1	711.2	1517.6
Xinjiang	60.0	65.0	69.3	81.6	49.6	51.7	829.6	1941.1	756.2	2039.2

Sources: (1) China Population: National (in Chinese), Chinese Finance and Economy Press, Beijing, 1989. (2) Lu Lei, Hao Hongsheng and Gao Ling "Table of Provincial Life-expectancy in China in 1990", Population Studies (in Chinese), May 1994. (3) SSB, China Regional Economy: A Profile of 17 Years of Reform and Opening-Up, China Statistical Press, 1996. (4) China Population Yearbook 1996.

Notes: (1) Literacy ratio in 1982 is for population aged 12 and over. (2) Provincial price indices used for adjustment of GDP per capita are those of retail prices.

Table 7. Trends in Human Development by Province, 1990-95

Province	Adjusted real GDP per capita (PPP$ in 1990 prices)		Adult literacy rate (%)		Combined first-, second- and third-level gross enrolment ratio (%)		Real GDP per capita (PPP$ in 1990 prices)	
	1995	1990	1995	1990	1995	1990	1995	1990
Shanghai	4846	4759	91.5	86.7	71.2	66.7	10901.1	5921
Beijing	4799	3028	92.1	89.2	73.1	67.8	7750.1	3028
Tianjin	4772	4023	90.7	88.4	67.2	63.0	6437.6	4023
Guangdong	4731	2108	88.6	84.7	60.1	54.5	5149.6	2108
Zhejiang	4720	2062	83.0	77.5	59.7	53.0	4932.4	2062
Jiangsu	4402	2216	85.4	77.7	60.2	53.2	4402.9	2216
Liaoning	4305	2830	90.7	88.8	57.5	55.1	4305.2	2830
Fujian	4312	1722	79.4	77.0	58.0	49.8	4312.9	1722
Shandong	3684	2167	82.4	77.6	57.0	50.0	3684.6	2167
Heilongjiang	3227	2069	89.2	85.6	56.7	53.9	3227.1	2069
Hainan	2999	1388	85.4	79.5	53.9	49.9	2999.8	1388
Hebei	2853	1669	86.7	78.4	56.5	51.3	2853.9	1669
Jilin	2776	1798	90.7	86.2	59.6	54.7	2776.1	1798
Shanxi	2189	1689	90.6	87.1	54.9	51.7	2189.8	1689
Xinjiang	2702	2039	86.6	81.6	52.0	51.8	2702.2	2039
Henan	2228	1309	84.1	77.4	54.5	47.5	2228.3	1309
Hubei	2404	1782	82.9	77.5	53.0	50.0	2404.9	1782
Guangxi	2071	1027	86.5	84.3	50.6	46.9	2071.5	1027
Anhui	2047	1333	80.6	66.5	55.7	47.3	2047.8	1333
Hunan	2003	1173	84.7	83.1	55.6	49.6	2003.3	1173
Sichuan	1930	1164	83.2	78.6	54.7	46.3	1930.9	1164
Jiangxi	1926	1650	81.4	78.9	55.8	51.7	1926.4	1650
InnerMongo	1856	1200	83.4	76.1	55.2	48.1	1856.4	1200
Ningxia	2021	1518	73.6	67.5	53.1	50.9	2021.1	1518
Shaanxi	1636	1342	81.7	75.0	55.1	51.8	1636.1	1342
Yunnan	1813	1367	70.6	64.4	51.4	45.3	1813.7	1367
Gansu	1381	1252	66.0	60.8	52.7	49.3	1381.7	1252
Qinghai	2034	1665	62.6	61.5	45.7	45.5	2034.6	1665
Guizhou	1121	878	70.5	64.3	51.1	46.3	1121.6	878
Tibet	1442	1404	38.5	31.7	32.9	32.3	1442.5	1404

Sources: (1) Lu Lei, Hao Hongsheng and Gao Ling "Table of Provincial Life-expectancy in China in 1990", Population Studies (in Chinese), May 1994. (2) SSB, China Regional Economy: A Profile of 17 Years of Reform and Opening-Up, China Statistical Press, 1996. (3) Data of National 1% Population Survey 1995, China Statistical Press , 1997. (4) China Education Commission, Statistical Yearbook of China Education 1995, People's Education Press, 1996. (5) China Population Yearbook 1996.

Notes: (1) GDP per capita is in 1990 prices. (2) Provincial price indices used for adjustment of GDP per capita are those of retail prices. (3) Life expectancy index is based on figures of provincial life expectancy in 1990

Table 8. Provincial Income Accounts in China, 1990

Province	GDP (in 1992 PPP$, billions)	Agriculture (as % of GDP)	Industry (as % of GDP)	Services (as % of GDP)
Beijing	54.04	8.8	52.4	38.8
Tianjin	33.55	8.8	57.7	33.5
Hebei	96.71	25.4	43.2	31.2
Shanxi	46.32	18.8	49.0	32.2
InnerMongo	34.45	35.3	32.1	32.6
Liaoning	114.58	15.9	50.9	33.2
Jilin	46.00	29.4	42.8	27.8
Heilongjiang	77.17	22.4	50.7	26.9
Shanghai	81.62	4.3	63.8	31.9
Jiangsu	152.84	25.1	48.9	26.0
Zhejiang	96.89	25.1	45.5	29.4
Anhui	71.00	37.4	38.2	24.4
Fujian	56.46	28.3	33.3	38.4
Jiangxi	46.25	41.1	31.2	27.7
Shandong	163.06	28.1	42.1	29.8
Henan	100.85	34.9	35.5	29.6
Hubei	88.95	35.1	38.0	26.9
Hunan	80.33	37.5	33.6	28.9
Guangdong	158.81	26.1	39.9	34.0
Guangxi	48.45	39.1	26.4	34.5
Hainan	11.06	44.9	19.6	35.5
Sichuan	127.99	35.2	36.1	28.7
Guizhou	28.07	38.5	35.7	25.8
Yunnan	48.74	37.2	34.9	27.9
Tibet	2.99	50.9	12.9	36.2
Shaanxi	40.36	28.2	42.0	29.8
Gansu	26.20	26.4	40.5	33.1
Qinghai	7.55	25.3	38.5	36.2
Ningxia	7.00	26.0	39.1	34.9
Xinjiang	29.57	34.5	30.5	35.0
National	2001.32	27.1	41.6	31.3

Sources: (1) SSB, China Regional Economy: A Profile of 17 Years of Reform and Opening-Up, China Statistical Press, 1996.

Table 9. Population Age Composition and Dependency Ratio, by Province (Sample Survey, 1995) *

Region	Sample Population				Dependency Ratio (%)		
	Total	Age 0-14	Age 15-64	Age 65 and over	Total	Dependency Ratio of Children	Dependency Ratio of The Aged
National	12366954	3306220	8232607	828127	50.22	40.16	10.06
Beijing	129009	25304	93588	10117	37.85	27.04	10.81
Tianjin	97040	20875	68195	7970	42.30	30.61	11.69
Hebei	662160	188241	430958	42961	53.65	43.68	9.97
Shanxi	316488	89846	207745	18897	52.34	43.25	9.10
InnerMongo	234917	61924	161952	11041	45.05	38.24	6.82
Liaoning	421365	90076	300652	30637	40.15	29.96	10.19
Jilin	266885	61281	190609	14995	40.02	32.15	7.87
Heilongjiang	380940	89349	274148	17443	38.95	32.59	6.36
Shanghai	145817	24996	104155	16666	40.00	24.00	16.00
Jiangsu	727334	160769	508060	58505	43.16	31.64	11.52
Zhejiang	444671	96682	309536	38453	43.66	31.23	12.42
Anhui	608435	169017	407820	41598	51.64	41.44	10.20
Fujian	332885	99928	211354	21603	57.50	47.28	10.22
Jiangxi	417343	126299	264364	26680	57.87	47.77	10.09
Shandong	896253	220099	609571	66583	47.03	36.11	10.92
Henan	935439	268096	605232	62111	54.56	44.30	10.26
Hubei	593583	173809	383617	36157	54.73	45.31	9.43
Hunan	658654	182408	429419	46827	53.38	42.48	10.90
Guangdong	705162	218047	436873	50242	61.41	49.91	11.50
Guangxi	466843	146514	289457	30872	61.28	50.62	10.67
Hainan	74250	23586	45958	4706	61.56	51.32	10.24
Sichuan	1163343	276430	801722	85191	45.11	34.48	10.63
Guizhou	3060419	110041	230503	19875	56.36	47.74	8.62
Yunnan	409505	115994	269513	23998	51.94	43.04	8.90
Tibet	24646	8723	14719	1204	67.44	59.26	8.18
Shaanxi	360934	104248	236050	20636	52.91	44.16	8.74
Gansu	250179	71187	168128	10864	48.80	42.34	6.46
Qinghai	49397	14018	33613	1766	46.96	41.70	5.25
Ningxia	52491	16572	33937	1982	54.67	48.83	5.84
Xinjiang	170567	51861	111159	7547	53.44	46.65	6.79

a) The dependency ratio for children refers to the ratio of children age 0-14 to population aged between 15 and 64; that of the aged refers to the ratio of those 65 and older to population between 15-64.

*The sample proportion was 1.04% of total population.

Source: Statistical Yearbook of China 1996, p. 73

Table 10. Employment by Province

	Labour force as % of total population	Women's share of urban labour force %	Labour share of agriculture %	Labour share of agriculture %	Labour share of industry %	Labour share of industry %	Labour share of services %	Labour share of services %	Real earnings per employee, annual growth rate [ii]
	1995	1995	1978	1995	1978	1995	1978	1995	1981-95
Beijing	53.5	37.0	28.4	10.6	40.1	40.1	31.5	49.3	6.1
Tianjin	52.0	39.9	n.a.	16.9	n.a.	48.4	n.a.	34.7	5.9
Hebei	52.3	32.8	76.9	51.4	13.9	26.1	9.2	22.5	5.1
Shanxi	47.5	31.5	65.1	43.5	19.6	29.8	15.4	26.6	4.3
InnerMongo	44.9	34.5	67.1	52.4	18.5	22	14.4	25.6	3.1
Liaoning	49.7	37.4	47.4	31.1	34.5	37.9	18.0	30.9	4.2
Jilin	48.4	34.0	49.3	44.8	31.8	26.7	18.9	28.5	3.2
Heilongjiang	41.9	33.5	53.0	36.8	29.4	34.1	17.6	29	2.0
Shanghai	54.3	39.2	34.5	9.2	44.1	51.4	21.4	39.3	7.1
Jiangsu	53.3	37.8	69.9	41.7	19.7	33.8	10.5	24.6	6.7
Zhejiang	62.5	33.2	56.8[iii]	42.7	31.2[iv]	31.4	12.1[v]	25.9	6.8
Anhui	53.3	31.5	81.7	60.7	10.3	17.9	8.1	21.4	4.8
Fujian	48.4	34.1	70.0[vi]	50.4	15.1[vii]	23.7	14.8[viii]	25.9	6.0
Jiangxi	50.7	31.2	77.2	55.4	13.0	18.1	9.7	26.5	3.9
Shandong	53.1	34.6	79.2	54.4	12.3	25.1	8.5	20.5	5.5
Henan	51.6	33.7	80.8	60	10.5	19.8	8.7	20.2	4.7
Hubei	46.9	34.1	77.0[ix]	51.1	14.1[x]	22	8.9[xi]	26.9	4.9
Hunan	54.9	31.6	78.4	61.4	13.4	16.3	8.2	22.2	4.0
Guangdong	53.2	33.1	n.a.	37.5	n.a.	28.6	n.a.	33.9	7.2
Guangxi	52.4	31.1	80.4	66.4	10.5	11.8	9.1	21.7	4.9
Hainan	46.3	32.0	79.5	60.7	8.2	11.7	12.3	27.5	3.8
Sichuan	55.9	32.2	n.a.	63.1	n.a.	15.9	n.a.	21	4.6
Guizhou	52.9	29.1	82.8	73.7	10.2	10	6.9	16.3	4.1
Yunnan	54.8	32.1	86.1	75.8	7.7	9.9	6.2	14.3	4.7
Tibet	47.4	27.1	79.4[xii]	77.2	4.7[xiii]	4.6	15.9[xiv]	17.9	5.5
Shaanxi	50.5	32.1	71.2	59.5	17.5	19.2	11.2	21.2	3.4
Gansu	47.6	31.6	75.1	58.4	14.7	17.5	10.2	24.1	4.4
Qinghai	47.0	32.7	71.0	59.9	18.6	18.2	10.3	22	2.8
Ningxia	47.5	33.0	69.9	58.9	18.4	19.1	11.8	21.9	3.5
Xinjiang	39.9	36.5	72.5	56.9	15.3	18.8	12.2	24.3	3.7
National	51.5	34.0	70.5	52.9	17.4	23	12.1	24.1	5.5

Source: China Labour Statistical Yearbook 1996; Historical Statistics of China's Provinces 1949-89; China Statistical Yeabook 1996

ii 1981-92 is deflated by overal retail price index; 1992-95 is deflated by cost of living index of workers. Both periods are based on 1980.

iii 1984.   iv 1984.   v 1982.   vi 1982.   vii 1982.   viii 1982.

ix 1979.   x 1979.   xi 1979.   xii 1988.   xiii 1988.   xiv 1988.

Table 11. Provincial Income and Inequality

Province	Urban Income shares, 1994		Rural Income shares 1995		Ratio of urban income per capita to rural (1995)
	Lowest 40% of households (%)	Ratio of highest 20% to lowest 20%	Lowest 40% of households (%)	Ratio of highest 20% to lowest 20%	
Beijing	27.1	2.81	24.4	3.60	1.82
Tianjin	26.2	3.15			1.83
Hebei			19.0	4.74	2.20
Shanxi	27.5	2.87	23.1	4.03	2.42
InnerMongo	26.9	3.07			1.99
Liaoning	27.3	2.82	19.3	5.89	1.88
Jilin	26.3	3.20	16.1	7.32	1.81
Heilongjiang	26.7	3.06			1.68
Shanghai					1.61
Jiangsu	27.1	2.91	23.1	3.86	1.71
Zhejiang	27.5	2.72	19.5	5.54	1.93
Anhui	27.1	2.91	28.1	2.67	2.61
Fujian	27.8	2.76			2.11
Jiangxi	26.7	3.16	28.3	2.62	1.98
Shandong	28.9	2.53			2.31
Henan	27.1	2.94	25.4	3.3	2.46
Hubei	27.1	2.92	19.7	5.13	2.39
Hunan	26.8	2.95	24.5	3.47	2.86
Guangdong	25.7	3.32	20.8	4.71	2.54.
Guangxi	27.7	2.75			2.97
Hainan	23.9	3.77			2.86
Sichuan	26.2	3.14	27.1	2.88	3.10
Guizhou	26.0	3.30	26.2	3.20	3.15
Yunnan	28.3	2.60	22.0	4.59	3.64
Tibet	.				3.72
Shaanxi	25.6	3.41	26.5	3.02	3.17
Gansu	.		22.4	4.28	3.29
Qinghai	26.5	3.30			3.02
Ningxia	27.0	3.13			2.92
Xinjiang	24.5	4.32			3.38

Sources: (1) Provincial Statistical Yearbooks for 1995; (2) 1995 Household Income Survey research conducted by international collaborative team under the auspieces of the Institute of Economics, CASS. (3) SSB, China Regional Economy: A Profile of 17 Years of Reform and Opening-Up, China Statistical Press, 1996.

Notes: (1) Income shares for the urban population are based on the Province Statistical Yearbooks for 1995; (2) Calculation of income shares of rural population are based on data from 1995 Household Income Survey.

Table 12. Natural Resources Per Capita: China in International Perspective

Resource	China's resource per capita as % of world average
Land area	32
Arable land	32
Forest	13
Grassland	33
Iron ore (proved reserves)	49
Copper ore (proved reserves)	29
Bauxite (industrial reserves)	33
Wolfram (industrial reserves)	225
Uncultivated land	31
Forest reserves	13
Fresh water	24
Coal (oil in place)	47
(Economically workable reserves)	40
Oil (oil in place)	32-64
Hydra-power (total reserves)	61
(Workable reserves for hydroelectric power)	81
Tin ore(proved reserves)	70
Rare-earth (industrial reserves)	338
Titanium (proved reserves)	100
Nickel (proved reserves)	25
Lead (proved reserves)	54
Zinc (proved reserves)	100
Sulphur (proved reserves)	85
Phosphorus (proved reserves)	52

Source of Data: Institute of Development, Rural Research Center of the State Council of PRC: A Choice for Modernization, Economic Science Publishers, 1987, p. 43.

Table 13. Environmental Fragility and Poverty, 1995

		East	Central	West
Cultivated land	% of national total	32.0	43.3	23.7
Agricultural output	% of national total	49.07	33.36	17.57
Rural population	% of national total	40.7	35.1	24.2
Typical province		Jiangsu	Henan	Gansu
Annual average	temperature deg. Celsius	15.8	13.0	10.0
Annual average rainfall	mm.	771	549	368
Cultivable land	ha/capita	0.065	0.075	0.164
Grain yield	kg/ha	5710.5	3934.5	2200.5
High income (>2000 yuan per cap)	% of rural pop	54.8	0.1	0.0
Low income (<500 yuan per cap)	% of rural pop	0.0	0.0	14.3
Arable land affected by natural disasters	% of total	43.1	51.5	91.5
Crop failure due to natural disasters	% of total	1.6	5.8	18.0

Note. Natural disasters include drought, flood, storms and low temperatures.

Source: MOA (1996a, 1996b).

Table 14. Population, Migration by Province, 1995 (in 10 thousand persons, %)

	Total population	Gross in-migration	of intra-provincial migrants	Gross out-migration	Net migration	Gross in-migration rate	Gross out-migration rate
Beijing	1256.6	135.8	66.9	86.6	49.2	10.8	6.9
Tianjin	945.2	49.4	27.0	34.9	14.5	5.2	3.7
Hebei	6449.7	144.3	89.3	134.4	9.9	2.2	2.1
Shanxi	3082.7	51.5	34.6	51.7	-0.2	1.7	1.7
InnerMongo	2288.2	99.4	69.9	96.3	3.1	4.3	4.2
Liaoning	4104.2	167.1	122.4	145.9	21.2	4.1	3.6
Jilin	2599.5	82.1	65.0	96.0	-13.9	3.2	3.7
Heilongjiang	3710.5	133.1	110.1	175.2	-42.1	3.6	4.7
Shanghai	1420.3	174.0	101.7	125.4	48.6	12.3	8.8
Jiangsu	7084.5	333.2	224.2	277.1	56.1	4.7	3.9
Zhejiang	4331.2	146.3	87.2	148.9	-2.6	3.4	3.4
Anhui	6023.8	90.1	62.6	138.5	-48.4	1.5	2.3
Fujian	3242.4	113.1	76.2	107.7	5.4	3.5	3.3
Jiangxi	4065.1	96.5	57.9	108.7	-12.2	2.4	2.7
Shandong	8729.8	205.5	148.0	189.0	16.5	2.4	2.2
Henan	9111.5	116.9	83.3	161.3	-44.4	1.3	1.8
Hubei	5781.7	123.3	90.3	130.8	-7.5	2.1	2.3
Hunan	6415.5	130.1	103.8	172.4	-42.3	2.0	2.7
Guangdong	6868.5	428.4	245.2	310.7	117.7	6.2	4.5
Guangxi	4547.2	96.8	82.9	138.2	-41.4	2.1	3.0
Hainan	723.2	23.8	13.3	26.1	-2.3	3.3	3.6
Sichuan	11331.3	278.9	209.6	354.8	-75.9	2.5	3.1
Guizhou	3510.6	65.5	46.1	86.9	-21.4	1.9	2.5
Yunnan	3988.7	91.3	68.9	95.3	-4.0	2.3	2.4
Tibet	240.1	7.2	3.5	6.7	0.5	3.0	2.8
Shaanxi	3515.6	74.3	56.5	85.7	-11.4	2.1	2.4
Gansu	2436.8	59.5	44.0	70.9	-11.4	2.4	2.9
Qinghai	481.1	20.3	14.7	22.6	-2.3	4.2	4.7
Ningxia	511.3	13.3	7.8	13.8	-0.5	2.6	2.7
Xinjiang	1661.4	91.6	31.3	50.1	41.5	5.5	3.0
National	120458.2	3642.6	2444.2	3642.6	0	3.0	3.0

Source: Yang Jianchun: Size, Direction and Structure of China's Population Migration -- An Analysis on the Data from the 1%

National Population Sample Survey, Research References, Vol. 2, 1997.